Memories, Milestones and New Horizons

Memories Milestones and New Horizons

Reflections on the Regeneration of Ballymun

Edited by Aibhlín McCrann

BLACKSTAFF PRESS

BELFAST

For the hands, hearts and minds creating
new horizons in Ballymun

First published in 2008 by
Blackstaff Press
4c Heron Wharf
Sydenham Business Park
Belfast BT3 9LE

in association with
Ballymun Regeneration Limited
Civic Centre
Main Street
Ballymun
Dublin 9

Edited by Aibhlín McCrann

Typeset by CJWT Solutions, St Helens, England

Printed in England by Athenaeum Press

ISBN 978-0-85640-835-9

www.blackstaffpress.com
www.brl.ie

CONTENTS

EDITOR'S NOTE   vii

Foreword   ix
CIARÁN MURRAY

Open Heart Surgery, E10 and the Emerging Sixth   1
DAVID PRICHARD

Rebuilding Ballymun   27
ANNE POWER

The Architecture of Ballymun   45
JOHN MONTAGUE

Driving the Vision of Regeneration   77
JOHN TIERNEY

The Greening of Ballymun   93
PETER WYSE JACKSON

Providing Effective Access to Legal Services   115
GERRY WHYTE

When All is Said and Done   137
MICHELE RYAN

Bridging the 'Town and Gown' Divide   153
RONNIE MUNCK AND DEIRIC Ó BROIN

Fostering an Enterprise Culture in Ballymun   167
RONAN KING

Ballymun: Future-proofing with a Green Community   183
DUNCAN STEWART

Linking Urban Regeneration and Sustainable Development   191
ANNA DAVIES

Ballymun: A New Town Once Again   207
CIARÁN CUFFE

A Horse of a Different Colour   223
ROBERT BALLAGH

Heights and Consequences   241
DERMOT BOLGER

The National Memory Town   259
JOHN WATERS

ABOUT THE CONTRIBUTORS   278
INDEX   283

Editor's Note

When I first conceived the idea for this collection of essays, I wanted it to be both an acknowledgement and a celebration of what has been achieved in Ballymun over the past ten years.

Working on the book has been a rewarding and stimulating journey, and many people have walked the road with me:

Ciarán Murray, who enabled the idea to become a reality;

Sheena McCambley, who brought a keen sense of intellectual rigour to the project;

Theo Dorgan, who shared his insights and experience of the publishing world;

Felix Larkin, who pointed out the potential pitfalls along the way and how to avoid them;

Ray Yeates, who used his considerable persuasive powers to great effect;

Patricia Scanlon and Sarah Millar, who listened and advised throughout the book's passage;

Cian Harte and Sinéad McKeon, whose quirky choice of images brought Ballymun to life;

Kai Wagner and Brid Hughes, whose back-room support and attention to detail were remarkable;

Helen Wright of Blackstaff Press, whose guiding eye assisted at every turn;

and Peter Finnegan, who provided a willing sounding-board and wise counsel.

I have been overwhelmed by the enthusiasm and generosity of response from the essayists who have endured a persistent editor with the greatest tolerance. Their voices truly mark the *Memories, Milestones and New Horizons* of Ballymun.

AIBHLÍN McCRANN

Foreword

Ballymun: A Town Reborn

This collection of essays was commissioned by Ballymun Regeneration Ltd to mark ten years of progress in rebuilding Ballymun. The various contributions reveal unique personal perspectives, recollections and insights into the changing faces of Ballymun as viewed by a diverse range of observers. You may, like me, not agree with all of the views expressed in the essays; however, collectively, they provide a rich tapestry of reflections for discussion and debate on Ireland's only really unique city neighbourhood.

Ten years ago when I wrote the foreword for the regeneration masterplan, entitled 'Ballymun is unique in many ways', I too reflected on Ballymun's difficult history, its vibrant community spirit and the opportunities to rewrite that history. The 1998 masterplan adopted a brave approach to redevelopment, retaining all the existing residents while rebuilding the town and putting in place all the social and economic infrastructure necessary to sustain the community. It remains, to this day, unique throughout Europe for the integrity of that process, and is in stark contrast to what happened in the 1960s, when families were forced to evacuate tenement buildings throughout Dublin city and uproot to the brave new world of modern living, in the newly built, edge-of-city high-rise housing estate in the green fields of Ballymun.

Forty-five years on, it is still easy to imagine the widespread panic and state of crisis that developed in Dublin city following the four fatalities that occurred when tenement buildings collapsed in Bolton Street and Fenian Street within a two-week period in June 1963. In a matter of weeks, hundreds of families were evacuated from dangerous buildings and Dublin Corporation (now Dublin City Council) and the Dublin Health Authority struggled to find accommodation on an emergency basis for homeless families.

The pressure on the government and Dublin Corporation to respond adequately to the housing crisis was enormous. It culminated in the collective decision in May 1964 to follow the UK and European model, in vogue at the time, for procuring public housing by adopting the low cost, quick-fix solution of prefabricated, system-built, high-rise housing. Following a speedy tendering process a four-year contract for the planning, development and construction of the Ballymun estate was signed on the 2 February 1965. Initially 36 high-rise blocks, comprising 2,820 flats including 7 fifteen-storey, 19 eight-storey and 10 four-storey blocks, together with 400 two-storey housing units were built in Ballymun up to the end of 1969. Subsequently a further 1,600 two-storey public housing units were added to the estate making Ballymun one of the largest public housing estates in Europe.

A great deal has been said and written in relation to the failure of the high-rise estates built in the 1950s, 60s and 70s. The Ballymun story featured in Dr Anne Power's seminal work *Estates on the Edge* as one of five symbolic case studies throughout Europe. Ballymun, however, best demonstrated the flawed planning and management, which ultimately led to its rapid and steep decline into a notorious ghetto. I have often described the original planning of Ballymun as being Ireland's version of apartheid; suffice to say that large-scale social housing schemes which were physically and socially excluded from normal city economic activity were doomed to failure from the start. Experience has shown that far more enlightened and integrated responses are necessary to create successful city neighbourhoods.

The brief which issued from the government when the regeneration project was officially announced in March 1997 reflected such visionary thinking by recognising that housing-based policies alone would not solve Ballymun's problems. The ambition for the project was encapsulated in one sentence of the press release which read 'The aim of this major social project is to get Ballymun working as a town which caters for all local needs and attracts public and private investment, provides employment and secures a better mix of housing in a rejuvenated physical environment.'

The regeneration of Ballymun has been a long and difficult journey into the unknown and at the time of writing is, as yet, an unfinished story. There was no script or template to follow in planning its rehabilitation. For those of us who have travelled this journey from the start, it has been the ultimate challenge and ultimate buzz; a roller coaster of emotions, as each new element of the project revealed untold stories of prejudice and betrayal, of misery and loss, of courage and conviction, of survival and ambition. These stories deserve to be publicly told, but, like most true life stories, are best left until the wounds are somewhat healed.

Ballymun is being transformed, with a renewed pride of place evident on every street. A wide range of quality new community facilities have been provided throughout the five neighbourhoods, with parks, playgrounds, sport and recreation facilities, and childcare and community buildings emerging around almost every corner. But perhaps the best measure of the progress that has been made can be gleaned from the community's own responses, which have seen Ballymun win upwards of thirty separate environmental awards and eleven Tidy Towns awards in recent years. These achievements were further underpinned in 2008, with Ballymun winning a Taoiseach's Award for Excellence for its Community Safety Strategy, which was also recognised when Ballymun Regeneration Ltd won the Vodafone Innovative Organisation of the year 2008. This year Ballymun also won the national title of Fairtrade Town of Ireland 2008, which is a remarkable tribute to how far this community has come, in leading the way for the rest of the country.

Another area where Ballymun is leading the way is in its approach to the development of the arts. Last year axis, our community arts and resource centre, staged 183 separate events and performances and attracted forty thousand new visitors to shows in Ballymun. In 2006 this small community theatre premiered Dermot Bolger's new play *From these Green Heights*, which was voted the best new play of the year. Similarly impressive has been the impact that our own Per Cent for Art commissions have made on the public generally, with many of the works being highly acclaimed for their creativity and public engagement. Artist Seamus Nolan's *Hotel Ballymun* saw the two top floors of the soon-to-be demolished fifteen-storey Clarke Tower converted into a temporary hotel for a six-week period.

In many respects the jury is still out on the success of the regeneration project with only about two thirds of the physical works completed to date. Certainly, continued commitment from the Government and Dublin City Council will be essential to see it through to completion, or else the hard yards gained may be to no avail. International experience has shown that it is important to sustain necessary supports well beyond completion of the physical works. Otherwise there is a distinct danger that the downward spiral of degeneration can re-emerge with all the investment put at risk.

Looking to the future there is still a number of large pieces that need to fall into place before the regeneration jigsaw is complete. The opening of the new IKEA store in 2009, delivering upwards of five hundred jobs, will make a profound impact on unemployment locally, while also making Ballymun a national destination centre. The planned Metro line through Ballymun from the airport en route to the city is the most exciting public transportation development in the last century, and will connect Ballymun to the city in a way that no other initiative could. Equally impressive are the plans recently lodged for the redevelopment of the shopping centre which will provide a unique shopping experience in retailing terms, as the scheme is essentially an open street-based development as distinct from the usual out-of-town, mall-style centre. Also in the pipeline is a research and development business park, which BRL hopes to promote and progress in the short to medium term.

The Ballymun Regeneration logo depicts the hand of the community reaching for a bright new future, a future that is now in sight, and hopefully one that will be a very real and tangible legacy from the days of the Celtic tiger.

CIARÁN MURRAY
MANAGING DIRECTOR, BALLYMUN REGENERATION LIMITED
ASSISTANT DUBLIN CITY MANAGER

Open Heart Surgery, E10 and the Emerging Sixth

E10: environment, employment, education and training,
empowerment, economics, energy, empathy, estate management,
evidence, exit

DAVID PRICHARD

A masterplan, as the name suggests, is often thought of as a fixed blueprint
for a physical project. By reflecting on the original ideas and intentions ten
years on, I will attempt to explain how the plan for Ballymun was
conceived as a planning framework for regeneration that set ideals but
allowed scope for evolution in response to inevitable but unpredictable
forces. Many of the ambitions in the masterplan foretell the six themes in
Dublin City Council's *Maximising the City's Potential: A Strategy for
Intensification and Height*, which sets out visions for the economy, society,
culture, urban form, movement and sustainability agendas.

It is sometimes said that masterplans are led by vision, commerce or
process. I believe all three drivers are needed, and it is the appropriate
balance that matters – otherwise, the document will collect dust on a shelf,
as many do.

Ireland's unprecedented economic success in the last fifteen years made
possible this huge undertaking of transforming the conspicuous and
notorious high-rise estate of Ballymun into a desirable district of North
Dublin. Fortunately, Ireland has only one such estate, whereas the UK
has over two hundred, and Europe hundreds more. The project team's
desire to understand regeneration and deliver best practice in all its facets
was summarised at the outset in our preoccupation with the four Es:

education, employment, environment and empowerment. That quest for best practice has led Ballymun Regeneration Ltd (BRL) to look to Europe and forge links so as to benefit from others' experiences of regeneration. In turn, Ballymun is much visited by outsiders, not just for the product or hardware represented by its physical regeneration, but for the comprehensive social regeneration programmes being managed by the highly committed staff at BRL who have had to establish them – indeed, invent them – because each regeneration project requires bespoke community programmes.

When the team commenced work in 1997, there were few guidance documents on masterplanning, and the word 'sustainability' was only beginning to emerge. Now, there are numerous books and endless checklists, and to further confuse matters, the term 'masterplan' is often interchangeable with 'vision', 'urban design' and 'development framework'. All of these terms are applied across the board from small-scale infill schemes to whole towns.

The often neglected ingredient for success in an initiative like the regeneration of Ballymun is the role of project champions. Without a project staff exuding passion, conviction and tenacity, even with a compelling case, there can be a loss of focus, ambition and time. The role of project champion calls for commitment that goes way beyond the usual day-job duties, and for a decade-long project can be likened to running a marathon rather than the sprint of the typical building project. BRL's staff have had to spend countless evenings in meetings to clarify issues and negotiate solutions with the increasingly wise, well-informed and ambitious residents. This part of the process requires patience, communication skills and empathy; after all, it is the residents' environment that has been turned into a noisy, messy, dangerous building site for more than a decade.

Ballymun covers over 760 acres, and was home to twenty thousand people in 1998. Its scale can be difficult to grasp except by comparison with, say, Fatima Mansions' oft-quoted eleven acres. Nearly all the lands are owned by Dublin City Council – the planning authority for the land of the existing homes – while the open fields fall within Fingal County Council's jurisdiction. While area, like population, provides a simple measure of scale, to comprehend the extent of Ballymun's deprivations requires a grasp of complex social factors that are difficult to measure. For there to be real and lasting change, the project had to be much more than just a housing renewal exercise. To ensure Ballymun grew into a more stable community, it needed to become something other than a satellite dormitory – it had to grow into a town with a choice of places to work, live and relax, in which people could move around easily and safely.

At the competition interview in 1997 for the commission to work with BRL in the preparation of the masterplan, I likened the impending trauma for Ballymuners to open heart surgery. The team was asked for its vision for Ballymun, and we said much of its dysfunctionalism was probably attributable to its lack of connections – physical, social and economic – and that these had to be dramatically improved. We empathised with the residents: we imagined they were tired of being surveyed, did not want to be conspicuous and probably dreamed of being like the rest of North Dublin. That was a social, not an architectural vision. One panellist asked me if changing the name was necessary if its notoriety was to be expunged. My response was that UK politicians had tried that with Windscale, and did renaming it Sellafield make Ireland feel any better? That said, what is now called 'branding' is significant, and for Ballymun the rebranding started with the early idea of emphasising the constituent communities' names. These were the existing five neighbourhoods of Coultry, Shangan, Silloge, Balcurris and Poppintree – represented by the five fingers in the hand logo of Ballymun Regeneration Ltd. Ballymun residents were proud of the name – it was the rest of the country that needed to change its opinion. With a project like this, we thought there was a risk that politicians might believe that a few big, quick ideas would solve the problem. It was reassuring that local politicians did appreciate that the complexity of the social issues required a multiplicity of overlapping solutions, and that the implementation process itself could make the community stronger – and its fabric and economy more stable and enduring – with residents' involvement and support.

In fact, the conspicuousness of Ballymun has increased since 1998, but in a different way: it is now a destination for various audiences and customers seeking civic and health services, motor tax, arts, leisure, hotels and – soon – IKEA, which will open in 2009. Hopefully, in the next three years, the long-planned shopping centre will be added to that list.

We were one of several foreign teams interviewed, and we had established a link with O'Mahony Pike Architects that enabled us to benefit from their local knowledge and national reputation for housing. My own experiences of large-scale renewal had been in London's East End, where I had led the planning application process for three estates of about five hundred homes each for the Bow Housing Action Trust. There, I had worked alongside two other experienced housing practices, Levitt Bernstein Associates and Pollard Thomas Edwards. Although we had designed several thousand new homes for UK development corporations (Warrington, Basildon, Milton Keynes and London Docklands) over the previous twenty-five years, Ballymun was by far the largest and most challenging residential commission my practice had ever undertaken. It required us to lead and employ the consultant team in a country we did not know, to be based on-site much of the time, and to work alongside the newly established BRL team. There was a deadline, too: the plans had to be based on extensive resident consultation, have broad stakeholder support, and be published by 31 March 1998 or the project would miss the deadline for significant tax-designation benefits. There is nothing like a deadline to galvanise everyone into helping each other achieve what, at times, seemed on the edge of the possible. The exhilarating six months of true collaboration between about forty people forged relationships that have endured.

Ten years on, Ireland now has much housing and renewal experience it can share with other countries. For a population of four million, the building industry has achieved (up until 2007) over 95,000 new homes per year, compared to the UK's population of sixty million and 165,000 houses per year. In terms of procurement and quality in this period, Dublin City Council has pioneered PPP (Public-Private Partnerships)-style delivery, and has insisted on high space standards in its document *Achieving Liveable, Sustainable New Apartment Homes for Dublin City*, as well as through renewal programmes with extensive provision of social facilities, such as in Fatima Mansions, where we revised the masterplan and are joint architects.

Ballymun was designed in the mid-1960s in response to an urgent need to rehouse inner-city residents living in derelict properties. It was constructed on open fields on the edge of the city, beyond the 1930s-to-1950s sprawl, where radial routes out of Dublin dissolved into the countryside. As with many such estates of that era, the high-rise Balency concrete system was used; 2,820 homes were built in the form of 7 fifteen-storey towers, 19 eight-storey spine blocks, and 10 four-storey walk-up blocks. After numerous reports considering alternative options, one tower and two spine blocks were extensively upgraded in 1995. Following an evaluation of that refurbishment, Dublin Corporation and the government committed themselves to rebuilding Ballymun through an integrated social and economic regeneration programme involving the demolition of all the high-rise flats over an eight-year time frame. Hence the establishment of BRL and the need for a masterplan.

The overriding desire of the team was to find bespoke proposals for the many problems facing Ballymun. Precedents established elsewhere may inspire but can rarely be transplanted as ready-made solutions – after all, that was the approach in the 1960s, which created this problem in the first place. The safety valve on work of this nature is the community itself – in Ballymun's case, the community was established, articulate and cautious about becoming a guinea pig for a second time.

The masterplan set out some simple-to-follow big ideas for the physical environment for each of the five neighbourhoods. The environmental agenda, agreed with residents, for each of the five neighbourhoods was to:

- Create a distinct identity;
- Provide local community facilities, such as shops, crèches, meeting rooms;
- Provide new parks and play spaces;
- Improve access and legibility by connecting cul-de-sacs and making new links;
- Improve internal space and energy standards.

In an article for *City* magazine, I summarised the masterplan intentions. The key ideas for improving the environment were also described in a series of critiques of what already existed and of the masterplan's response. I will now revisit these and add some more.

MOTORWAY: SAVIOUR RATHER THAN SCOURGE

When the northern section of Dublin's M50 orbital motorway opened in 1997, the Ballymun Road – which used to trickle out to the countryside – suddenly had its own junction, which is used to access the airport. Adding a motorway environment seemed for many residents to make matters bleaker, and some wanted a Ballymun bypass to avoid the through-traffic.

What the M50 did was make Ballymun Road a key radial artery into Dublin. The M50 and, to the east, the northbound M1 demonstrated the development corridors that motorways become, albeit that many of these have unattractive 'big shed' land uses. The M1 is the road spine to the Dublin–Belfast economic corridor, which will be of increasing regional significance in a peaceful twenty-first century. The M50 created an impenetrable edge to the north of the masterplan area. The nineteenth-century railway corridors leading into cities overlook backyards; motorways often do the same, so we wanted the approach to Ballymun to set a better example.

In 1998 a business park was planned for those fields in Fingal, but there was a slowdown in the office market in 2001. Advanced infrastructure planting planned for the motorway edge is only just beginning – it is a pity to have missed out on ten years' tree growth. A tall building (at the time, we favoured an apart-hotel) was proposed to give this motorway junction an identity, and some such emblem is still needed. The first IKEA store in the state is visible from the M50, so Ballymun will soon become a national destination.

The masterplan could only control one quadrant of the motorway junction. Metro North – the rail line from the city to the airport planned since 2005 – will run up Ballymun Road and cross the motorway beside the junction. A comprehensive vision for all four quadrants is essential to prevent these pieces of national infrastructure becoming new barriers to the integration of these large land banks into North Dublin's valuable airport fringe.

TOWN PLANNING: CREATING PLACES RATHER THAN SPACES

Arriving in Ballymun in 1997, one was greeted by a huge roundabout with windswept pedestrian underpasses surrounded by a cluster of seven tower blocks. Spine blocks radiated out, and beyond were carpets of two-storey houses, not as conspicuous as the towers but many in poor condition. The overall impression was of windswept grass with a few trees and horses roaming the pock-marked, muddy verges. The isolation and lack of connection was accentuated by the surrounding unstructured open space, perceived by some adjoining neighbours as their *cordon sanitaire*. To make matters worse, overhead electricity pylons ran along two boundaries, thus creating an aggressive 'electric fence' and compounding Ballymun's severance from neighbouring Glasnevin and Santry. One of the first major infrastructure expenditures was the undergrounding of those cables, which won back development land and removed potential concerns about building new homes close to sources of electromagnetic fields.

A sense of enclosure had to be achieved on Ballymun Road to transform it into a street with town-like buildings leading to a recognisable centre. A streetscape has been achieved at the southern and northern ends, but the middle will lack form and identity until the slab blocks are removed and new kerb-hugging development proceeds. Wherever possible, new homes with road and footpath connections have been built on the wasteland boundaries to help dissolve the existing physical and social divisions.

The landscape strategy was crucial to creating familiar and valued parks to replace the useless swathes of muddy grass. Building on these swathes of land was controversial with the residents until it was understood that better-quality spaces would be provided and that they would be able to retain their community ties by moving to new homes close to their old flats.

ROAD HIERARCHY: MAKING CONNECTING STREETS RATHER THAN CUL-DE-SACS

The original road hierarchy reinforced the built form, with wide roads radiating from the central roundabout leading to dead-end estate roads that in turn led to residential cul-de-sacs. That road system thwarted community integration, prevented efficient bus services, and spawned alienating and difficult-to-find addresses – it was a thoroughly illegible and unnavigable estate.

The roundabout formed the terminus of the suburban dual carriageway and divided the community in two. It had pedestrian subways that were not justified by the pedestrian movements or even by today's traffic volumes. The residential cul-de-sac layouts had roads parallel to the estate roads, generating still more verge space and compounding the diluted and separated pattern of settlement.

The masterplan advocated several new short link roads, converting the long cul-de-sacs into through routes, thus improving the connection between communities. These link roads are now built. New signage to the villages also helps to establish the communities' boundaries and individual identities.

We proposed replacing the roundabout with a crossroads, and allowing through-traffic movements to be prioritised without reducing capacity.

Ballymun Road has been traffic-calmed and will become a more conventional town main street. This idea challenged traditional road-engineering interpretations, but we are in an era when the car's supremacy is being questioned, and precedents have been established in some of Dublin's main streets, which carry similar volumes and have a strong character. The coming decade will see quieter, smaller and cleaner cars, so the masterplan ambition of a pleasant, walkable Main Street is not as difficult to achieve as some think.

The creation of Main Street was seen as key to giving Ballymun a new identity. New destination land uses were sought and have been delivered. Building active street frontages for retail, civic and commercial buildings, expected to serve a community of thirty thousand, will create a sense of arrival in a proper town, rather than just another dormitory.

TRANSPORT: PUBLIC SYSTEMS RATHER THAN PRIVATE CARS

Car ownership in 1997 was very low, due to a combination of low incomes and poor security. Car parking provision has a major impact on the quality of housing layouts, and to justify the proposal for low provision, BRL has actively supported improvements to public transport services. Bus routes have been adjusted but still do not serve some of the districts to which Ballymun residents need to travel for work opportunities.

In 1999 the exciting new transport lifeline for Ballymun was the LUAS tram system. Ballymun was to be on the northbound line to the airport, and so the masterplan reserved land for it and identified a route serving the existing community which led to the existing bridge over the M50 at Silloge. BRL was pleased with the prospect of the LUAS route since it would connect Ballymun to the major new citywide network. In combination with the new motorway junction, the LUAS would place Ballymun on the main axis between city and airport.

The Main Street development framework we designed in 1999 also took account of the LUAS, and it was agreed with the Railway Procurement Agency (RPA) to run it not in the middle of the road – where it is unpleasant for customers to wait – but to split it and run it beside the pavements like a bus service. However, by 2005 the RPA was committing to the heavier Metro system for the airport link. At first, it was proposed to run it on the surface up Main Street, which would have destroyed all the investment made in bettering the environment; fortunately, that, and the proposal for an overhead option, were short-lived. In 2007, it was agreed that the Metro will run underground with a station in the Ballymun Plaza and another serving the M50 lands. With the downturn in 2008, there are concerns that the Metro project may be vulnerable to delay and cost savings, but it is a national imperative to have a city–airport rail link, and Ballymun will benefit from it. In sum, Metro North will finally connect Ballymun with the city fabric and economy.

COMMUNITY: CONNECTED AND FOCUSED RATHER THAN UNSERVED AND ISOLATED

Residential communities need a visible focus – ideally, one with all the classic ingredients of places to meet, shop, learn, play and worship – and they must have public transport links to employment. The original retail provision was all in the 1970s shopping centre, which was laid out as an inward-looking pinwheel plan. Displaying its service yards to the visitor, and with little parking, it was unappealing and inaccessible for passing trade. It worked for a while in the 1970s, when spending power was higher and before the advent of large out-of-town shopping centres, but by 1998 the spending power in Ballymun was very low, with a large number of shop units empty or occupied by community support organisations. The few remaining shops inevitably offered less choice, and goods were frequently more expensive than at nearby retail centres. The isolated neighbourhoods were served by improvised container shops offering limited and expensive stock to a poor, vulnerable and dependent community.

A vibrant town centre was planned, and most of the civic facilities are now built: the axis arts and community resource centre, the leisure centre, the divisional headquarters of both the Health Service Executive and An Garda Síochána, and the new garda station. The pool and the civic offices have been operating for several years. If only there had been a way to start the retail redevelopment sooner, it would by now be established. The downturn in the economy will naturally affect the retail sector, and this could prevent the shopping centre opening before the completion of Metro North because that construction will entail cut and cover-up the length of Main Street.

The existing schools and churches have been anchors for the communities, especially during the turmoil of renewal. Demography has changed and there is overcapacity in some schools, and with new energy standards and changes in education, there may well be consolidation and need for new buildings.

The scale and time span of the Ballymun regeneration project highlights the need for a multi-agency coordinated approach between housing, social and health services. The need for joined-up thinking is obvious yet still presents significant challenges because agencies have different agendas and priorities.

CORNER SHOPS RATHER THAN CONTAINER SHOPS

In 1997 local convenience shopping was provided by twenty-seven unlicensed container shops that had set up around the neighbourhoods. These responded to the needs of the 'benefit' community of home-bound single parents by offering snacks and corner shop produce as well as cheque-cashing and credit, but goods were not cheap. The strategy has been to replace these with traditional parades of shops well located for passing trade. These are now built – with apartments above them – in Coultry and Shangan, and Silloge is nearing completion. The post-war UK new towns included local shops and located them for ease of residents' access on foot – this was laudable except that they do not capture passing trade. We planned for both. The nature of retailing is constantly changing, and the one-stop shop now embraces most needs. The co-location of these local shops near bus stops, parks, surgeries and schools has helped secure their viability and create the focus each neighbourhood needs.

In contrast to the previous cul-de-sac layout, the new through-road network has helped those parades win new passing trade. The Shangan neighbourhood centre was located to assist integration and serve more affluent neighbours from Santry. Sadly, the proposed link is still not agreed, demonstrating that social perceptions can take a generation to change.

Apartments over shops were proposed and have been built; such locations are ideal for small and elderly households. Shops provide a focus; community rooms for the many active groups in Ballymun can be added, and, most important of all, there are crèche facilities that can liberate single parents to pursue other activities.

IDENTIFIABLE NEIGHBOURHOODS RATHER THAN ONE SPRAWLING BALLYMUN

Despite their anonymous concrete world, Ballymun residents had created the communities of Coultry, Shangan, Silloge, Balcurris and Poppintree. They ran community forums that proved to be one of the key conduits for consultation during the masterplanning period and subsequently. Those neighbourhoods had no clear focus – no beginning, no centre, no end – all had the same towers and spine blocks, except Poppintree, which was comprised of two-storey houses and had a young, ill-defined park. So the design challenge was to re-plan those neighbourhoods around community facilities, to make well-defined places – around a park, row of shops, road junction, existing school or church – and carefully reinforce existing facilities that worked well. This ambition to create urban villages – or parishes – was and is a recurring goal for designers working in suburbs.

During the consultation stage, we were surprised to learn that over one hundred and fifty groups met regularly, sometimes in empty flats. They were the optimistic sign of an active, self-supporting survivor community. Replacement meeting rooms have been provided, and the nature of their use will change since many residents now have jobs, homes and gardens to maintain. In the Coultry housing scheme, these rooms were located on street corners, and designed so they could be converted into apartments in due course. The existing parish churches and schools remain the focus of much activity and support in the community. The intervening years of upheaval during building works has placed additional demands on these invaluable support networks.

Any of the early-phase sites for new homes were road verges and SLOAP (a 1970s expression: Space Left Over After Planning!) between the existing houses and flats. Intrinsically more complex to design and develop economically, it was upon this land that new homes were to be built prior to demolitions, which was essential if the community was not to suffer the disruption of moving twice.

LEGIBILITY: DISTINCTIVE AND DIFFERENT PLACES RATHER THAN UNIFORMITY

We thought the new road hierarchy and road naming would help establish an identity for each neighbourhood. An early idea in the re-planning period in 1997 was to introduce new link roads leading from Main Street directly into each community – so each could be signposted separately. These link roads now lead to new places, such as Coultry Park, and pass the convenience shops and school. This improved legibility has helped visitors, and has created attractive addresses rather than the previous dehumanising block numbers. Several of the original roads extended over two kilometres, turned through 270 degrees and had wide grass verges that made finding addresses maddeningly difficult and dangerously slow for emergency services.

The new homes are predominantly suburban houses. The small clusters of apartments have their own front doors to the street rather than shared lobbies that are expensive to manage and keep secure. Most of the new homes have two, three or four storeys, and many have mono-pitch roofs that help create an urban scale, along with the parking, which is mostly on-kerb rather than on-plot.

All the scheme designs place emphasis on strong corners, and this helps legibility and navigation. The length of streets, the choice of names and the location of front doors are all crucial ingredients to making convivial and safe neighbourhoods. BRL has involved the residents in the choice of street names that sometimes capture historic references.

Concern for secure back gardens has led to nearly all the housing schemes being designed with no exposed-flank garden walls. Pedestrian-only lanes or alleys have been eliminated, and all street frontages have frequent doorways to animate and help security.

PUBLIC OPEN SPACES: RAILED PARKS RATHER THAN VERGES OR FIELDS

The swathes of unstructured open space provided spare land, and enabled the first replacement homes to be built without demolitions and the consequent need for residents to move twice. This was extremely helpful in terms of programme delivery, but was initially controversial with residents, who valued the quantity of open space rather than its quality. In 1997 the horses had grazed on what little planting there had been, and the 'parks' were barren and unappealing. In Ireland, the word 'park' is used for any small, open space; the useful English word 'common' has no currency because of the history of land ownership. We promoted the principle that parks should have railings and gates, like many traditional town squares; for the residents, however, gates were associated with private rather than communal space.

In 1997 there were several local football clubs using over thirty pitches that were generally poorly drained, casually maintained and had no changing rooms. The provision of properly laid-out pitches with new club rooms was a priority for BRL.

There was a startling lack of equipped play areas in 1997; the original ones had long since been devastated by vandalism – encouraged by locations that were not overlooked or easily managed. The masterplan identified playground locations that could be overseen, were on main pedestrian routes and would serve the needs of different age groups.

The parks built in Coultry and Balcurris have turned out to be completely different to the Poppintree neighbourhood park. Here, the residents' ambitions and involvement has led to more European-style parks – open and unfenced – with sophisticated land forms and planting schemes, an exciting array of outdoor rooms and atmospheres, and many extra facilities for different age groups to play. The long-term maintenance commitment is very different from the parks department's standard budget allowances, so new management methods are being put in place. In the UK, the Commission for Architecture and Built Environment publishes guidance notes for developments, and its recent *Start with the Park* document promotes the view that new neighbourhoods should be focused on quality outdoor spaces. This is an example of Ballymun experience and solutions foretelling formal best-practice guidance.

SECURITY: FRONTAGES TO PUBLIC SPACE AND DOORS ONTO THE STREET

Graffiti and break-ins were common around the existing open spaces because side walls and back gardens abutted public space. The masterplan proposed that all public parks should have driveable edges with housing frontages facing the park. This results in the creation of attractive addresses overlooking parks, and helps to make the parks feel safe.

Much has been written in the last three decades about the virtues of people having their own front doors. Communal entrance halls are often a source of management problems, and the elimination of unpossessed space has been the mantra of housing designers everywhere.

BALLYMUN ROAD: A TOWN MAIN STREET RATHER THAN A DUAL CARRIAGEWAY

The housing renewal programme was the *raison d'être* of BRL and the imperative behind the 1998 masterplan. Main Street posed a much more complex set of commercial and logistical dynamics, and became the subject of a separate development framework prepared by my team with BRL in 1999. The character and quality of this street would depend upon the road design, and Muir Associates was instrumental in advancing the planning and technical processes for the new road network, traffic-calming devices and integrating the LUAS.

The exceptional development opportunity in Main Street results from land ownership being almost entirely with Dublin City Council, which is also the planning authority. BRL won special tax incentives in 1998 that have helped deliver private investment in Main Street's hotels and retail outlets.

The urban design intentions were to achieve a mix of uses, enclosure from the street, active frontages, a beginning and an end, and two public places: the Civic Plaza at the south end would be a hard, active, bustling place, whereas the north-end square would be green, tranquil and passive. In its interim pre-Metro-station format, the triangular Civic Plaza is currently formed by two enclosing sides. It is developing a character, has a welcome grassed surface and hosts a weekly farmers' market and other events organised by axis arts centre.

In 1999 we anticipated that the Main Street framework would have to accommodate a variety of potential outcomes, and the robustness of that proposal has certainly been tested. The factors of timing and sequence of land-parcel releases have had profound implications on the outcome and interim conditions. The tax incentives granted only applied for three years, so there was an urgency about liberating key sites, sometimes in advance of the dates generated by the logic of the housing-renewal programme. The urgency to deliver the leisure centre meant that the planned surface car park for the shopping centre was built upon in 2002. Coincidentally, the shopping centre was acquired, and the new owners – Treasury Holdings Ltd – had a very ambitious city density, shopping mall, mixed-use scheme approved.

The Main Street framework anticipated transforming the street from each end simultaneously. The north end stalled after the hotel was built because the new-build programmes slipped for other reasons, and so the slab blocks are still to be vacated. BRL has been able to consolidate some of the smaller land parcels, and wants to attract a civic function, such as law courts. That would expand the destination uses and attract legal-related offices, increased spending power and another audience to Ballymun. However, it appears now that this may not happen.

So in 2008, Main Street – the emerging sixth community – is still evolving. The vacant middle is disappointing, but is key to enhancing the town's appeal. Perhaps the best offer for the middle may not be identified and built until after Metro North. That will be the next development trigger, and could coincide with the next market upturn.

SHOPPING: INCREMENTAL RENEWAL AND GROWTH RATHER THAN MAJOR NEW CENTRE

We anticipated that retail renewal for Ballymun was going to be slow and incremental until new employment and new residents with greater spending power moved in, thus providing an incentive for retailers to invest. We believed retail in that context to be a follower, not a leader. Retail would also provide much-needed new work opportunities for residents. We thought the land won back from elimination of the huge roundabout could provide more frontages on to Main Street and offer more visible car parking so as to capture passing trade. Those ideas were not to be.

As mentioned above, the first Treasury Holdings scheme was based on the now-outdated enclosed-mall format. Fortunately, the current scheme is exploring open streets in the manner of our recent urban-design work for Castlethorn at Adamstown Central – the new town in west Dublin. The proposed density of the Treasury development and presumption of mostly car-borne customers generated a proposal with several decks of underground parking and numerous residential storeys above. If only there had been a more incrementally deliverable design, we might not still be looking at the backs of the seventies shops. The timing and outcome are unknown now the market has changed and while Metro North is awaited, but retail and employment beside the station will be the lead sectors in the next wave of economic regeneration.

CIVIC FACILITIES: TO SERVE NORTH DUBLIN RATHER THAN JUST BALLYMUN

We understood retail development and understood that shops do not work on both sides of a busy main street. Therefore to create a new balance of function across the street, we promoted civic facilities on the east side; an arts and community resource centre, town hall and library were on the wish list in 1998. The first two are complete; the new library will now be in the west-side retail development and so is still to come. The axis arts centre was first to be funded, and was built by 2001, followed shortly afterwards by the civic offices. The triangular shape of the Plaza was derived from the new street layout and the pragmatics of land being liberated after demolitions. It feels too large at the moment, but when the shopping centre is built and Plaza Station opens, there will be a lot of activity and a high-quality landscape.

Additional employment and public service opportunities negotiated by BRL for the Civic Centre were the motor-tax office, new Health Service Executive offices, a primary health-care centre and the new police headquarters; the latter has recently opened.

This concentration of civic functions has been criticised as a continuation of the heavy local authority presence that typified old Ballymun, but the independent and local management of the functions, together with their dilution with other private and commercial development, avoids any disadvantage. Leadership of urban renewal with state investment is essential, and prepares the context for the private sector to follow.

The great advantage of these regional facilities is that they encourage visitors who, historically, have avoided Ballymun. It is vital that these visitors see a changing Ballymun if they are to overcome their prejudices and spread a positive message.

PUBLIC ART: COLLABORATIVE AND RELEVANT RATHER THAN APPLIED AND OBSCURE

The role that publicly accessible art can play in urban life had been better appreciated during the 1990s in the UK than it was in Ireland. That role is multifaceted: it can be of celebration, involvement, enticement, amusement – as well as presenting information. All too often, art has been applied retrospectively to public spaces; that was not the Main Street framework's attitude to public art, however. We saw it as an embedded, parallel process; adding an unexpected dimension to regeneration, and enhancing community pride.

We thought that involving artists at the early stage would represent a sound investment while the scheme was building. Once the first wave of housing renewal was in train, spending time and money on art collaborations did not seem to the residents as potentially frivolous or untimely as it would have done before. Interventions by artists offer good value: when done well, they attract attention from not just local, but national and international audiences. BRL grasped the opportunity and launched Breaking Ground, an innovative public art programme, which soon became the largest Per Cent for Art Scheme programme ever undertaken in Ireland. A high profile for the whole project has been achieved with competitions, displays of ideas by artists working on-site, published reviews and so forth. Artists working on-site became an asset for local schools to exploit for project-based and skill-based work.

When we drafted the plan, we wrote that the project must learn from the mistakes of the previous era, when Ballymun gained its own 'Stonehenge' – the nickname for some standing stones on the spoil heap created from digging out the roundabout, which were not respected. We emphasised that artists' interventions needed to be inspired by the local context, to involve the residents and to be perceived by them as relevant. The precedents we cited were in Cardiff Bay and Lewisham, where artists brought delight to very practical objects such as signage, seating, surfaces and balustrades. Reflecting on the success of John Maine's work in Lewisham, we felt one key place for an artist's involvement would be Main Street. As the Ballymun Road is soon to be dug up for the Metro, perhaps this idea can be given a second chance.

Thanks to such projects as Breaking Ground, the value of cultural development in regeneration is better understood.

THE ARCHITECTURE: LOCAL INSPIRATION RATHER THAN FOREIGN TRANSPLANTS

In 1998 we observed that 'foreign' design ideas transplanted from other cultures can work, but may need several generations before they are accepted, or may fail catastrophically, as was the case with the original Ballymun. In the last decade, with a buoyant Irish economy enticing returnees and other nationals to Ireland, there has been an outburst of new ideas and approaches. Ireland has embraced a European – indeed, global – outlook. In the UK, the recent history of social housing reveals the arbitrary nature of some designers' imagery, and combined with the residents' perception of being guinea pigs for designer ambitions, this makes appearance a serious issue that haunts housing design.

My team's design for the first-phase homes derived its layout from Dublin's nineteenth-century residential suburbs. The scheme is a gently curving terrace overlooking Coultry Park, and its imagery reinterprets the Dublin architecture of terraces, steps and railings, and the layout hierarchy of park, street, mews and close. The projecting front steps lead to apartments with their own front doors on the landing, and so eliminate the need for internal entrance halls with their associated problems. The homes have front gardens for display and privacy; these were kept short in length so as to avoid the temptation to cut down railings and park in front.

We knew that a concentration of one household type in one location is not ideal, so in mid-terrace and end-terrace conditions we planned apartments. The ground-level end-terrace corners were designed to provide local meeting rooms, but could become a corner shop, office, or be converted into an apartment.

In contrast to the formality of the brick-clad terraces bounding the park, the mews cottages behind are two-storey, wide-frontage houses, with coloured-render elevations inspired by nineteenth-century Dublin examples. Here, the road and pavement surfaces are combined with other calming devices to make the mews a safe place for children to play.

LAND PARCELLING: STREETS SHOULD UNITE, NOT DIVIDE

An early mistake made in the UK new towns was to divide up the development lands using the roads as boundaries. This resulted in a world of road-engineers' verges dividing and isolating hamlets of residential developments. Roads are the way we discover and explore towns, so they must be thoughtfully designed and possessed by their adjoining buildings to help create a particular identity, rather than the everywhere and nowhere of most suburban road networks. Hence, the masterplan recommends that housing development land parcels should straddle roads. Design teams on adjacent parcels should work together and coordinate common elements where adjoining parcels share a boundary. Likewise, open spaces such as parks and greens should be designed in conjunction with their overlooking properties, not as a separate exercise – and perhaps by the same design team. This ambition has been difficult for BRL to deliver because the old road network has dictated land availability.

IDENTITY: CREATING PLACES RATHER THAN A COLLECTION OF SCHEMES

To maintain confidence and continuity of relationships within each neighbourhood, we thought there needed to be one coordinating architect for each who would be responsible for organising the separate teams of designers. Their role was to ensure variety and consistent attention to quality since the housing sites might range from small infill sites of five-plus to ones of over a hundred homes, with the emphasis on more smaller schemes wherever practical. The criticism of this method is that it spawns too much variety, but we thought this could be avoided by the careful choice of designers and by selecting a palette of materials and details to share within a neighbourhood.

The innovative and experimental housing percentages we promoted were distributed across the housing sites to maximise the richness of interpretations, and this has avoided enclaves of 'funny' houses.

Giving each community an identity was one of the key goals of the masterplan, and the new parks are the most dramatic success of this aim. Five parks are now in use, though their landscapes require time to become established before they will really look the part they undoubtedly play. Parks management by local rangers is an essential dimension to their success because the designs are a far cry from the gang-mower friendly flat grassland of so many estates. These parks have well-equipped play areas for different ages; shelters; interesting land forms; feature lighting; swales; and diverse planting, all of which require supervision and maintenance. Each park is a big investment and makes a profound impact on the neighbourhood by establishing the strong focus that unites the community. House values are also enhanced by these amenities.

ENERGY: INDEPENDENT CONTROL RATHER THAN INCLUDED IN RENT

With advice from Dublin-based Codema – an advisory agency specialising in energy and sustainability – a series of energy analyses were undertaken to enable BRL to reassure residents that their heating bills would not increase when they moved to a new home. Residents had been used to a district heating system, the cost of which was included in the rent. The existing system had the familiar problems of poor control, intrinsic wastefulness and high maintenance costs. With several housing-ownership and management regimes being proposed, an individual home-by-home heating system was preferable. Codema developed a clear picture of the energy purchase options for the project and for the residents, and established that it was possible to heat space and water to higher standards than before for the same expenditure. Energy poverty is likely to return, however, given the economic downturn and the significant increases in gas and oil prices, and this puts even more emphasis on raising insulation standards and using renewable energy sources.

We saw the project as an opportunity for experimentation and research into the benefits of varying energy-saving strategies. We were also anxious to monitor the outcomes as we were aware that the technical benefits are often not achieved due to human factors, such as the complexity of control systems.

With this in mind, and with funding from the European Union Regen Link project, we undertook to incorporate a number of what were then regarded as experimental features in Irish social housing, such as solar collector panels, ground-source heat pumps and grey-water recycling, among others. These were monitored during the first twelve months to assess the benefits. There were both successes and failures, and some features proved to be more suitable than others. Those which typically functioned well were those that were robust, unobtrusive and required minimal user intervention. Included for the first time in social housing in Ireland were high-efficiency condensing gas boilers, higher than best practice insulation standards, low water-usage fittings, and sustainably sourced timbers in all of the replacement homes, thus further reducing the heating and resource demands of the new housing units. The masterplan for the new Ballymun has been reviewed and updated to take account of the increasing standards demanded by building regulations, and to ensure a continuation of the higher-than-best-practice standard.

BRL is currently honing its strategic approach to sustainability by further developing objectives and targets in relation to social and environmental matters.

SUSTAINABILITY: NOT JUST FOR NOW, BUT FOR OUR GRANDCHILDREN

The concept of sustainability was new in the late nineties, but is becoming more and more relevant as the analyses of our carbon and water footprints make us embarrassed by the distortions that characterise our Western economic model. In 1997 the Department of the Environment published *Sustainable Developments – A Strategy for Ireland*; land-use planning is identified as a significant element in that strategy, and urban regeneration is a key policy objective. Ballymun offered an opportunity to identify criteria, choose indicators and establish targets over time frames.

The early test of the residents' belief in the need to diversify tenure was the debate over the allocation of 'spare' homes in the first wave of the new build. The outcome was a resounding commitment by the residents to make the spare homes available for sale to outsiders. There is also an acceptance that land should be made available to private house builders. The processes of empowerment and self-management, together with more private investment and enterprise, have been key to Ballymun's version of sustainability.

CONSULTATION: EMPATHY TO ENGAGE, NOT JUST PRESENT A FAIT ACCOMPLI

It was not easy to consult with a community of twenty thousand during the masterplanning exercise. The existence of long-standing organisations and groups – the Ballymun Task Force, the Ballymun Partnership and the neighbourhood forums, to name but a few – provided the initial structure through which to contact the community. The range of consultative methods included planning days, focus groups, design groups, working groups, public meetings, newsletters, public exhibitions, feedback questionnaires and surgeries for one-to-one discussions. The process has continued and evolved as the scale of issues reduces from town planning down to play areas, house plans and resident choices within new homes. But though the physical issues seemed possible to resolve, the more intractable community development issues will be ongoing beyond the life of the renewal programme.

It is obviously impossible to please everyone, but articulating likes and dislikes is a fundamental element in making the process and decisions overt and comprehensible to all. The time, thought and energy put into the process by residents has been remarkable, and will surely help the community take ownership of many difficult decisions.

The role of women in the project has been most inspiring for me, and prompted the quote beside my sponsored tree in the Amaptocare installation, which is part of the Breaking Ground public art programme:

> I salute the women of Ballymun. You have held the community together. You have been not just home makers but community makers and town makers. You have made time to engage in forging the future of your community and your town for your children's future. You have patiently endured living on a building site for years. May you and your families reap the reward of your commitment, belief and pride in Ballymun.

HOUSING TENURE: A DRAMATIC SHIFT IS NEEDED

The tenure mix is shifting towards 60:40 owner:social rented from a starting point of 20:80 in 1997, when the national figure was 80:20. The increased densities resulting from Metro North will enable future sites to help deliver this change of mix more quickly. BRL has been alert to the demand for special-needs housing, and the voluntary housing sector helps to deliver this. A tenure diversity strategy limiting any additional social housing in the area has been adopted by the board of the company and the local area committee of the City Council.

EXIT STRATEGY: PLAN THE END FROM THE BEGINNING

It seemed rudely premature in 2000 – at the beginning of a decade of work – even to raise this matter. However, to achieve real sustainability, there should, by definition, be no need for a special agency like BRL at the end of the programme. This assumes, however, that the regeneration process is complete, and that the area is self-funded and self-managed by community and business organisations. The organisations and their roles over the project period have evolved, but they should not be self-perpetuating, as is the case with too many bureaucracies. In the UK new towns all powers were transferred back to the local councils once the main programmes were complete. In Ballymun, however, I suspect the residents will fear losing the locally based and responsive management they have experienced with BRL. In the case of Ballymun – with its vast scale and the comprehensive town-like systems – there is perhaps a need for a continuing housing and community management organisation constituted on a for-profit trust basis to be the caring estate managers. The responsive and democratic structure that manages the enlarged and matured Ballymun housing stock will be the crucial factor in determining its future, and in ensuring that history does not repeat itself.

SUMMARY

The physical environment of Ballymun is improving, but the community remains socially challenged. BRL continues to identify gaps in the provision of support services, and is developing innovative responses and forging partnerships with statutory and voluntary agencies so as to sustain such initiatives beyond the time frame of reconstruction.

The palpable satisfaction expressed by residents in their new homes is matched at community level with success in the National Tidy Towns competition, which would have been impossible a few years ago.

Ballymun has the most ambitious local authority-commissioned arts programme in the history of the state under the government's Per Cent for Art Scheme. The Breaking Ground programme is providing an 'opening for art in all forms to be made in different contexts and with new publics'. Its four strands of engagement with the community, with the built fabric, and through events and education are already internationally known, and establish new links, a new image and a source of pride for Ballymun.

These goals are being met, but the incremental nature of the development means the interim conditions can look quite chaotic. The puzzle pieces are revealing the bigger picture around Coultry Park, Balcurris Park and Main Street – the latter is, in fact, the sixth community of Ballymun, providing district-wide facilities.

This constant evolution of the masterplan has been managed by BRL's site-based team. Their role goes way beyond project management, architecture and construction programming, because they devise and deliver the 'soft' – and more difficult – non-construction projects that flow from the social and economic agendas.

The most dramatic urban-design achievement is the transformation of the dual carriageway and roundabout into Main Street and the Civic Plaza. The south and north ends of Main Street are in place, but the middle is vacant as demolition of the slab blocks is awaited, together with their replacement by more employment land uses that will contribute to this becoming a real town.

The overall coherence of each neighbourhood has yet to be achieved, and largely depends upon the planned but unbuilt schemes, as well as a maturing landscape and thriving community facilities. Understandably, the current status of construction gives a patchy impression. The challenge for multi-phased projects like Ballymun is that the last phases – the last few pieces of the puzzle that make sense of the picture – must be the jewels in the crown.

Most schemes are of under seventy-five homes, which is a consequence of several factors, such as availability of sites, the phasing of demolitions, the desire for architectural variety, the construction companies' capacity and risk reduction. In contrast, the private sector has no qualms about much bigger schemes being undertaken by a single designer, which can have a profound impact on the diversity of the built form.

Unlike the UK development corporations of the 1970s, where the chief architect dictated the colour of brick and roof tile for each neighbourhood so as to achieve an overall coherence, BRL has been consciously more liberal and encouraged greater diversity, as is the cultural tradition. No doubt for reasons of economics, the prevailing materials are bricks for front facades, with extensive use of render for other features and rear elevations. BRL's in-house landscape team has designed the town-wide palette of hard surfaces, street furniture and soft landscapes.

Design codes could, perhaps, have been useful for each neighbourhood.

New Hall village near Harlow in Essex is quoted as an example of the successful use of codes, but its village green is poorly enclosed by three different architectural styles. As with all design guidance, the outcome still relies upon the maturity of the designers to look beyond their individualistic mark, to tune into the context and to collaborate with each other.

If the construction costs and complexities of inner-city renewal are compared with new-build projects on green-field sites, it is easy to see the appeal of the latter. Councils and those providing funding must appreciate that specific skills and varying budgets and timescales are needed for regeneration, and that the problems to be tackled are usually not solved by new hardware but require the coordinated inputs of other agencies and budgets to enable the community to flourish.

This brief review has been about the hardware of the regeneration. Ballymun's education, training, employment, and community and cultural development programmes are very impressive, and it is these that will deliver the socially sustainable community that new buildings can only host.

NOTES AND REFERENCES

Anne Power, *Estates on the Edge: Social Consequences of Mass Housing in Northern Europe since 1850* (London, Routledge, 1993).
Ballymun Regeneration Ltd, Ballymun Masterplan, 1998.
Ballymun Regeneration Ltd, Ballymun Main Street Development Framework, 1999.
David Prichard, 'On the Edge', *City*, vol. 4, no. 1, 2000.
David Prichard, 'The Importance of Place Making', *RIAI Urban Regeneration Issue*, 2005.
Dublin City Council, *Maximising the City's Potential*, 2007.
Tom Mitchell, 'How to Make Room for Housing', *Architects' Journal*, 13 March 2008.

Metropolitan Workshop is responsible for preparing the recent Adamtown Central urban design with Castlethorn Construction, the Swords masterplan with Fingal County Council, and the Liberties LAP with Dublin City Council and John Thompson and Partners.

Rebuilding Ballymun

Stepping into the Future

ANNE POWER

I first went to Ballymun in 1968 after a year and a half of living in America at the height of the American civil rights movement. I had been living in one of the worst urban 'ghettos' I have seen, on the inner West Side of Chicago – still the most segregated city in the US. My brief involvement in the American civil rights movement, coinciding with Martin Luther King's 'End Slums' campaign in Chicago, shaped my optimism about the human capacity for both altruism and self-help, but it made me realise that degraded conditions could overwhelm the human spirit. I wanted disadvantaged communities in our rich but sometimes brutal Western societies to fare better. Nothing I saw in Britain or Ireland after I returned could compare with the shocking conditions I witnessed first-hand in American inner cities. That formative experience drove my ambition to live in an inner-city community in London and work with local people to make things better.

I had two small children at the time of my first visit to Ballymun, and my sister-in-law invited me to see her work in the area, organising community self-help groups. As a pioneering community worker, employed by the area health authority, she was organising mothers' groups, enlisting fathers and setting up children's play activities in the basement of Pearse Tower. So she took me to see what she was doing with the families. The pre-school play groups, after-school clubs, parental support, mother's gatherings, and networks of friendship and exchange were movingly significant to those involved, but they were dwarfed by the mounting problems and by the threatening and uncared for spaces outside.

When I arrived in Ballymun, I was immediately struck by the pristine conditions, the gleaming white blocks rising sharply – majestically, some said – out of the green plain. However, the efforts of the area health authority to support the several thousand young mothers with small children who were moving in were not a match for the shock that new residents experienced on finding themselves with so much unusable space and so few community supports. It was an alien environment and people were being plucked out of established communities into isolated, separate and dislocated boxes, with few social networks.

The slightly damp and musty smell of new concrete is still with me. The flats in the high blocks stood in stark contrast to the surrounding low-rise homes of outer Dublin, but they also contrasted vividly with the crowded terraces and tenements of inner Dublin that I was far more familiar with, and where more traditional patterns of support still prevailed. Social problems were emerging almost from the birth of the estate, and these mounted in intensity with the passing of time.

We now know that young mothers simply do not flourish in such an alienating environment, and moving people away from 'slums' was a bitter and costly experiment in improving family conditions. Such large-scale building was driven by a belief that there were major housing shortages in Dublin, and that a rapid 'return migration' of émigré Irish families would overwhelm the city – squeezing particularly the poorest and worst housed – as the Irish economy showed signs of picking up.

The dreams of a 'brave new world' were never to be realised in Ballymun as the economy did not recover in the seventies. Irish people continued to go abroad, and the estate quickly became unpopular, hard-to-let and transient, rapidly losing many of its earliest residents in the flats to low-cost owner occupation in subsidised houses. The Irish government had, from its foundation half a century earlier, strongly supported owner occupation, and over 80 per cent of the population, almost regardless of income, already owned their own homes. The government virtually gave away council housing to the occupants even though the state had paid the full capital cost of the homes. Most Irish council tenants seized upon the

Tenant Purchase Scheme – as this concession was called – and, as a result, more council houses were sold than were retained for renting, accentuating the pressures on cheap renting.

Ballymun was to be an exception to this widespread sales policy. Rather than buying council flats, residents were encouraged to accept a 'transition grant' to move elsewhere. Dublin Council, backed by the government, used the increasingly unpopular flats – as they fell vacant – to accommodate vulnerable households that were unlikely to be able to buy. Included in this category were single parents, single homeless people, discharged mental patients and other difficult-to-house and vulnerable groups. Meanwhile, the two thousand or more houses that formed part of Ballymun could be bought under the Tenant Purchase Scheme, and were therefore generally more popular, more settled and less socially polarised.

The Irish government's generous cash grants to help those people stuck in flats – those who could buy and wanted to get a foot on the ownership ladder – created an accelerating exodus from the estate by the more stable families. This opened up the opportunity for housing many more formerly homeless and vulnerable people.

Ireland was more generous and, in a social sense, more progressive than Britain or other European countries in committing itself to rehousing homeless single people. But it failed to recognise the social consequences, imagining that concentrating the groups in need of most support together in a vast, new, unsettled estate would actually work to solve problems, rather than create them. The estate began a slide from which it did not fully recover. It was a social experiment that failed as soon as it began, and I saw this already being played out on that first visit forty years ago.

AN ACCELERATING SPIRAL

By the time I returned to Ballymun in 1980, I had gained ten years' experience in developing community-based housing cooperatives among tenants in inner London as a way of countering slum clearance and as a tool for developing small-scale, street-based, renovated housing for rent. The idea was to retain the old community spirit but to give low-income families the chance to live in a repaired house, and, where there was room, to convert large renovated houses into two or more units. Most alternatives to clearance and rehousing into large, new estates seemed preferable to the loss of community support that was happening in the poorer areas of London and other cities. But building small, self-help cooperatives of low-income tenants was a slow, costly and laborious process, requiring strong commitment. It also required government and community recognition of the significance of small-scale, community-based solutions.

Because of the visible impact and popularity of this work – originating in Islington but quickly spreading to other boroughs and cities, particularly Glasgow and Liverpool – in 1978 I was asked by the British government to help involve communities in the urgent task of turning around the most difficult council estates in the country – some high-rise and gigantesque, but the majority rather standard flats and houses. By the mid-1970s, the British government had realised after a thirty-year period of mass building that clearing 'slums' and building new council estates would not on its own resolve our housing problems. Much more was needed.

The work of the Priority Estates Projects, as the programme was called, ran through the 1980s. It showed that a targeted approach to particular estates immediately made problems more manageable. By adopting a problem-solving approach, we were able to tackle the most serious problems, and reverse some of the worst conditions in some of the poorest estates in the country. Conditions could be transformed by a combination of a local management office with a local repairs team, direct on-site supervision and maintenance of the local environment and common areas, and by the involvement of residents in helping to determine priorities and in developing community resources. Crucial to the success of this method was a dedicated estate budget ring-fenced to meet all local costs while allowing some discretion as to how problems might be solved. We argued for many shifts in practice, including local beat policing, the constant people-based supervision of open spaces, schemes to involve children and young people in upgrading efforts, and special support programmes for mothers with small children and for the elderly.

The Irish government heard about this programme and invited me to come and visit some of Dublin's most challenging areas, including Ballymun.

My revisit to Ballymun under official government auspices was coloured by both the insights I had gained by working with small community groups to develop community-based solutions and, more recently, by a new understanding of large-scale bureaucratic systems. My experience of working directly with the British government and local authorities in large cities exposed to me some of the harshest community problems created by the government's thirty-year obsession with the construction of mass council estates.

My reaction to the Ballymun that I had last seen as a pristine but precarious social experiment fifteen years before was one of shock and even horror at some of the conditions. It was massively run down, poorly maintained and its many common areas were neither cleaned nor cared for. There was harsh graffiti everywhere; spaces were unguarded, uncared for and part of the vast no-man's-land left by the Corbusier 'streets in the sky' design. Lifts, garage doors, entrances and stairwells were worst. I sensed a menacing atmosphere, even though the residents were friendly and anxious to help. The bare, windswept, littered open areas suggested a complete lack of management control. The estate's precarious housing resources were used mainly to shelter people excluded from mainstream society.

The managers in the city council explained to me that the predominance of single parents, single homeless men and psychiatric patients – among them heavy drug users – was driven by the lack of other places to house needy groups due to slum clearance and the closure of old hostels, coupled with the availability of space in Ballymun.

The estate seemed to me to be an impossible social, physical and organisational cocktail, like many mass high-rise estates I had seen all over Europe. But the acute social problems were greatly accentuated by inadequate local management and repair, the unclear responsibility for the large open spaces, and the totally inadequate support for particularly vulnerable people. These local problems were constantly reinforced by government policies and incentives, along with unwieldy government systems and the striking inefficiency of council housing management.

I argued long and hard for a change in focus, in the structure of management and in the attitude to the community. Apologising for my outsider status, I responded to official questions with strong views but without a blueprint. My desire to learn from other countries over-rode my apprehension at speaking out of turn, and I explained as honestly as I could how I saw the situation. In Ireland, the genuine search for answers seemed to come up against a deep-set fear of changing the way things were done.

The truth was that other countries, particularly the UK, were grappling with remarkably similar problems, were confronted with similar blockages and were facing inevitable change. Policy makers and politicians I met around the UK, Europe and the US experienced an almost overwhelming sense of powerlessness in the face of the vast, failed experiment that the builders of social housing had created on the back of the political ambition to fulfil the grandiose dreams of utopian, brutalist architects.

In my meetings with Ballymun residents at that time, I heard about a lack of work, a high turnover of tenants, high crime rates, children not in school during school hours, open drug trading and substance abuse, vice and violence, poor police–community relations, and a deep cleavage between Ballymun's community and the rest of the city. Media headlines did not help, but the estate's residents largely concurred.

Ballymun's reputation as a 'bad and failed place' had spread far and wide. Yet in spite of so much bad news, there were at least ninety known community groups in the estate, and their struggle to make Ballymun better was nothing short of remarkable. The groups were organised and manned by committed tenants and community activists, some of whom had moved to the estate specifically because they wanted to help, but most of whom emerged as leaders from the houses and flats of the estate itself. The groups were drawn from many parts of Ballymun, but some key local leaders lived in the houses.

The groups seemed to involve themselves in every issue, from organising young people's and children's activities to running first Communion dress-making classes, from providing advice on legal rights to fighting for community spaces and community programmes. There was an impressive locally run credit union and an evocative Association of Horse Traders. The driving mission of most groups was to create a 'better Ballymun', which some had as their slogan. The City Council worried about how to reconcile the ambitions of community groups with the daily pressures of problems. It allowed community groups to proliferate without a clear mechanism for responding, other than by providing spaces in empty flats at ground-floor levels for activities, and sometimes by providing funds, very much like the original Pearse Tower initiative.

A deep-set Irish government fear of privatisation hindered the adoption of the British model of estate renewal supported by the Thatcher government. Tenant management, housing associations and cooperatives were viewed as a form of shadow privatisation in spite of their innovative, community-driven, bottom-up style. The community efforts in Ballymun could not overcome the political and bureaucratic hurdles to restoring marginal communities to viability. I left Ballymun and Ireland, shocked by the level of polarisation, poverty and decay that I saw in council housing there. Ballymun and other poor estates of flats and houses I visited stood out in even starker contrast to the neat streets of owner-occupied housing where the majority lived then in Britain.

EUROPE'S NON-PROFIT LANDLORDS

Throughout the 1980s, many European housing practitioners, including visitors from Ireland, came to visit the Priority Estates Projects in the UK. I was shocked to learn that across Europe, mass housing estates – involving seventeen million homes on post-war modern estates – were experiencing similar problems. I decided to visit the places causing so much angst, and learn from their efforts in trying to reverse conditions. Between 1986 and 1993, I came to realise through my European search that local management, repair, resident involvement, reinvestment, security, social investment and physical upgrading all combined into an almost magical 'patchwork' remedy. There was no single solution – rather, multiple solutions had to be stitched together, or 'joined up', on the ground. When this was done, places began to work. Even the most chaotic and decayed blocks could be 'managed out of' trouble with the right inputs.

Ireland provided an interesting contrast with other European countries because of its high level of owner occupation. Also, the Irish government – with its commitment to council housing, and in response to intense community activity that seemed to emerge in disadvantaged estates – was keen to participate in this trans-European 'voyage of discovery' and to learn from it. I recorded my main findings in a book, *Hovels to High Rise: State Housing in Europe since 1850* (1993), which documented the European-wide post-war drive to clear slums and build anew.

Continental Europe, however, adopted very different approaches to social housing than the UK and Ireland. On the Continent, there were diverse providers rather than a single council landlord, resulting in large injections of charitable, trade union, employer, cooperative and private finance delivering many examples of community-based and cooperative structures, but also ensuring a diversity of styles, ideas and outcomes.

Overall, this more varied, more non-profit approach resulted in much more careful management, more investment in repair and a stronger sense of control over social conditions, and worked to prevent the kind of deep polarisation that both Britain and Ireland were experiencing. However, 'strong management' could not alter the fact that all European countries were going through a period of fast social change, with rapidly rising unemployment, inward migration, loss of industry and a growing skills mismatch. These wider trends were accompanied by the rapid growth in lone-parent families, inequality and workless households. One widespread consequence was that youth disaffection, crime and disorder were increasingly concentrated in large, modern, peripheral estates.

Within this broader European perspective, Ballymun was doing badly, but it was not alone in facing extreme decline. Nonetheless, while most European social landlords made concerted efforts to diversify their estate communities and to hold on to better-off in-work tenants for the sake of economic and social stability, Ballymun's problems were accentuated by government efforts to help households that were more established to move from the flats. The continuing priority given to the most vulnerable and marginal households in letting the empty flats simply reinforced the trend towards a lack of viability.

A NEW BROOM

In 1993, following the publication of *Hovels to High Rise*, I came back to Ballymun in pursuit of my quest for solutions to the Europe-wide problem of giant concrete housing estates. I wanted to see how it was faring given that it had seemed one of the very worst estates among the hundred or so I had visited. My Europe-wide survey included four difficult estates from five countries, with one extreme case study from each, where conditions were seriously unravelling. Ballymun became my Irish case study.

The extreme estates in the other countries – France, Germany, the UK and Denmark – were also turbulent, chaotic, dislocated and unpopular within their own context. The patchwork of remedies I had found earlier tackled the physical, environmental, organisational, social and financial problems of these estates simultaneously. Through a multi-pronged approach, social landlords developed hands-on, locally attuned remedies that levered in major reinvestment in the physical structures and environments of estates.

In Ballymun, a serious proposal emerged to pilot the refurbishment of a limited number of blocks in one area, with close resident involvement, strict supervision and a conspicuous upgrading of the environment surrounding the blocks. Although this was expensive compared with the original construction cost of the now thirty-year-old buildings, it was far cheaper than the full cost of demolishing and replacing the concrete flats. It would offer high security, close management, major repair, community amenities and the retention of the close social networks within the established blocks. Residents were closely involved in this experiment, and reported greatly increased satisfaction at the end of it.

The progress of the refurbishment reinforced the belief that a better Ballymun was possible, and that residents were part of the solution rather than the principal cause of the problems, as some had come to see it. However, the experiment was handicapped by outdated bureaucratic restrictions on some essential details of the upgrading. For example, some internal pipe work and roofs were faulty, but neither could be fully replaced for legal and technical reasons. The original contract made the builders, not the council, responsible for replacement of structural and design faults over a thirty-year period. Despite the fact that the builder had long since disappeared into bankruptcy, that the thirty years was almost up, and that the council had failed to ensure the essential repairs over decades, the government stuck to this limiting clause in the contract.

The refurbishment nonetheless produced an attractive environment – more popular, easier to maintain and more secure. Positive resident feedback and staff enthusiasm for the new conditions created momentum for change, and Ballymun seemed set for a makeover that would echo the experience of European partners on similar estates. The groundswell of support for a turnaround coincided with a national surge in economic growth. Ballymun's location near the airport and the housing pressures in the Dublin area led to vastly more radical proposals to demolish the whole estate, literally changing the face of Ballymun forever. Ireland's growing fame as the 'Celtic Tiger' of Europe called for a dramatic reshaping of Dublin's 'eyesores'. Ballymun was emblematic of the poverty, mismanagement and mistakes that the country wanted to leave behind.

A masterplan for rebuilding Ballymun in phased rehousing for all existing residents was immediately popular among tenants, but relied on doubling the number of homes and funding many new amenities. Nonetheless, it proposed a far more humane approach to urban design than the original towers, with their cellular homes.

By 1998, when the grand plan was agreed, no one the length and breadth of Europe would have advocated Ballymun's original design with its far-reaching social consequences. At the same time, there was a strong argument for keeping in place the community that had grown together while fighting for a better Ballymun. It would have been a truly painful, heavy-handed and almost certainly undoable process to replace both the place and the people in a single act of destruction and dispersal. But the 1998 'clear and build' proposals had several intrinsic hurdles to overcome. First, it was pulling in two directions by trying to keep all residents *in situ* while simultaneously aiming to bring about a social and economic transformation of the estate, yet leaving in place the intense poverty of many residents and the accumulation of deep social problems. Secondly, it relied heavily on public funding, and assumed that the transformation over time would attract private investors. Thirdly, it grossly underestimated the actual costs and timescales of a total demolition-and-rebuild scheme, while relying on misleading information about the cost of renovation. They showed the projected cost of rebuilding as lower than the demolition and refurbishment costs of the pilot blocks, yet experience from Britain and Europe, documented in my book on mass housing, *Estates on the Edge: Social Consequences of Mass Housing in Northern Europe* (1998), suggested that these estimates were at best inaccurate.

It quickly became obvious, due to the complexities of the scheme, that the timescale for operating such a complex, three-way process between the city, the community and private enterprise would be far longer than the eight years allowed for by the government of the time and in the original plan. Concerns were brushed aside in the enthusiasm to go for a total solution, another New Jerusalem.

On the other hand, a turning point in this plan was the decision by Dublin City Council (DCC) to create a wholly-owned company, Ballymun Regeneration Ltd (BRL), in order to drive and deliver the complex social, economic and physical investment programme on the ground. Built into BRL's funding plan was the potential to attract private investors as the regeneration scheme progressed, and to reinvest proceeds from increasing land values, new enterprises and the sale or rent of private developments at market rates into community facilities, programmes and support. This gave BRL a strong incentive to diversify the estate, and to bring about social and economic regeneration alongside physical rebuilding.

A BETTER BALLYMUN

Over the ten years since BRL began its work, an enormous amount has changed for the better. At my latest visit in 2008, two thirds of the blocks – including all but one of the highest towers – had been demolished, and only one third remained. Over half of the planned new council housing has been built as replacement homes for existing residents, and the overwhelming majority of the community has opted to stay and win their prize of a new home – the majority with gardens. This speaks volumes for the 'community spirit' that was engendered by the condemned flats.

Many changes have been introduced that are transforming life in Ballymun. A few struck me particularly strongly. Families have gained homes that they can control directly, unlike the exposed communal entrances and staircases of the old blocks. Many new play areas have been incorporated into the small housing developments that make up the new Ballymun 'estates'. An impressive diversity of designs and layouts is being tested with the aim of breaking up the monolithic character of the estate. At the same time, the five original neighbourhoods of Ballymun have been maintained using the same names in order to retain a sense of identity and continuity. Each neighbourhood has its own park, neighbourhood centre, shops and community facilities, generating a sense of belonging very quickly within what are otherwise very new areas. People seem to like the new Ballymun. One resident pointed out that 'it's more like normal streets and neighbourhoods now, with everything a bit different'.

Many social services have expanded: there is now a full-scale police station covering the whole district, sharing an impressive building with the social welfare offices. A community safety strategy is in place, jointly negotiated and accounted for by BRL, DCC, An Garda Síochána and community representatives. About seventy residents come every six weeks to independently facilitated open community meetings with senior staff from the three agencies in order to work through the problems of the community and to hold the gardaí to their commitments. Crime is still a very big problem, and there is a hard core of 'prolific' young offenders who are very hard to reach. But in spite of a spate of gun crime related to gang activity in nearby areas, Ballymun has so far escaped any major incidents.

An innovative activity programme is beginning to attract the young 'hard core' lads away from inevitable trouble. Yet trouble is often etched in their histories, and it will require remarkable staying power and understanding to lift them out of patterns set in their childhoods and family backgrounds. The schools in Ballymun still perform below the national average, and many estate parents send their children elsewhere at primary and secondary level. But this type of activity programme, run in concert with the schools, may limit some of the most acute problems. I was told there is a need to double the number of places available for young people on these programmes.

An ambitious arts centre opened early in the regeneration effort – in 2001 – as part of the new 'town centre', so as to provide a community magnet where children, young people, adults and the elderly could enjoy social as well as artistic activities, offering creative ways of bringing people together in a setting where trained organisers were on hand to help. The axis arts and community centre houses a community café, a two-hundred-seat theatre, a dance workshop, an arts and crafts centre and many other facilities, including the offices of community organisations. Over a thousand people passed through its doors during the third weekend in September 2008.

The theatre pioneers the work of local artists and offers local groups the chance to express themselves. It showcases local, national and international talent, and attracts audiences from all over Dublin who are keen to experience the 'new Ballymun' at first hand. Dermot Bolger, an internationally renowned local playwright, has written a trilogy portraying Ballymun, and this has been performed in the axis theatre to the acclaim of the theatrical community and arts reviewers.

There is plenty of room for expanding and attracting more 'punters', but the record of axis so far challenges the cynical attitude that the arts cannot work for low-income communities. The artistic focus is intensified by

Breaking Ground, the Ballymun Regeneration Per Cent for Art commissioning scheme that champions multimedia, innovation and community engagement. In 2007 the *Hotel Ballymun* project caught the public imagination: the top floor of the Clarke Tower – one of the last remaining tower blocks in Ballymun – opened its doors to the public in the form of a unique short-stay hotel. Commissioned by Breaking Ground, artist Seamus Nolan enlisted the help and support of Ballymun's vibrant network of community groups and worked collaboratively towards the conversion of the former flats into short-stay hotel rooms. Nolan reconsidered the utopian architecture of 1960s Ballymun and encouraged the practice of salvaging and re-imagining objects, spaces and resources from the past and reusing them inventively to meet contemporary needs. He also curated an eclectic programme of art, music, seminars and social events on-site.

Another landmark initiative was BRL's commitment to sustainable development and environmental care. This programme includes collaborative action directed by BRL and involving the local authority and many voluntary projects in Ballymun. It promotes a cleaner, greener area, as well as energy efficiency and best-practice waste management initiatives. A partnership between BRL and the National Botanic Gardens converts food waste from residents' kitchens into usable compost for Dublin's parks, including those in Ballymun.

I visited a community garden created by an award-winning residents' group in Poppintree. This group helps elderly people in warden-sheltered housing to maintain a community garden that is now producing some of its own vegetables. The group also worked with others in local environmental care to the point where numerous National Tidy Towns awards went to Ballymun from 2006 to 2008. I was particularly struck by the furniture recycling workshop: not only saving and reusing unwanted items, but producing beautiful stripped-pine 'antiques' out of old-fashioned junk furniture, and reupholstered 'period' armchairs out of soiled and grimy rejects. BRL hopes to win government support for a new Rediscovery Centre that will bring home to people both the urgency and the beauty of saving the environment.

There are many other experiments in social and environmental sustainability that deliver local services. For example, the Aisling project provides after-school and holiday programmes for children who are vulnerable to pressures and distress at home. Special projects deal with issues relating to substance misuse, more marginalised groups and other social needs. Young people's activities are pulled together in several centres, including the Reco café and youth centre, where over five hundred young people a day are able to enjoy not just fun and games but healthy food and access to learning. The idea of wholesome snacks and lunches – cooked on the premises by a local chef – appeals to both secondary-school kids and to local workers. It is becoming a start-up business as well as a community café, and its wholesome basic meals are delicious.

A groundbreaking collaboration championed by BRL is the integration of advice, legal and mediation services in a partnership between the Community Law Centre in Ballymun, the Legal Aid Board, the Citizens' Information Service and the Family Mediation Service. BRL facilitates the coming together of these groups to offer a service to residents that I believe will provide alternative remedies to legal disputes, assist family cohesion and ultimately strengthen social fabric in Ballymun.

THE FUTURE

There are some strikingly obvious breakthroughs waiting to happen which BRL is considering. One is more sustainable transport. For example, Ballymun, a flat area that is less than a mile across, and only four miles from the centre of Dublin, could be a 'biking town' for the energetic. Safe bike routes have been facilitated throughout the area, all connected to its busy Main Street and the bus lanes into the city centre. Nothing would put Ballymun on the map as a truly sustainable and accessible urban neighbourhood more quickly than this. A protected bike route to the city centre along the inside of the already functioning bus lanes would begin to put Dublin on a par with Freibourg, Strasbourg, Copenhagen and Amsterdam. A full-blown cycling scheme could attract young people, advance the health of the community, and reduce traffic and environmental impact more broadly. It would also create much quicker and cheaper access to opportunity.

The bus lanes have already helped create better public transport links into the city, and the dream of a metro link through Ballymun to the airport is shaping scaled-up ambitions for the next phase of work. More immediate, more deliverable and more environmentally sustainable methods of moving around could be set in motion now, in the form of dedicated cycle lanes and 'fast track' bus lanes.

While Ballymun is now caught on the fringe of an almost gridlocked city centre, with a weak public transport infrastructure, there is room at least to try some cheaper and more deliverable innovations. After all, it was virtual gridlock on London's roads and sardine-like conditions on London's Underground that drove a doubling of cyclists and a big rise in bus passengers in the last few years.

Still to be surmounted are some big social barriers. Attracting more diverse income groups with varying backgrounds and lifestyles into Ballymun is crucial to the public-private balance of the remaining investment to be made. The aim of the regeneration is explicitly to make the area more socially mixed, more diverse and more integrated into the city. At the moment, the new-build areas are still overwhelmingly council housing. It should not be too difficult to make Ballymun more socially and economically integrated, given its location near the airport and its proximity to the city centre. The huge improvements already carried out should make it possible for private renting, and cooperative and co-ownership housing to attract young professionals paying market rents, and for new owner-occupied housing to become much more diverse. Local community representatives support this mixed approach as long as it does not prevent or further delay the legitimate rehousing of all the remaining families on the estate. But it is currently difficult to expand the supply of private housing fast, in part because of the overriding dominance of council housing and also because the economic climate deters investment in new housing.

It is hard to see an easy way forward for the second half of BRL's plan in the current environment, but continuous marketing of the opportunities in Ballymun should eventually prevail over doubts, and attractive facilities and moderate costs should generate new demand. Meanwhile, some of the starkly concentrated problems in Ballymun may be diluted and should gradually filter away with the realisation of a more broad-based community. An IKEA store is about to open here, and this may create a snowball effect as it is extremely conspicuous and considered a real catch. Further plans include a major new retail centre in the heart of Ballymun in addition to the giant IKEA.

WHERE NEXT FOR BALLYMUN?

BRL's impressive achievements will bear fruit over time, but the remarkable progress in Ballymun needs to be buttressed, gradually expanded and consolidated. It may be easier to attract investors in lower-cost unsubsidised housing for 'more average' workers than to try and subsidise these costs through the hope of higher-end and luxury housing that simply may not arrive. Creating more 'intermediate level' housing – affordable housing that covers its costs with a modest margin – would lead to a broader, more workable and more realistic social mix than replicating the extreme of wealth and inequality that Dublin, like London, has witnessed in recent years.

The current climate of cash shortages and lack of confidence in grandiose ambitions raises the vexed questions of the renovated pilot blocks and other remaining flats. Certainly, some of the surviving medium-rise blocks could be refurbished to a high standard both outside and in, and this would make them attractive again. The difference lies almost entirely in the maintenance and repair deficit, the lack of colour, and the intense neglect of the communal areas of the blocks themselves. Seen through builders' and designers' eyes, these remaining blocks, if carefully refurbished, could blend in with the new blocks that have been built along Main Street.

If options that are more flexible were considered, the people living in the remaining blocks should gradually be rehoused into on-site new homes as they become ready, and the remaining empty blocks that are structurally sound should be reassessed. They could gradually be restored, with the ground floors converted into commercial and social enterprises, as has happened in France and Germany. Thus, a more diverse community would flow organically from a mix of building forms, costs, styles, periods and activities, as happens in a real town. The ground has now been laid for a more diversified and flexible approach to regeneration, and while I recognise that these ideas may not win friends everywhere, it is crucial to revisit this question in the light of current economic problems.

Dublin can learn from other cities. Several planned demolitions of 1960s concrete council blocks in the UK have been suspended by developer interest in their conversion to super-modern 'apartments' for both purchase and rent. Urban Splash's flamboyant conversions in Birmingham, Bradford and Manchester have paved the way for recycling monumental and sometimes despised buildings and blocks. In Germany and France, a mix of partial demolition/partial refurbishment is restoring large concrete estates to viability.

The dedicated BRL team has made Ballymun a unique ferment of ideas and activity. It has driven social innovations and supports without which families would fare badly in the current climate. The most urgent next task may be to create a Ballymun management company with Dublin City Council as a major partner and local interests strongly represented, borrowing from the European model of non-profit, arm's-length companies. If all partners in Ballymun's regeneration were to pay proportionately into the maintenance of Ballymun, then the environment and services of Ballymun could be maintained to a high standard and immediate repairs constantly carried out on site. The Ballymun management company could, over time and with the backing of Dublin City Council, take over the management of the new housing areas in order to integrate systems and services on the ground. With close attention to the needs of residents and patterns of occupation, the management company would perform the core task of making Ballymun viable. The current fragmentation of responsibility between BRL and Dublin City Council for local environmental services, management and maintenance, could evolve into the more integrated system of local control and supervision that seems necessary.

The costs, timescales, social mix, essential social and organisational supports, and the imperatives of sustainable development tell us that Ballymun needs a dedicated team, ring-fenced resources and a multifaceted, flexible approach. This comes more easily at arm's length from central bureaucracies. Continuing innovation in management and participation would help Ballymun see through its unique experiment in community development, social regeneration and environmental rescue over the coming decade. It will not be a rapid process, and at least a further eight years should be allowed to deliver the latest and most tricky stages of the plan. The risks in today's climate are enormous because nobody knows the future of the financial markets and the international banking system, nor the future trajectory of energy use and population pressures. But Ireland needs affordable housing, and Ballymun will flourish in the future if this avant-garde project is allowed to 'learn by doing' and adapt to new imperatives.

The Architecture of Ballymun

The Fall and Rise of an Iconic Dublin Suburb[1]

JOHN MONTAGUE

There is a photograph of Ballymun on the Internet with an accompanying caption that speaks volumes about how Ballymun was/is sometimes perceived: 'A Housing Project north of the city: do not go here on foot. This is a bad area.'[2] (Figure 1) The image forms part of a website describing a

Figure I

pilgrimage made to U2 sites in Dublin by an American fan, and is even more evocative of the negative sentiment demonstrated in the text. The digital photo was taken from the back seat of a moving car that sailed swiftly around the roundabout that used to be the inappropriate central hub of Ballymun. We can see the seat-belt strap and the distorted colours of the intensely blue sky through the tinted windows. The iconic and brutal shape of Pearse Tower overlooks and dominates the rest of the scene behind the curving barrier of the roundabout itself. This visitor is not stopping to visit one of the 'Seven towers, but only one way out' referred to in U2's 'Running to Stand Still', but is speeding through the estate with the windows firmly closed.

Of course, Ballymun's reputation for toughness has been happily promoted by some of those who live there. But Ballymun is a sometimes brutal environment that has engendered a brutal response from some of its residents. Over the years, there has been desperation, neglect, violence, despair, destruction. The appearance of the place is evidence of a form of environmental self-harming – with all of the psychological implications – that some children and young adults compulsively engage in. Endless breaking, wrecking and burning is carried out by a minority of the residents on the homes (flat complexes, for the most part) and open spaces of all of the rest of the residents. In terms of the statistics of law and order, this is fairly low-level stuff; it cannot be emphasised enough that only a very small percentage of the residents engage in this destructive behaviour, yet the entire community is consequently stigmatised (Figure 2). The concrete canyon of flats, the stairwells and the lifts are plastered with the signs of fires, broken doorways and windows, and a palimpsest of confusing graffiti: 'Johnner is a scanger', 'MB is gay!', 'If you're reading this, you're gay', 'Moo!', 'Fuller Daryl Dempo Mark 07', 'No cash, no hash. No mun, no fun.', 'Kelly is a tramp', 'Karina is a leasbean'.

Why are things this way? It seems very hard to escape the reasoning that it is the architecture itself that is at the heart of the problem. There is poverty, and the chances of gaining employment in the 1980s and 1990s were compromised by the very stigma of Ballymun as an applicant's address. But poverty alone is not an explanation for this self-harming behaviour. Indeed, during the economic recovery of the last decade, when unemployment rates plummeted, much of this environmental self-harm continued unabated.[3] So what was wrong with the architecture? In the very first place, the vast majority of the population of this country does not live in high-rise concrete flats. Ballymun was marked out as different from its beginning: an iconic ghetto. Its population was a displaced one, removed to the fringes of the city territory from the mostly eighteenth-century tenement houses of the inner city into what were arguably concrete tenements.[4] The severing of the relationship between community and place, and the breach of people's relationships with one another, amounted to a traumatic schism – a disconnection from the past.[5] On the other hand, it is widely reported and remembered that the flats themselves were initially a huge improvement on previous living conditions, and the views over the city, the underfloor heating, the sometimes endless supplies of hot water and the generous size of the flats were things greatly appreciated by the earliest residents. This has to be balanced against the endless maintenance problems, of broken lifts, water mains breakages and other psychologically destabilising irritants for the flat-dwellers in particular.[6]

Some policy decisions also had an effect on the temper and stability of this vulnerable community. Most notorious was the Surrender Grant Scheme of 1985, a nationwide plan introduced by the Department of the

Figure 2

Environment; this affected all local authority estates, not just Ballymun. It was objected to not only by tenants' groups but by Dublin Corporation itself. In a misguided attempt to bring into circulation more local authority housing, a grant of £5,000 was offered to people who wanted to leave council flats and buy their own houses. This seemingly benevolent scheme meant that, for the most part, the best-off and most well-established residents were being encouraged to move out of these estates. Ballymun lost many of its community leaders and those who naturally gave a sense of stability to the area. A report by Threshold (the National Housing Organisation), quoted in Robert Somerville-Woodward's excellent two-volume history of Ballymun,[7] detailed some of the more unfortunate consequences of that policy. Communities where unemployment was high lost many of those people who had jobs. Income levels dropped and services in the area deteriorated. Vacant houses and flats were vandalised. Perhaps the greatest impact on Ballymun was that an already fragmented community now had to deal with the introduction of other marginalised groups. In contrast to the strict selection procedures used for the earliest tenants, Ballymun had now become a 'sink estate'. New residents included vulnerable single-parent families from all over the city and country, single homeless people – many of whom were older and/or unemployed – and 'those with alcohol and drug problems and people with mental illnesses who had recently been released from an institutional environment'.[8] The latter group arrived as a result of the so-called back-to-the-community drive that was popular among psychiatric-care policy makers at this time. Good in principle, without the back-up services it was bleak and depressing in practice: the rows of flats became pigeon lofts for former residents of St Brendan's in Grangegorman and St Ita's in Portrane.

But this article is about, for the most part, the architecture, and it is the relentless, repetitive, unsympathetic quality of the flats that remains at the brutal heart of the social and physical environment of the old Ballymun. This is not necessarily specific to the Ballymun flats themselves, but more to do with the very nature of high-rise, mass-produced, industrially built, local authority estates. Popular throughout Europe from the 1950s, it would appear that such housing complexes were not introduced into this country until this modernist experiment had more or less run its course elsewhere. This, in fact, is not true. The equally problematic Robin Hood Gardens in

London – designed by the Team 10 pioneers, Alison and Peter Smithson – was started after the completion of Ballymun in 1972. The debate about its preservation is a live one. Both architects and social historians argue that it was the use of Robin Hood as a 'sink estate' rather than the quality of the architecture that brought about its failure.[9] It is the belief of this author that there is something inherently alienating about machine-made, modular, repetitive modernist architecture per se. However, much of the valiant thoroughness of social design – integrated playgrounds, social facilities and landscaping – envisaged by some of the 1960s 'new brutalist' pioneers was passed over in the execution of the 1960s Ballymun project.

HISTORY

In the first instance, Ballymun is a slight geographical misnomer, albeit one which predates the construction of the local authority estate in the late 1960s. An examination of earlier townland maps shows that Ballymun was, in fact, a townland north of Santry Demesne, rather than to its south and west, as it is now. John Rocque's 1760 county map of Dublin records a place called Ballymount[10] in this location, as well as a Sillock to its west (again, a good deal north of the current area known as Silloge), with a Poppintree and Ballycurris closer to their current locations. Ballymun may be roughly translated as 'the townland of the thicket' – a kind of lower-grade scrubland.[11] These townlands have real historical significance, as they predate the Anglo-Norman invasion of the twelfth century.[12] The field markings – from which some of the later roads took their shape – often followed the ancient lines of hedges that were in some cases many hundreds of years old. The area in which the local authority housing estate was built remained almost exclusively rural until the 1960s, although some private housing estates had been built to the south and east of the future area, as shown by an aerial view of the planned development taken from the east (Figure 3). The name Ballymun (from the townland further north) had been appropriated to this area before the Corporation estate of the 1960s. It had none of the stigma attached to it that later would lead to its renunciation by the residents of Ballymun Avenue.[13]

The new estate of tall flats came about as an idealistic gesture of the late 1960s, and as a response to a real crisis in social housing. It was intended to be the single-largest housing development in the history of the state. In an

Figure 3

advertisement feature that appeared in the *Irish Press* in 1969, its developers were given the heroic title of 'the to-morrow builders'![14] During the 1950s and 1960s, there had been a considerable decrease in house building both by Dublin Corporation and the private sector, which matched a general downturn in the economy.[15] This compounded the housing shortages and the problem of the massive slums in Dublin and in other towns in Ireland. In 1963, however, two disasters brought about a new sense of urgency. On 2 June 1963 number 20 Bolton Street collapsed, killing Mrs May Maples and her husband John. Only ten days later, two little girls were killed when a building in Fenian Street collapsed on top of them. Here is how it was reported in the *Irish Times*:

> Two children, on their way to buy sweets, were killed by tons of rubble, when two four-storey houses collapsed in Fenian Street, Dublin, yesterday, shortly before 4 pm. The 17 occupants of the two tenements escaped injury, although some of them were in one of the buildings at the time. The two children killed were Linda Byrne (8) of 24 Holles Street, and her inseparable school friend Marie Vardy (9) of 11 Holles Street.[16]

There was a public outcry, with marches through the streets of Dublin exhorting the Corporation to clear out these slums and demolish the dangerous buildings. A declaration of a Dangerous Buildings Emergency forced 900 families and 326 single persons to evacuate. This naturally threw into stark relief the extreme state of the housing crisis.

The Department of Local Government and its minister, Neil Blaney, were drafted in to deal with what was seen as a national problem, not just a Dublin one. Dublin Corporation produced a report that suggested that there was a need for ten thousand new dwellings outside of the normal building programme, which had been running at two to three hundred per year – a fraction of what was needed. Blaney expressed an interest in system building – that is, a kind of production-line prefabrication of building components that theoretically could speed up production and reduce costs. Study trips were made to Copenhagen, Stockholm and Paris. In the end, the governmental National Building Agency was given the task of overseeing the process of finding a contractor who could see the massive project to fruition. A site belonging to Albert College School of Agriculture was purchased from UCD, and was divided in two by Ballymun (later,

Figure 4

Glasnevin) Avenue – the part to the north being for the new estate, and that to the south being set aside for the National Institute for Higher Education (Figure 4).[17] The portion north of Ballymun Avenue – approximately 212 acres – was an awkwardly shaped site divided in two by the Ballymun Road – an ancient northern highway – that ran past Dublin Airport in the direction of the Naul in north County Dublin. By far the larger portion of this new area was to the west side, and with the later addition of lands in Poppintree, this disparity between east and west in the present Ballymun is even greater.

In July 1964 a decision was made to build three thousand new dwellings at Ballymun. Submissions were sought from interested and qualified parties. This was to be a mixed development, though predominantly of flats, the maximum height of which was to be fifteen storeys. Astonishingly – given what emerged – the avoidance of monotony was emphasised. Five distinct communities with attendant facilities were to be designed. Silloge, Balbutcher, Balcurris, Coultry and Shangan. Each was to have 'a focal point of community and as much individuality and character as the system allowed'.[18] There were eighty-nine submissions, from all over Europe, the UK and Ireland. Thirty were shortlisted, and these were in turn whittled down to six. Criteria included a proven record at system building – very rare in Ireland at this time – and a definite Irish component. In November 1969 the contract was awarded to the three-company consortium of Cubitt Haden Sisk. Cubitt had experience in the two proprietary systems of flat and house building that were to be used. Haden was an engineering firm with an office in Ireland, and Sisk had been building houses in Ireland since 1949 and had a proven track record, which included the construction of Liberty Hall, then the tallest building in the country.

Two separate construction systems would be used for the building of the flats and the houses: the Balency et Schuhl system for the flats, and the Lowton–Cubitt system for the houses. The house system was developed by Lowton Construction Group Ltd, which was based in Warrington, Lancashire. The technique was relatively new, and its primary feature was that the roof trusses, the roof and the first floor could be supported on metal frames that covered and protected the works below them. Most of these homes were up to 960 square feet – or 90m^2 – much larger in area than the standard Corporation house. These were five-room houses, designed in different plans to accommodate different family sizes and types.

The Balency et Schuhl system used for the flats had been developed by the French firm of that name, and was used under licence in England and Ireland by Holland, Hannen & Cubitt. Based on automobile manufacturing, the plant for the production of the precast elements of the new buildings was located north of Ballymun, where Musgrave's was later built (Figures 5, 6 and 7). As can be seen from the archive photographs, the factory had sections of open roof that facilitated the removal of the prefabricated concrete sections for the new building. These pieces were hoisted by cranes from the moulds on the factory floor onto trucks which transported them the short distance to the site. Note the massive moulds, which, when the concrete was dry, tilted and opened to facilitate the removal of the sections. One of the real advances in this method was the way in which the services were integrated into the moulded sections. These included vertical technical blocks containing the plumbing, water supply, gas pipe work and the vertical heating mains, as well as the mechanical ventilation ducts. The floor slabs contained the heating coils and electric wiring. This system method was to make the construction of the flats much cheaper than would have been the case had they been built on-site by traditional means. The later cutbacks regarding installation of planned amenities in the area suggest that the savings were not as intended.

The system approach – which seeks to build with as few components as possible, and for as many as those components to be repeat components – led to the anonymous, repetitive appearance of the Ballymun flats. By definition, these 1960s buildings lacked a human touch – that is, the *trace de la main* advocated by Peter Rice in his important work on the usually overlooked role of the engineer in the design and humanising of architecture.[19] These buildings were consistent with the machine aesthetic of mass-produced, planar and undecorated elements that were part of the visual language of the international style. A previous generation of architects in Ireland had subscribed to modernism – with some degree of grace – and their work was more commonly associated with public buildings such as schools and hospitals. Among their better buildings was the nearby Collinstown (Dublin) Airport, designed by Desmond Fitzgerald and the Board of Works. Generally, the emphasis was on flat-plane, horizontal designs, with white walls, strip windows, and a stoical casting-off of what

Figure 5

Figure 6

Figure 7

was seen as the decorative baggage of historical styles. This distillation of what was essential, and a renunciation of the ephemeral, could, in the hands of lazier or less-talented architects, lead to terribly monotonous, albeit righteous, ugliness.

None of this emerged, of course, from a vacuum. The 1950s and 1960s saw a host of flat complexes for social housing being built in the UK. The planning and architectural ideas of the French modernist genius Le Corbusier were a central influence. The use of rough-cast concrete by August Perret and, later, Le Corbusier – known to them as *beton brût* (raw concrete) – was an early source for a later style of architecture aptly titled 'brutalism'. Corbusier's Unité d'Habitation – a high-rise apartment complex in Marseilles – was a case in point. It combined Corbusier's ideas of huge, single monolithic structures for multiple dwellings, and which utilised the crude type of raw concrete. A brilliant concrete monoblock on gigantic fin-like stilts, the detailed internal planning of the ingeniously interlocking apartment units in the Unité, with single and double-height internal spaces in every flat, and views to both sides of the building – among many other innovations – were generally overlooked by other architects and planners, who gladly subscribed to the mass-production convenience for the construction of often monstrous buildings. These included the repetitive, modular concrete Robin Hood Gardens in London (1969–72) by the architects Peter and Alison Smithson – members of the breakaway modernist group known as Team 10, which was noted for the austerity and single-mindedness of their 'new brutalist' works – and the notorious Hutchesontown Area C high-rise complex designed by Sir Basil Spence in the Gorbals in Glasgow.

Arguably, these are buildings programmed with intellectual and aesthetic – as well as good – intentions. But issues of maintenance and lack of facilities were not the only reason that these complexes failed. There is the sense of alienation engendered by the unsympathetic quality of the materials themselves, as already alluded to. A more fundamental problem can be found in what might be termed 'vertical communities'. Gaston Bachelard, in his *Poetics of Space*,[20] speaks of the consequent lack of rootedness in dwellings that do not reach the ground, as it were:[21] 'In Paris there are no houses, and the inhabitants of the big city live in superimposed boxes. They have no roots and, what is quite unthinkable for a dreamer of houses, skyscrapers have no cellars. From the street to the roof, the rooms pile up one on top of the other, while the tent of a horizonless sky encloses the entire city.' Ironically, despite the exterior height, apartments are generally confined to horizontal compartments, so that the traditional choreographies of indoor life are diminished by the absence of storeys and their different domestic meanings: 'Home has become mere horizontality. The different rooms that compose living quarters jammed into one floor all lack one of the fundamental principles for distinguishing and classifying the values of intimacy.'[22]

The fact of people stacked in separate horizontal a(com)partments one on top of another brings about another type of problem not outlined by Bachelard: this is to do with the lack of passive surveillance, the well-meaning watching-over that takes place between neighbours. If you can never see your neighbour, your sense of security is undermined. It is an aspect of social psychology that we address one another eye-to-eye on the level. Living in such intense proximity requires a form of unspoken social contract. People naturally watch over their neighbours' behaviour as well as their property, and in this way some kind of social order is preserved. If you cannot see your neighbour, because s/he is stacked somewhere unknown, and unseen, above your head or below your feet, your sense of security is automatically undermined. When you hear a scream in the night in a normal arrangement of dwellings, you look out of your window, across the street, into someone's garden, in search of the disturbance – a light on, a car window smashed, and so on. In a block of flats, the cry could be coming from anywhere below or above. It could be a cry of ecstasy or joy, of fear, of fun, of desperation, but from where no one can tell. To find out, you have to risk entering the communal street of the stairwell and shared front-balconies[22] from which there is no retreat, no direct route to an outside open space. All of this can lead to fear and insecurity, as well as an unwillingness to get involved, with the consequent effect on community. In turn, this insecurity is compounded by the impermanent nature of occupancy common to the Ballymun flats, especially since the 1980s, as described already. You very often do not know your neighbour, or, at least, many of your neighbours, despite the fact that you share so much space with them: stairs, entrance, lifts, open ground.

The other most common type of vertical community in modern

societies are prisons. The sleep-inducing effect of the under-floor heating,[24] the numbing effect of heroin, hash and alcohol addictions, the encircling wall around the whole estate, and the Panopticon-type[25] design from the roundabout to the five areas of the estate all gave Ballymun some of the qualities of a low-security prison. In the days of the poor bus service and huge unemployment rates, many in Ballymun stayed in their flats all day, and never got much further than the shopping centre.

Returning to the issue of concrete *brût* buildings themselves, it should be pointed out that much more satisfactory work was carried out in the UK and in Ireland, but these tended to be high-status cultural commissions, such as Ahrends Burton and Koralek's Berkeley Library in Trinity College Dublin (1961–7) and John Johansen's American embassy in Ballsbridge (1962–4). However, it was from a less imaginative working through of the modernist vision that the conception for the Ballymun flats came about. The architects were Arthur Swift and Partners, a Glasgow firm that had previously designed the uninspiring Glasgow bus station, which included a fairly tall building of concrete interrupted by an anonymous grid of apertures for the windows. Why, it might be asked, were Dublin Corporation's own architects, or, indeed, a more sympathetic native architectural practice, not involved? The developer-led design approach advocated by the government as a means of saving money forms only part of the answer.[26] Photographs of the original models for the Ballymun flats survive, and even in what must have represented an idealised projection – judging from the oversized trees – one finds it hard to be bowled over (Figures 8 and 9). The model of the proposed fifteen-storey tower shows two rectangular-planned sections joined at the centre by a service and circulation shaft that included the two sets of stairs and two lifts. The eight-bay facades on either side included a balcony for each of the six flats on each floor, alternating with two pairs of two windows, and a single window on the end. The modular, or repeating design, had all the effect of a vertical ratchet, and resembles closely the completed buildings as they survive today (Figure 10).

In terms of the overall plan for Ballymun, the proposed shopping centre was to have been the single unifying object at the heart of the town. Since the construction of the shopping centre in Coventry as a replacement for the medieval town lost during a severe German bombing campaign in the

Figure 8

Figure 9

Figure 10

Second World War, these ready-made town centres also represented a quick-fix solution to the problems of so-called new towns. These once-off, ready-made, covered town spaces were a much more practical means of bringing a commercial and civic infrastructure into place at the lowest cost and at the quickest rate. However, being built as a single unit – in this case, in the same drab concrete clothes of the flats – the shopping centre lacked the character and interest of towns that had emerged through historical process. Another important planning principle for Ballymun was the separation of roads and footpaths into two independent systems. As befitted the futuristic mood of the time, Ballymun was envisaged as a motor-age town. To facilitate this, vehicular and pedestrian routes were to be separated – an idea that found its source in Radburn, New Jersey, which was built as a new town in 1929. This explains why so many of the roads in Silloge in particular – the first area to be constructed – have no footpaths along them.[27] This results in the sometimes alarming experience for car drivers of mothers walking with push-chairs and buggies on the road. The town was also to have been an important visual statement of Ireland's modernity, as viewed by visitors landing at nearby Dublin Airport (Figure 11). This was to be read from the sky, as Michael Scott's shamrock-shaped Irish pavilion was in New York's 1939 World Fair. An aerial image (of the original

Figure 11

59

designers' model) shows this to be neither visually arresting nor particularly legible. The design consisted of two broad C-shapes back to back, with the ring of the seven towers around the shopping centre in the middle, alongside the second, and confusing, centre of the roundabout to its east. Finally, perhaps the only locally meaningful tag given to the flats was the naming of the seven towers. Following closely on the heels of the 1966 fiftieth commemoration of the 1916 Rising, each was given the name of one of the seven signatories to the 1916 Proclamation: Thomas Clarke, James Connolly, Eamon Ceannt, Pádraig Pearse, Joseph Plunkett, Seán McDermott and Thomas MacDonagh.

PRESENT REDEVELOPMENT

There are those who make important arguments against the Irish and English 'addiction' to house-with-front-and-back-garden dwellings, and speak of the advantages of the European model of city apartment living. In terms of the advantages of high densities and the consequent positive effects on the delivery of services, not to mention the negative effects of the untrammelled urbanisation of the Irish landscape, the need for increasing densities is a compelling argument. But Ballymun was always a high-rise, low-density estate. The regeneration was possible because of the huge, open, poorly managed prairie lands between the flats, which were to leave ample room to build houses for all the flat-dwellers *and* to increase the densities. European apartment complexes are effective for a variety of reasons, none of which are present in Ballymun, nor, indeed, in many of the new developments in inner-city Dublin. There is a social tradition in Europe of living in towns in medium-rise apartment complexes that are well served with amenities and which feature the types of security features not present in the Ballymun flats in particular. That there was a need for these things was illustrated by the introduction in the early nineties of the concierge system into Balbutcher Lane and Joseph Plunkett Tower, as a first experiment in regeneration. Street-level doors with buzzer entry systems (operable from each flat) were introduced,[28] and the 'internal streets' of balconies and stairwells were 'semi-privatised', with all of the increased sense of security that this implied.

There can be a balance between the need for increased densities and a pleasant housing environment that does not involve high-rise mono-block flats. The early-twentieth-century Dublin Corporation scheme at Church Street, designed by the Dublin city architect, C.J. McCarthy, combined just such a high-density approach 'built to a traditional urban pattern of streets and squares in a familiar and legible way'.[29] Some aspects of this more compact *urban* pattern, rather than the 'Garden City' *suburban* one of the needlessly expansive but innovative Marino,[30] are currently being attempted in the present regeneration of Ballymun.

One of the most potent lines of argument that had been made by some of the already housed residents of Ballymun against the regeneration – that is, the housing of those still in the flats – was that all of the green spaces in Ballymun would be lost to the new houses. From the point of view of area covered, this was for the most part true, though there will be three reasonably large and newly landscaped parks with new play and leisure facilities, as well as a series of small 'pocket parks' in the new estates.[31] However, the former green areas were not green spaces as we like to think of them: benign, health-enhancing havens such as the Phoenix Park or St Stephen's Green. For the most part, they were nothing more than land left behind between the flats – covered in grass for sure, but by little else. Poorly tended and unregulated, these areas left little opportunity for children to hide, to make huts or to draw on anything that might define their play. All human interaction – be it child's play or adult's – has been given form, if not generated, by the spatial definition given by architecture. Citing such examples as the agora in Greece, the forum in Rome and the piazzas in later Mediterranean cities might sound high-blown, but the effect of the absence of spatial definition can be viscerally demonstrated by a look at an aerial view over the east side of Ballymun taken just before the regeneration began (Figure 12). Here, we see a single, vast open space, greater in size than six or seven football fields, without hedge, rock, path or wall, or any other defining man-made or natural features other than the great cliff-like sweep of the spine blocks of Coultry Road. Into this, every day, spilled the children of over five hundred flats, and here they attempted to eke out some kind of individual, separated play space. During the summer, the intimidating scale of what was, after all, one single space drove all but the toughest indoors. The rest kept their heads above water in the packs that dominated the scene. Unregulated, unsupervised – the parents were generally multiple floors removed from the scene – over a long summer,

Figure 12

anarchy could escalate to a *Lord of the Flies*-type frenzy. It is no wonder that countless parents in the Ballymun flats kept – and keep – their children indoors or on the front balconies when not in school.

However, almost as if in a dream, a decision was made that all of this architectural and planning misery was to be radically changed. Blown away and replaced. Regenerated. This regeneration is well underway, having begun in earnest in 1998 with the development of the masterplan and its carrying out in the years since then. The details of this, and how the decision was made, will no doubt be treated in greater detail elsewhere in this volume. What surprises, from a resident's point of view, is that such a radical proposal seemed to be entertained at all, never mind decided upon. These kinds of bonanza-like decisions just did not happen. Many residents laughed at the final question in the periodical surveys that asked whether they wanted this, that, or another thing – or last, whether to just blow up the whole lot. It appeared like a cruel, sardonic joke because no such thing would ever be entertained. No one in the Corporation thought so, either. For sure, groups such as the Ballymun Housing Task Force[32] and others had campaigned vigorously for the renewal and restoration of the flats for many years. Their most important success before the regeneration was, arguably, the experiment in refurbishment that took place in the flats of Joseph Plunkett Tower and Balbutcher Lane, together with the upgrading and landscaping of the areas outside. However, the appearance of structural cracks almost immediately after work was finished, and the continued danger of falling concrete, contributed to the surprising decision to demolish all the flats and to replace them with houses.[33] The 1993 Craig Gardner Report on the works in Balbutcher Lane and Plunkett Tower – and options for the future – noted that the cost of demolishing the flats and replacing them with new houses and apartments would be some £15 million cheaper than a complete refurbishment of the existing buildings.[34]

Whatever about the rhetoric in the masterplan and, since then, about a community-wide participatory design process – which at the start was based only on a number of open days and questionnaires – an ambitious plan was nevertheless put in place that has real meaning and a vision for the future of Ballymun.[35] In the first instance, the roundabout[36] – the then meaningless hub of the town – was to be replaced with a real main street formed by domestic, commercial and civic buildings facing directly on to the street on either side. This was to be founded on a civic plaza instead of the vehicular roundabout and dual carriageway of former days. The dark and unsavoury underpasses were done away with. The reduction in the widths of the carriageways and the median, as well as other traffic-calming measures, put some manners on the car. The dowdy, run-down shopping centre was to be replaced by a real town centre, with flagship retail units, restaurants, cinema and bowling alleys. Alone among all of the ambitions, this has met with the least success to date, although negotiations between interested parties and the City Council continue. On the other hand, there have been some notable successes, with the early introduction into the centre of the town of axis – the theatre and community resource facility – followed by the splendid Civic Centre and a new hotel. These form two sides of a triangular plaza that will be completed by the new town centre when it is built. On the other side of the road, a brilliant new swimming pool and leisure centre – with a curved roof and glass wall to the street – was a bonus not originally envisaged in the masterplan. All of this gave a human scale to the centre of the town, where the resident pedestrian was given some equality with those in cars, who previously were mostly passing through.

Arguably the most important success was the creation of a host of new neighbourhoods and micro-neighbourhoods, with a colourful and invigorating variety of houses. Each of the five Ballymun areas – represented by the former flat conglomerations of Coultry, Shangan (on the east side), Silloge, Balbutcher and Balcurris, and Poppintree (on the west side) – were to have their own dedicated community facilities within neighbourhood centres. These buildings incorporate meeting rooms for the five neighbourhood forums and other groups, and offices for the delivery of services, as well as small neighbourhood shops. These are backed up by currently ongoing development of the three larger parks (Coultry, Balcurris and Poppintree), as well as the completion of a number of pocket parks distributed around each estate. This decentralisation was a very positive first step, and represents an important balancing against the dominating effect of the depressing shopping centre, with its two notorious super-pubs, numerous betting shops and chemists, and dowdy supermarket.

Most ambitious of all – and that which has, perhaps, caused most problems in the micro-management of its delivery – is the very large number of architectural schemes that were commissioned for the houses. Instead of the traditional approach of a once-off and endlessly repeated single-house design spread in endless multitudes – as in former local authority housing estates – no single scheme in the new Ballymun was to be much greater than approximately one hundred houses. In turn, each of these schemes was founded on a great variety of house types.

Although some of the houses respond to the not-unexpected demand from the flat-dwellers for a traditional type of house – with pitched roofs, chimneys and fireplaces, and front and back gardens – there are also a number of schemes of modernist approach, with flat roofs and deeply cut square apertures set in white or coloured rendered walls. Throughout, the emphasis has been on colour, and on a variety of textures and materials, profile and heights, within and between different schemes. A very fine and much envied group is the housing estate at Woodhazel, with its sympathetic use of a warm ochre brick, varnished-timber detailing in the high-quality doors and windows, deep overhanging eaves, and metal-grilled balcony surrounds. Here we see Rice's *trace de la main* – that is, the visual evidence (or trace) of human craftsmanship that was so absent from the machine-made rough-cast concrete of the flats. This is architecture on a human scale. There are the numerous nooks and crannies; ideal for children's play on a smaller and more individual plane, with places to make little huts or play hide-and-seek and kick-the-can, or the small make-up games of fantasy that had become so unusual in the overpowering spaces around and beneath the flats.

Another signature scheme – one which fulfils literally the desire expressed by many of the flat-dwellers for houses of traditional appearance – was that designed by BRL architects in Coultry Way (Figure 13). A vernacular, or Dublin-type, of garden-city design common in some of the smaller Edwardian streets in, say, Ranelagh, with continuous high-pitched roofs and tall chimneys, and angled brick courses under the eaves interrupted by projecting gabled bays to the streets, all linked by overhanging tiled porches, given a wholly new appearance by brightly coloured pastel renders of purples, yellows, lime green and red ochres, and generous squared timber windows. A recent photo shows the degree to which these have been settled into by the earliest of the new Ballymun residents, bedded-in with plants and creepers, and even finished off by

Figure 13

latticed *faux* shutters around the windows by one enthusiastic resident (Figure 14).

The delivery of all this has been painful for many – residents and practitioners alike. Never before has such a large-scale building site been developed while the residents remained *in situ*. This is one of the most noble aspects of the regeneration, and puts a stop to the old pattern of moving the problem to some other location on the outskirts, and thus breaking up communities once again. This necessarily causes great discomfort, however. Some moved into their new houses within a year or so of the publication of the masterplan. Despite the terrific progress, however, many others continue to languish in their flats ten years later, while a host of unanticipated delays have held up the overall completion of the project. There is also a variety of quality in the new houses, which is only to be expected given the desire for a variety of design. Some residents have had to move into smaller premises than they had previously occupied in the flats, although in general the internal planning of the new houses and apartments is a vast improvement on the flats that are left behind in terms of effectiveness and comfort, as well as in actual floor area. Some

Figure 14

neighbourhoods work better than others, and there is a difficult bedding-in period for nearly all those who moved from flats which had continuous heating and hot water, and easily accessible and low-responsibility garbage chutes. There are others long since housed in the older Ballymun who must watch on as the flat-dwellers are housed in spanking new dwellings, and while the environment of some of the older estates continues to stagnate. All have had to suffer, too, under the enormous infrastructural development that took place over the first five or so years of the development, when all of the streets were undone and rebuilt. Almost nothing that was established from the past was to remain, and this caused understandable discomfort to many. Old routes and well-beaten paths disappeared overnight.

Despite the apparent slowness of it all, the rate of progress and radical transformation is nonetheless remarkable. We have had the experience of seeing computer simulations of the new Main Street turn into almost identical reality within a short number of years. What seemed like fantasy images of new housing estates bear startling comparison to their built realities, which followed on very quickly after the plans (Figures 15 and 16). This appeared interminably slow for those who had to trudge through the dusty and mucky paths and stretched and obstructed routes from home to bus stop, shop or work. In the greater scheme of things, however, the change has been a relatively speedy fulfilment of something that only ten or more years ago none of the residents could have hoped for. Indeed, it is hard to believe that the Edward Hopper-like photograph by BRL's Eamonn Elliot of the new Civic Centre is not one of its earlier computer simulations, when it is in fact a real-life photograph taken of the completed Main Street (Figure 17).

CONCLUSIONS

Much of the chronology of the early development of Ballymun, and some of the ways the utopian dream unravelled in the 1970s and after, has been outlined by Sinéad Power,[37] and by Anne Power in a chapter in her book on European social housing in the twentieth century.[38] A good deal of work remains to be done on the details of the 1960s development itself, as a seminal and iconic, albeit failed, architectural and planning project, as well as the historical and planning circumstances by which it came about. All of

Figure 15

Figure 16

the original plans and construction drawings, for example, have been retained.[39] An argument may, indeed, be made for the preservation of at least one of the blocks – most obviously, the last standing of the original seven towers (Joseph Plunkett Tower) – as historical artefact, although all of the issues connected with its suitability as housing remain. Important work also needs to be done in documenting the long and turbulent history of the countless community groups and individuals who stood up and voiced the concerns of residents against the backdrop of systemic, if not cynical, neglect.[40] A more forward-thinking attempt at community participation has been attempted since the onset of the regeneration, and with mixed results. A much more human and, for the most part, open approach has been taken. However, in some cases, the 'yes' to requests and the agreements between residents and officials that are *not* followed through or delivered upon can be even more frustrating than the answer 'no' – or simply no answer – of former years.

Finally, the experience of living through the regeneration, while frustrating for many, is a constant source of pleasure and excitement for a resident interested in buildings and stimulated by visual and spatial change,

Figure 17

Figure 18

Figure 19

as much as it is for the boy inside him who wonders at big yellow diggers, cranes and other oversized mechanical toys. An overlooked visual wonder of the place is the elusive archaeology of a complex and fleeting present. Because many of the new buildings are being constructed alongside those that remain but are scheduled to disappear, there are extraordinary views of combinations of buildings that will last for only the shortest of times. It is a thrill to capture and record some of this kaleidoscopic wonder as it comes into being and just as quickly disappears (Figure 18). There is also the sculptural abstract quality of what is left behind: the weathered and stained Balcurris flats before demolition, or the extraordinary innards of the towers as the front walls of the hundreds of former flats were peeled away by the crunching machines to reveal the dayglo honeycomb of lived lives within (Figure 19). Finally, there is a sense now among the regenerated and the nearly regenerated that we can commit to something that we think will last. The move for most, after spilt tears, is a really joyful thing. In the summer months, the new houses quickly become a wonder of colour with flush new gardens and hanging baskets. It is a wonder to think how we will get on at all when it is over. When there is no more regeneration, we may all be bored out of our minds!

NOTES AND REFERENCES

1   This article came about as a result of a paper given by this author at *Hotel Ballymun*, the art installation by artist Seamus Nolan in Thomas Clarke Tower before its demolition. I am grateful to Seamus for the opportunity. Thanks are also due to Ellen Rowley of Trinity College Dublin, who read an earlier version and made many useful suggestions that have been incorporated into this article. However, all errors or any bias in interpretation are the responsibility of the author alone.
2   http://u2exit.com/u2audio/u2dublin/images/ballyflats.jpg (viewed 6 May 2008). The injunction not to go to Ballymun has been crossed out but maintained, showing a very fair historical progression in the development of the website and of Ballymun.
3   It might be argued that many are on low-paid jobs, and that a hardcore of long-term unemployed people has been missed by the recent rise in the economic circumstances of the country. Nevertheless, a lift in many people's financial circumstances in Ballymun has been evident, and has certainly raised the mood on the estate greatly; that, and the prospect and unfolding of the regeneration.
4   As Tom Baker ironically narrated in the pilot episode of the BBC TV series, *Little Britain*, 'Working-class people in Britain are stored in buildings like these.'
5   'Arguably, the only major achievement of "planning" in the city was to decant the

former working class to the periphery, out of sight and out of mind. The pattern of extended family relationships that sustained people during the worst period of slum-dwelling in the inner city was broken and, although the quality of housing was better, it is already clear that this dislocation represents a sociological timebomb.' Frank McDonald, 'Ireland's Suburbs' in Annette Becker, John Olley and Wilfried Wang (eds), *20th-century Architecture: Ireland* (Munich & New York, Prestel, 1997), pp. 49–53.

6   Ballymun is made up of both high-rise flats – 10 four-storey spine blocks, 19 eight-storey spine blocks and 7 fifteen-storey tower blocks – and houses, the latter built over the years in a series of phases as the estate has expanded.

7   Robert Somerville-Woodward, 'Ballymun: a History, *c.* 1960–2001' (unpublished report for BRL, Dublin, 2002), pp. 149–52.

8   Ibid.

9   Richard Rogers and Anne Power, 'Estate of the Art', letter to the editor, *Guardian*, 20 June 2008, http://www.guardian.co.uk/artanddesign/2008/jun/20/architecture.housing (viewed 18 August 2008).

10 Rocque was a French Londoner who made a few errors in transcription, and we can safely assume that it was Ballymun to which he referred.

11 Thicket being 'a dense growth of shrubs, underwood, and small trees': *Oxford English Dictionary*, 2nd edn (Oxford, Oxford University Press, 1989).

12 Thomas McErlean, 'The Irish Townland System of Landscape Organisation' in T. Reeves-Smyth and F. Hamond (eds), *Landscape Archaeology in Ireland* (Oxford, 1983), pp. 315–39; Robert Somerville-Woodward, 'Ballymun: A History, *c.* 1600–1960' (Dublin, unpublished report for BRL, 2002), p. 4.

13 Some time in the 1970s, the residents there changed their street to Glasnevin Avenue so as to escape the negative connotations of the Ballymun flats.

14 *Irish Press*, 31 July 1969.

15 A good deal of the historical background in the following three or four paragraphs is founded upon the second volume of Robert Somerville-Woodward's excellent and extensive unpublished archival report, 'Ballymun: a History, *c.* 1960–2001', op. cit., and upon Sinéad Power, 'The Development of the Ballymun Housing Scheme, Dublin 1965–1969', *Irish Geography*, vol. 33, no. 2 (2000), pp. 199–212.

16 *Irish Times*, 13 June 1963.

17 The National Institute of Higher Education later became the present Dublin City University.

18 Sinéad Power, 'The Development of Ballymun', op. cit. p. 204.

19 Peter Rice, *An Engineer Imagines* (London, Artemis, 1994), p. 63, *passim*.

20 Gaston Bachelard (translated by Maria Jolas), *The Poetics of Space* (Boston, Beacon Press, 1989), pp. 26–7.

21 The building from the exterior obviously reaches the ground, but each horizontal apartment does not.

22 Bachelard, *The Poetics of Space*, op. cit.

23 In Ballymun, what in other contexts are known as 'streets in the sky' are comprised

of short landings of between four to six flats, without access to the full range of exits and openings that normal streets enjoy. It should be acknowledged here that the 'streets in the sky' designed by the Smithsons – who coined the phrase – were much more extensive, and gave access to a greater part of the complex.

24 Like those who live in an institution, people in the flats have no (thermostatic) control over their own heating: they can equally swelter under an oppressive winter sun (with the heat on full blaze) or freeze on a windy day during the period of the summer when the heating is ritually turned off for the whole season.

25 The Panopticon was a prison designed by Jeremy Bentham in the late eighteenth century, in which a series of wings were built like spokes of a wheel around a central hub, from which all of the corridors to all of the cells could be monitored from a single location.

26 Sinéad Power, 'The Development of Ballymun', op. cit. p. 204.

27 Ibid. p. 209. The Radburn principles were jettisoned in the later phases of the development.

28 I have been told by one of the earliest residents of Ballymun that all of the stairwell entrances originally had very fine timber doors. These were all robbed out of the neighbourhood – even before the new flat-dwellers first arrived – to be used as fancy garage doors. Not one of these original doorways has survived in any of the flat blocks.

29 Eddie Conroy, 'Centre and Periphery: Housing in Ireland' in Becker, Olley and Wang (eds), *20th-century Architecture: Ireland*, op. cit. pp. 55–9.

30 Marino was laid out and built by Dublin Corporation in the late 1920s.

31 At the time of writing, much of this landscaped amenity is already in place or under construction.

32 Earlier known as the Ballymun Task Force, and in recent years as the Ballymun Neighbourhood Council. It produced, among other documents, a comprehensive proposal for the renewal of the flats themselves in July 1988: 'A Programme of Renewal for Ballymun: An Integrated Housing Policy'.

33 At the time, this was to have been confined to the 7 towers and 19 eight-storey spine blocks, but was later extended to the four-storey spine blocks.

34 Somerville-Woodward, 'Ballymun: A History, *c.* 1960–2001', op. cit. pp. 186–7.

35 The *Masterplan for the New Ballymun* (BRL, Dublin, March 1998) was created by the architects in BRL in consultation with MacCormac Jamieson Prichard, and O'Mahony Pike Architects and Urban Designers, alongside a number of other consultant landscape designers, urban economists, community development experts, and town planners, among others.

36 The roundabout in Ballymun was built around a deep basin crater of walkways – part of the Radburn planning separation of pedestrian and vehicular traffic. It had been excavated at the time, and the earth was transferred to the south where a great hill separated the main road from the houses being built in Sillog(u)e Gardens. On top of this was a piece of randomly commissioned art, known locally as 'Stonehenge' for its menhirs and modernist concrete lumps that the children climbed all over and older ones scored drugs in. When the regeneration project sought to refill the roundabout

crater, builders took the earth from 'Stonehenge' back to where it had come from. The new Gateway red-brick housing estate – with its two patinated copper and glass (gateway) towers standing guard over the entrance to this new modern town – was built there in its stead.

37 Sinéad Power, 'The Development of Ballymun', op. cit. p. 204.

38 Anne Power, 'Portrait of Ballymun, Ireland, 1966–95' in Anne Power (ed.), *Estates on the Edge: The Social Consequences of Mass Housing in Northern Europe* (London, Macmillan, 1997), pp. 240–65. Another important recent assessment can be found in Ellen Rowley, '*Hotel Ballymun*: A Site for Reflection in the Heady Days of Regeneration', *Architecture Ireland*, no. 228 (June 2007), pp. 66–9; Mark Boyle and Robert J. Rogerson, 'Third Way Urban Policy and the New Moral Politics of Community: A Comparative Analysis of Ballymun in Dublin and the Gorbals in Glasgow' (Strathprints, University of Strathclyde Institutional Repository, March 2006), http://eprints.cdlr.strath.ac.uk/681/ (viewed 22 July 2008).

39 Housed in the National Archives, this large body of material has yet to be assessed in any detail.

40 A successful oral history project has been sponsored by BRL and is ongoing.

Driving the Vision of Regeneration
Six Themes for a Sustainable Ballymun

JOHN TIERNEY

Urban regeneration programmes have been a significant element in Dublin City Council's development strategy since the early 1990s, and have contributed greatly to the reappraisal of many parts of the city as attractive and vibrant places to live and work. The process of urban renewal goes back much further than this, however, and can be seen as an ongoing concern in the city's development since at least the establishment of the state. Among the city's most significant 1930s architecture, for example, are the social housing projects of the south inner city. Recently restored, they were part of a slum clearance programme that would, for much of the last century, be the determining factor in the council's intervention in the historic core of the city.

The modern idea of 'urban regeneration' signifies much more than specific site redevelopment. It is an integrated programme of social and economic interventions encompassing government, local authority and private investment. The idea of regeneration is both reflected in, and supported by, many of the developments that have taken place in our society since the early 1990s. It has been underwritten by the prosperity and population growth that puts new demands on the urban environment, by a social consciousness that supports opportunities for disadvantaged communities, and, of course, by the simple recognition that many quarters of our city had fallen into serious states of disrepair, and required creative strategies to revitalise them.

UNIQUELY AMBITIOUS

Even in the context of a pervasive culture of renewal, the regeneration of Ballymun must be reckoned as uniquely ambitious and distinguished in its scope. It is widely acknowledged as the largest project of its type in Europe, and its remit to transform an area of major disadvantage was confronted by a distinct set of challenges. Not least of these is the fact that Ballymun, only forty-five years ago, was a green-field site peripheral to the city centre, and therefore possessed none of the more obvious advantages of an 'old city' brown-field site. But the very scope of the challenge has motivated all who have been involved in it from the very beginning. It has presented all stakeholders – government, Dublin City Council, Ballymun Regeneration Ltd (BRL), and the community, among others – with the rarest of opportunities: a project with the potential for a legacy on a grand scale, and the prospect of transforming a community beset by disadvantage by putting it on course for an empowerment that will yield positive dividends for generations to come.

With so much construction work taking place throughout Dublin over the last decade, the sheer scale of the regeneration process has been, perhaps, easier to underestimate than it might otherwise have been. Were it a stand-alone town, Ballymun – with a projected population of thirty thousand in 2013 – would be one of the largest in the country. Yet it has been built – or rather, rebuilt – from scratch since 1998. But Ballymun is, of course, not a stand-alone project. As Dublin City Council aspires to support this newly confident community and celebrate its achievements over what has easily been the most exciting decade of its history, its role and its relationship with the Greater Dublin Area (GDA) are at the forefront of our considerations.

Suburbs are frequently defined by what they are not rather than by what they are. Seen as neither the country or the city, they are visualised, at their simplest, as an 'in-between' space, a holding pattern of dwellings at a distance from the major resources of the centre, with a quality of life provided for by access to the city centre and a satellite network of public spaces. The popular perception of the suburb can be best summed up by the title of the classic novel by Milan Kundera, *Life is Elsewhere*. But successful suburbs defy so cynical a description. Most have, particularly in the Irish context, a traditional village or town centre at their core. Though it may appear to have submerged its identity into the greater urban whole, the local centre remains a hugely important nexus of community engagement – one that is consistently renewed in a changing economic and social context, and providing the sense of autonomy that is critical to a positive sense of identity.

The lack of such a community focal point was well attested to as being central to the failure of the original Ballymun project, and, from the beginning, it was recognised that creating a viable town centre would be one of the great challenges of regeneration, and that only by a multi-disciplined approach would it succeed.

INTEGRATION

The purpose of this essay is to locate the regeneration strategy of Ballymun within the context of the emerging development strategy for the city in general, and, in particular, to assess it against a new measurement index now being used for development projects taking place in Dublin. In benchmarking Ballymun in this way, our aim, very explicitly, is to highlight the connectivity between the new town and the older city, and to celebrate what is a critical juncture in the evolution of both. A strong relationship between the part and the whole is not a 'bonus feature' of the development process but is critical to it. We have, thankfully, left behind an era when quick-fix solutions to the issues of marginalised communities had currency.

And it is well to remember, from the outset, the context in which the histories of Ballymun and Dublin are intertwined. Though the suburb was built on the periphery of the 1960s city, its population belonged to its centre. There are many ironies in Dublin's history, but none greater than the fact that the streets and squares designed to house its most privileged citizens in the eighteenth century would, soon after, become cells of misery for its most disadvantaged. Well into the 1960s, tenement life continued in Dublin as it had in the nineteenth century, with shocking levels of deprivation. When the government was finally persuaded to construct a new place to accommodate tenement dwellers, it did so with little regard for even the most basic amenities.

Given the opportunity regeneration presents, our obligation is to recognise that a sustainable community is an engaged and connected one – its vision, its objectives and its ambitions are in harmony with the city to which it belongs.

THE SIX THEMES

While it is generally recognised that the mistakes of Ballymun occurred in the context of poor planning decisions made across Europe at the time, this should not mask the significance of local factors, particularly if they are still a cause of concern in 2008. It is a simple fact that planning for Dublin's future has not been an explicit part of government policy. There is no government department designated to consider the needs of Dublin, or, indeed, any of our cities. The thinking has doubtless been that Dublin, as a natural concentration of wealth and resources, can 'take care of itself', but the failure of this approach is amply demonstrated by under-performance in many critical areas of urban planning. So the time has come for a rethink. The GDA is, by virtue of status and population, of extraordinary importance to Ireland. It is the country's only economic region with international standing, and as the Irish economy enters more uncertain times, the need for a strong Dublin to drive economic growth has become more important than ever. This role should not be seen as a competition for resources with the rest of the country but, rather, as a competition with other city regions of the world. Dublin's successes are the successes of the entire country and its economy.

The onus is on local authorities to take responsibility for planning growth and development. Historically, they have been criticised for not doing this as well as they could, but many issues are beyond the control of the local authority. The complaints generally follow a familiar pattern, and centre on what might be called 'lack of vision'. One of my priorities when working with the elected members is to develop a holistic and sustainable approach to the future development of Dublin – one that can be benchmarked according to a variety of critical factors. The future Dublin – a place we aspire to make a vibrant, compact and creative city – demands a new approach; one that will, I believe, make the planning and development process much easier to understand and to communicate. Already, this approach has facilitated a more open discussion with councillors, developers and the public about what development is being proposed, and how individual projects fit into the city of the present and the future. This holistic approach is governed by six themes that are best visualised in the form of a circle (see Figure 1). Later in this essay, I will explain in more detail the policies and strategies by which each theme is explicitly supported, but for the moment it is enough to say that each signifies a vital element in the city's well-being, and that it is only by their relationship to each other that their optimum value is realised.

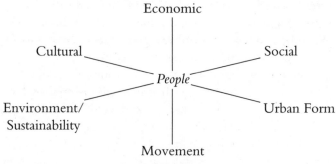

Figure 1: The six themes

All development and framework development plans produced by Dublin City Council are now proofed against the six themes, and in the case of major planning applications, developers are asked to do the same.

ASSESSING THE MASTERPLAN

The masterplan for the regeneration of Ballymun was published by BRL in 1998. As befitted a project of such scale, it was an extensive and ambitious programme, informed by wide-ranging consultation with the local community and representatives of business, education and politics.

A review of the masterplan was undertaken in 2006. The aim was twofold: to assess whether the regeneration was fulfilling its objectives according to the themes of sustainable development as set out for the GDA, and, if not, to ascertain what interventions were needed to address any shortcomings in a timely and focused way.

The outcome of this process was, I am happy to note, an extremely positive one. The strategy of Dublin City Council and the approach to regeneration taken by BRL were seen to show a great deal of concordance. The review process found that BRL had demonstrated, from the beginning, an integrated and multi-disciplinary approach to urban regeneration – one that was flexible enough to adapt and develop according to new inputs and best available advice. BRL was supportive of the analysis process, and sought to address issues that were raised in the review.

THE ECONOMIC

Though I have described the six themes as holistic and integrated, it is no accident that prominence is given to the economic. A community that is not economically sustainable has no foundation on which to build any of the other positive elements of its identity. This is true on both a macro and micro level, and one of the most obvious consequences of not focussing on Dublin as an economic powerhouse for the county is the lack of an integrated economic strategy for the region. Dublin City Council is now addressing this issue, and working towards an economic strategy for Dublin.

At a more local level, our framework development plans serve an additional function as economic drivers, encouraging, where possible, economic niches to develop in particular areas. Temple Bar is the most obvious example of success in this regard, where a thriving community lives side by side with an economic hub that focuses on cultural services. The Retail Cores Plan is another initiative, designed to ensure that Dublin city centre retains its pre-eminent position as the country's prime retail area.

The economic aspect of Ballymun's regeneration presented particular challenges from the beginning, as there was little historic context to work within. Geographically, the suburb's key strength is its proximity to the airport and its connection to the M50, but a range of barriers have prevented it in the past from taking full advantage of its location. Tax incentives and the Integrated Area Plan, implemented under the Urban Renewal Act 1998, were among the first measures employed to attract private investment and to kick-start the local economy. But the masterplan recognised that economic development could only happen through addressing underlying social concerns. It was important to ensure the new opportunities were shared equitably, and that local people affected by long-term unemployment were equipped with the skills needed to re-enter the market. Equally, it recognised that if Ballymun was to integrate within the broader GDA economy, employment opportunities should attract newcomers, too.

Infrastructural developments were also identified as a priority, and the masterplan bears the hallmarks of close cooperation with local transport authorities. An assessment of these initiatives are set out in the 'Movement' section of this essay.

The opening of the state's first IKEA store, expected in mid-2009, is a further positive, and will ensure a great many new visitors to the suburb, as well as creating many new local jobs. However, it is the economic activity in the fabric of the new town that will fundamentally drive and sustain this local economy. The particular emphasis put on Ballymun Main Street mirrors Dublin City Council's own vision for centralised, street-focused shopping districts, and a great deal of work has gone into creating a diverse and attractive environment. Main Street is today home to two hotels, a 324-bed-space student accommodation hall, a state-of-the-art leisure centre, axis arts and community resource centre, civic offices, a primary-care health centre, a new garda station, social welfare offices, a money advice centre and a nursing home. Over five hundred private apartments and a range of new retail units have also been created there. In 2009 the redevelopment of the shopping centre will commence in conjunction with the Metro station, and will further accelerate retail development on the street. Ballymun's challenge is to create a hub of economic activity that makes the best use of its location and the new accessibility projected for it. The attraction and generation of new businesses is a process that will grow by its own momentum, but Dublin City Council is satisfied that the groundwork and supports necessary to provide an attractive level of services and real employment opportunities have been put in place through the masterplan.

THE SOCIAL

As Dublin grows into a more culturally diverse city with a higher population, the social aspect of urban development is one for which focused and dedicated planning becomes increasingly important. A series of projects have been developed to support the framework planning process in this regard, including Making Neighbourhoods and Access Dublin – the newly established integration unit. Dublin City Council is also placing a huge emphasis on sport, arts and culture as mechanisms for building communities and supporting natural integration from the ground up.

Building strong communities is clearly a greater challenge in some areas than others. Across Dublin, there are housing estates and social housing complexes – often in fantastic locations and supported by strong local amenities – that simply have not integrated into the broader community in the way they should have.

One of the most difficult obstacles to overcome in the process of social regeneration is mindset – the expectations we acquire from our surroundings and which influence our interpretation of them. As advocates of urban regeneration, we need to be particularly conscious of this issue. The mindsets of the communities we work with need to be understood, but, equally, the expectations and understanding derived from our own backgrounds are relevant. If we are using the tools and resources of urban planning to change lives and help people realise their full potential, we must be conscious of the unspoken expectations we bring to the task. This involves constant reappraisal of our approach.

The social dimension was, from the very beginning of the Ballymun regeneration process, recognised and interpreted in the broadest possible sense to include housing, education, health and recreation facilities. It was also understood that new resources and new facilities could not be considered complete without programmes to support their maintenance in the long term.

In 2003 a further community sustainability strategy was developed to promote innovative ways of tackling ongoing issues in the community, and BRL is currently reviewing and renewing the social strategy to identify priorities for action and targets that need to be achieved over the remainder of the programme.

EDUCATION

The provision of high-quality childcare facilities and services was identified as being of particular importance in Ballymun, and BRL has provided a mentoring and business development service to childcare providers. It is also carrying out research to calculate the number of childcare spaces required as Ballymun grows and prospers.

The masterplan sought to identify ways of enhancing primary and secondary education in Ballymun, and, recognising that many adults in the area are at an educational disadvantage, has forged an active partnership with the National College of Ireland and with local training agencies to support adult education opportunities.

More recently, partnership with DCU (Dublin City University) has ensured that the university provides a third-level-access centre in the area. This is combined with outreach activities, and is geared to enhancing third-level participation in the Ballymun area. A partnership approach is also being adopted with the VEC (Vocational Educational Committee).

SPORTS AND LEISURE

Access to sports, leisure and recreation facilities are important for all communities, and throughout the regeneration process, the emphasis has been on the development of programmes that engage the widest possible section of society. A particular challenge – though not exclusive to Ballymun – is the use and respect of recreation facilities and spaces by young people. The development of social capital in the form of volunteering and other levels of participation offers a further means of integrating the community, and a series of initiatives to enhance this process will follow from the Dublin City Council review.

HOUSING

In building homes for thirty thousand people, the creation of a strong, safe and sustainable community is an overriding priority. Among provisions identified as necessary are more facilities for special needs, and housing for the elderly, homeless and other vulnerable communities. Partnerships with agencies such as the Health Service Executive and the Homeless Initiative will be further developed in the coming years, and the ability of the voluntary housing sector to respond to special needs will continue to be facilitated.

SAFETY AND WELL-BEING

The masterplan identified safety as a quality influenced by many factors, including urban design, estate management and individual and group behaviour. Policing and local government are the twin agencies with responsibility for a safe Ballymun. With the assistance of local residents, BRL has led the development of an action-based, problem-solving, agency partnership approach. A community safety forum called Safer Ballymun has sought to achieve reductions in levels of crime, environmental crimes and anti-social behaviour, and to facilitate improvements in area management. A three-year community safety strategy is currently being implemented with the active support of the community. This year the strategy was awarded the Taoiseach's Award for Excellence in Public Service. Further supporting the safety agenda, a town–wide CCTV system will provide real-time monitoring and supervision of the five neighbourhoods and the town centre, and is planned to be operational by the end of 2008.

The social and community objectives set out in the masterplan have been, and will continue to be, achieved through creating a framework for actions that offer an attractive 'buy-in' for the community. Success in this regard is, perhaps, the fundamental benchmark by which the quality and achievement of regeneration of Ballymun will be judged in the future.

THE CULTURAL

The cultural wealth and services of a city are now widely acknowledged as important measures of value not just for tourism, but for the quality of life of those who live and work within that city. Dublin has a rich cultural legacy, but is rich, too, with possibilities of further development. The city boasts one of Europe's most successful examples of culture-led regeneration in Temple Bar, and there are many more initiatives being progressed. The Parnell Square plan, for example, has already developed the Hugh Lane Municipal Gallery into a world-class facility, and, close by, the old Ambassador cinema will soon provide a worthy home for the city library. At local level, the framework plans now facilitate much greater interaction with developers regarding the cultural elements that should be in place as part of planning proposals.

The opening of the axis arts and community resource centre in 2001 fulfilled one of the central objectives of the Ballymun masterplan, and it is now a thriving centre of excellence for arts and cultural activities. Its engagement with the business community has recently been recognised at the Allianz Business to Arts Awards, where its artistic director won the Champion of the Arts category.

The Breaking Ground Per Cent for Art project, launched in 2002, supports arts projects undertaken by local, national and international artists in Ballymun. Like the axis arts centre, it has been distinguished by attracting artists of excellence in a wide variety of media, and also supports the broadest community participation. These cultural resources have played an important role in changing outside perceptions of Ballymun; and both the potential for the arts in the area, and the community confidence and self-esteem engendered by engagement with the arts have been shown to be considerable.

THE ENVIRONMENT

Sustainability is a buzzword of our time, but the issues behind it are very real. Carbon emissions and the protection of the environment are concerns that require awareness and changes of behaviour at individual and community level. Dublin City Council is currently developing a project called Sustainable Dublin. Starting with a period of review in which every aspect of our operations will be examined, it will develop into a more dynamic interaction with the community and with relevant agencies in the city. Dublin City Council estimates that 4.23 million tonnes of carbon dioxide are emitted in the city each year. To reduce this to an acceptable level will entail profound changes in practice and technological innovations, together with the development of renewable energy sources. Our Climate Change Strategy and Energy Action Plan will assist in driving the necessary change.

As part of our strategy, we are also demanding much better energy performance from the new buildings we provide, and we are prioritising prevention and recycling in waste management. Our objective is to see over 50 per cent of domestic waste in Dublin being recycled by the end of 2009.

It is testament to the farsightedness of the Ballymun masterplan that the environment was a strong focus for action from the beginning. Of course, there were practical reasons for this, not least the sense of civic pride that good public maintenance cultivates. To date, Ballymun has won some twenty-eight environmental awards, including five National Tidy Towns category awards.

Environmental action must be a community-led activity, and BRL has encouraged ownership of the area's environment, and liaises directly with Dublin City Council and its partner, Global Action Plan, in developing action-based, results-orientated community programmes. Furthermore, Ballymun's contribution to sustainability is now expressed in the innovative environmental features of its new homes. These have been praised by environmentalists as leading the way on sustainable living not just in the Irish, but in the European context. A renewed energy and environmental strategy is being developed with funding received under the European Union Image programme.

A local five-year biodiversity plan aligned with the Dublin City Biodiversity Action Plan is also underway, while an innovative new waste management facility, the Rediscovery Centre, is being developed in partnership with Dublin City Council's engineering and waste-management departments. Currently awaiting approval from the Department of the Environment, Heritage and Local Government, this is envisaged as a civic amenity site, a resource recovery centre and an educational facility that will demonstrate excellence in waste prevention, reduction, reuse, recycling and recovery. Supporting it, a number of pilot projects have been established, including a furniture and paint recycling scheme and a community composting project; a further opportunity to give 'destination Ballymun' a national profile, it is also important as a current and future opportunity for community employment, and has been selected and accredited as a Discover Science Centre under the National Discover Primary Science initiative.

As Dublin City Council prepares to engage in a new and far-reaching conversation on sustainability issues – issues that will impact on every community and individual within the city – the developments in Ballymun are playing an important role in advancing the engagement process and thereby providing a template for other communities in Dublin and beyond.

THE URBAN FORM

As Dublin grows, it must develop into a more consolidated city. Our research has shown that high-density, mixed-use urban areas are the most sustainable means of supporting this growth, and have been the focus of recently developed government guidelines in spatial planning.

A compact city is a connected city and a competitive city. It can sustain its character and support a creative economy, thereby providing jobs and building strong local communities.

Dublin is currently a low-density city, which has been rightly criticised for the extent of its urban sprawl. As we move towards new solutions to deal with this, the issues of height and density will become central to the debate. Recognising the concerns many have about raising families in apartments rather than houses, Dublin City Council has adopted a policy entitled *Achieving Liveable, Sustainable New Apartment Homes for Dublin City* (2007). The alternative – of continually extending the commuting miles of our population – is simply unsustainable, and for an increasing number of reasons.

The physical redevelopment of Ballymun, on the surface, appears to run counter to this theme. The most obvious and striking manifestation of the project was the demolition of a total of 36 of the fifteen-, eight- and four-storey-flat blocks which were, for many, the epitome of urban deprivation in Ireland. However, the original design of Ballymun had little to do with the urban form needed to sustain viable communities. Unsupervised and poorly utilised public spaces, a lack of civic and social resources, and the sense of segregation felt by those living in the tower and spine blocks all contributed to an environment that was not socially viable.

The masterplan recognised that healing the scars created by a dysfunctional urban environment required the development of neighbourhoods where buildings, functions and spaces related to each other in an understandable way and on a human scale. However, a sustainable density of housing was also a key objective. It is now recognised that a minimum of fifty units per hectare is required to keep shops, buses and other local facilities within walking distance of one another in urban communities. While densities vary throughout the regenerated Ballymun area, a direct correlation is maintained between density and the support for facilities such as shops, schools and community facilities. Along Main Street, densities of at least one hundred units per hectare are being achieved, and these have been recognised as appropriate to Ballymun's designation as a 'prime urban centre' in the Dublin city development plan for 2005–11.

NEIGHBOURHOODS

The new urban form of Ballymun now connects the previously separate neighbourhoods of the town. Each has its own centre, designed at a higher density than the surrounding residential layouts, and accommodating services and facilities with accessibility in mind. Architecture and urban design bring a distinctive sense of character to each neighbourhood. Communal areas have been minimised through the provision of separate entrances at street level, and, supporting the community strategy, the rental income from the shop leases is retained locally as a subvention for the running costs of public buildings. Dublin City Council is encouraged to see that approximately 15 per cent of the new social units provided to date have already been purchased under the Local Authority Sale Scheme.

A great deal of thought has gone into creating spatial experiences that will meet the recreational needs of all age groups: urban squares, parks, sports and recreational facilities of different sizes and character. It takes time for such spaces to mature and to fully fulfil their function as community resources, but Dublin City Council believes the regenerated Ballymun will convincingly answer the question about the relationship between open space and urban density.

MOVEMENT

One of Dublin's biggest and, certainly, most debated challenges relates to transportation. The number of vehicles in Dublin grew by 93 per cent in the period from 1990–2005. Aside from the pressures of congestion, the cost to the environment is an increase of 170 per cent (1.1m tonnes) in CO_2 emissions over the period. So we need to develop a more compact urban form, not only to shorten journey time but to make the car increasingly redundant as the urban transport of choice.

When Transport 21 is implemented, the impacts in the GDA are estimated to be as follows:

- 175 million extra public transport users by 2016;
- 75 million extra suburban rail users;
- 80 million extra LUAS/Metro users.

People will be able to travel from the city centre to the airport in seventeen minutes, the length of Quality Bus Corridors (QBCs) will be doubled, and a number of major park-and-ride sites will be established on the periphery of the city.

A key objective of the masterplan was to bring greater connectivity to Ballymun, recognising that a well-developed transportation infrastructure is fundamental to fuelling and sustaining economic growth. The masterplan and Integrated Area Plan highlighted the strategic resources available to Ballymun: the M50, the M1 corridor, and proximity to Dublin port (through the port tunnel) and the airport. The provision of a Metro line in Ballymun will transform its relationship to both the city centre and the airport, and can be expected to play a major role in stimulating public and private investment in the area.

Internally, important improvements have been made to the road network to such an extent that little evidence of the old road plan now remains. The old Ballymun roundabout was eliminated, Main Street was narrowed and new junctions were added to connect the five neighbourhoods. Significant traffic-calming measures have been put in place, and safe parking is provided with all housing units. Neighbourhoods are now much more easily accessed from Main Street, and neighbourhood traffic has slowed greatly, enhancing the sense of safety for residents in each area.

BRL is continuing to work with Dublin Bus and the community to improve bus services in the area. Improved connectivity and permeability throughout Ballymun have helped address many of the isolation problems experienced in the past, and will be an important driver for the future prosperity of the town.

CONCLUSION

The creation of a truly sustainable urban area was the central objective of the BRL masterplan unveiled in 1998. It recognised that a blueprint for physical redevelopment was not enough, and that urban regeneration depended on the integration of economic, social, environment, cultural, and urban form and movement elements. It is a strategy that has evolved with the support of Dublin City Council, and has benefited from ongoing policy and operational interventions. Further supported by the integrated and holistic approach Dublin City Council is now applying to planning issues, I am confident that we have a road map for future development, and a project whose outcome will be greater than the sum of the parts. As Dublin grows and develops, the lessons from the Ballymun regeneration project will also provide valuable templates for the future development of other communities.

I would like to congratulate BRL and the Ballymun community on their achievements on the tenth anniversary of this project. There are many elements of the masterplan yet to be implemented, but I believe we can speak with confidence of a sustainable community with the resources to shape its own destiny, which will contribute richly to the cultural fabric of Dublin now and in the future.

The Greening of Ballymun

Promoting Gardens, Gardening and Nature Conservation in
Ballymun as an Essential Part of Urban Renewal

PETER WYSE JACKSON

Shortly after I was appointed director of the National Botanic Gardens in Glasnevin in 2005, I was invited to visit Ballymun to help judge the gardens competition that had recently been launched. This was the beginning of what was to prove a productive partnership between the National Botanic Gardens and Ballymun Regeneration Ltd, and which continues to develop today.

My first impression on visiting Ballymun to assess the gardens was one of surprise that there were so many of them. This was not the urban desert that perhaps I had been expecting. Instead, I found a small but thriving local gardening community. We visited the different parts of Ballymun – Balcurris, Coultry, Poppintree, Shangan and Silloge – and assessed around fifteen gardens each year for what became an annual event. Ballymun does not have a long history of involvement in gardening, and so finding keen gardeners in the area was a considerable pleasure and eye-opener.

The purpose of this essay, therefore, is to outline not only my own ideas about what gardening can contribute to community regeneration, but also to suggest ways in which gardening in Ballymun and elsewhere can help to make our environment more sustainable. Some aspects of the work of the National Botanic Gardens in Glasnevin are discussed, as these may provide helpful guidance for Ballymun. The close links that have developed between the National Botanic Gardens and Ballymun Regeneration Ltd are also detailed. My own concerns about plant conservation, the promotion of native plants and environmental sustainability are also considered.

HISTORY OF GARDENING IN IRELAND

In discussing the development of gardening in Ballymun, it may be useful to touch on the history of gardening in Ireland in general, as this will provide a context for the topic of gardens in Dublin's urban setting. Ireland has a long history of gardening. Some of the earliest gardens in Ireland were probably those associated with Christian monastic sites in medieval times, where those living in the monastic community would grow a wide range of food plants and herbs, needed not only to supplement their diets but also to provide a source of medicinal herbs used to treat a wide variety of ailments. In more recent centuries, gardening in Ireland has been most often associated with large estates and the 'landlord class', where extensive pleasure grounds, walled gardens and designed landscapes were laid out, in some cases tended by dozens of gardeners.

Gardening around the more humble homes of tenant farmers was much less developed, and essentially consisted of subsistence farming and raising plants for food, thatch, cash and other utilitarian purposes. Plants needed for medicine were, by and large, collected in the wild. Plants grown for decorative and ornamental purposes were few and far between – a luxury that few were able to afford. For small farmers, all the land they had that was suitable for cultivation was used for crops. I have a very old and small country cottage in County Kerry that I use for holidays. When I bought it, I wondered about recreating the garden of this semi-derelict property. However, a local man reminded me that right up to the 1950s, all the land around the house was cultivated for growing potatoes, almost to the back door. My cottage, like so many small country houses, never had a garden. The traditional cottage gardens often associated with country cottages of rural England were not a typical part of the Irish countryside. In Ireland's larger towns and cities, gardening was more or less a preserve of the middle and upper classes, who could afford to hire gardeners and labourers to look after their gardens and estates, and to create decorative gardens, vegetable plots and fruit orchards surrounding their suburban houses.

Gardening in Ballymun has not, in general, come from a continuing tradition passed down from parents to their children. It is much more recent in origin – discovered as a pleasure and new hobby for many residents, and nurtured as part of Ballymun urban renewal. As noted by Simon Cocking,

> Due to the regeneration of Ballymun, many residents of flats are now moving into new houses with both front and back gardens. For a large percentage of these residents this was the first opportunity to have a garden. For several enthusiastic residents of these new houses their dream was to make their own gardens beautiful and to help their new neighbours to do so too.[1]

Gardening for pleasure has been encouraged throughout Ireland during the last few decades, as people have had more leisure time and disposable income to spend on plants, patios, garden furniture and decorations, and conservatories. There is now a great range of gardening programmes on television, and there are plenty of gardening events, such as the annual Bloom gardening festival held in the Phoenix Park, and the many new displays at the National Botanic Gardens. All of these developments help to encourage a growing interest in gardening and make it an accessible hobby for anyone.

WHY GARDENING?

During the Middle Ages, it was believed that human origins were to be found in the garden, a place where the weather was forever mild and flowers and fruits were everywhere abundant – the original Garden of Eden. Despite the biblical flood that Noah escaped in his Ark, the Garden of Eden was thought to have survived somewhere in the world.[2] Throughout the fifteenth and sixteenth centuries – the Great Age of Discovery – many explorers thought they could rediscover the Garden of Eden, and it was generally thought to be in the tropics, where the plants and forests grew all year around. As the sixteenth century came to a close, no authentic Garden of Eden had been rediscovered, and people began to think of recreating 'paradise' through the garden. Early botanic gardens were created in Europe, and exotic plants flooded into Europe from around the world, stimulating and supporting the development of major public and private gardens.

Many writers in the past have written about how gardening is an expression of an unconscious desire to create a paradise on earth –

recreating one's own Garden of Eden. Some of the earliest botanic gardens in Europe were created in the late Middle Ages not only to grow useful plants (particularly for medicine – the earliest botanic gardens were associated with universities and used for instructing students of medicine), but also for their religious and spiritual significance. Almost four hundred years ago, the founders of the Oxford Botanic Garden, for example, described its purpose as 'the glorification of God and for the furtherance of learning'.

It is worth therefore reminding ourselves of why people like to garden. Many people find it therapeutic and it helps them to relax. Unconsciously, perhaps, people are attempting to create their own Eden. Others find that gardening can be very good exercise, too. The ability to grow plants can be very satisfying: raising plants from seed, and bringing them through the seedling stage to flowering and fruiting; growing plants from cuttings; growing, harvesting and eating one's own produce from the garden. Creating a space around the house that is beautiful can be very rewarding. The best and most passionate gardeners are those who are driven by an emotional love of what they do, rather than by the practicalities of keeping the area around their houses neat and tidy.

Some years ago, I was involved in a simple survey enquiring of people why they liked to garden. These were some of the answers I received:

'I like to grow my own vegetables and herbs for the kitchen.'
'I have created a place of peace and tranquillity in my garden where I can block out and forget the busy urban life I have to lead most days of the week.'
'I am interested in plants and wanted to grow a range of plants I have seen on television from around the world.'
'I garden because I like to have a tidy and neat plot around the house.'
'My garden is a place where we like to sit and entertain family and friends, especially having a drink in the evening or weekend barbecues.'
'Because gardening gets me out of the house into the open air.'
'I love roses and love having my garden full of colour.'

Above all, people like to garden because it is a pleasure. Creating a garden is part of making one's own space, a *sanctuary*, away from the other cares of the world.

PROMOTING GARDENING IN BALLYMUN

Gardening and improving the nature-based environment in Ballymun has been recognised as a priority ever since the earliest days of work in the regeneration of the area. The new *Biodiversity Action Plan for Ballymun*, published in 2008, notes that the regeneration plan will provide 6,856 dwellings of which 4,400 will have gardens.[3] People who live in a beautiful environment are much more likely to care for and appreciate it than those who live in a bleak urban environment without green spaces, gardens and natural areas. The work to promote and improve the gardening landscape and the urban environment in Ballymun through regeneration and schemes such as the Garden Action Team initiative is greatly to be welcomed. A key element of the success of this work has been in helping to ensure that many more homes in Ballymun have space where people can create their own gardens and grow plants. The Garden Action Teams have provided a selection of plants (trees and shrubs) to new householders to encourage an interest in gardening. It is a very significant achievement in Ballymun that now almost all of the gardens of new houses have been planted. The *Biodiversity Action Plan for Ballymun* notes that a good selection of shrubs that attract and support wildlife are being planted in these gardens, such as species with berries like hawthorn and *Pyracantha*, which attract birds, and ones rich in nectar to feed insects, such as lavender.

THE BALLYMUN GARDENS COMPETITION

Participating in the judging of the Ballymun Gardens Competition has given me a wonderful opportunity to visit and appreciate many attractive little gardens throughout Ballymun. Judging the competition has never been an easy task, and to make it less subjective, a series of criteria were developed that were used to assess the gardens visited. These criteria, given under the five headings below, also provide a useful guide to how interesting and appropriate gardens may be developed to meet the needs of local householders, and could also be used as practical guidelines for home gardeners.

1 LAYOUT

Does the design and layout of the garden complement the building, and is it in keeping with the house? Is the garden well thought out and well designed to meet the needs of its users? Are the paths well made and suited for the purposes for which they are intended? If the house is modern, does the garden have a contemporary feel? If the garden is needed for various purposes, does the layout provide for these? Some gardens are used to entertain in, to grow food, for children to play in, to exercise pets and a variety of other purposes – a well-designed garden will often have specific areas where these different activities can be accommodated, or at least incorporate into the design a means for such uses to be compatible.

2 PLANTS

Has a variety of different plants been used in the garden? Is the choice of plants compatible with the space available and their situation? It is remarkable how many small, suburban front gardens in Ireland contain trees that are potentially huge forest trees that could, at worst, completely engulf the small house they are adjacent to, and damage and undermine the foundations with their vigorously growing roots, or, at best, block the light from front rooms. I have seen very many small front gardens with a sickly monkey-puzzle tree or overgrown 'dwarf' conifer that are more at home in the temperate forests of South America or China than in suburban Ireland. Are plants used in the right situations? For example, are plants that need sun being grown in shady situations, and vice versa? Has the garden been planted with an imaginative range of plants according to their colour and variety? Are there plants in the garden that will provide colour and interest throughout the year?

3 HARD LANDSCAPING

What materials have been used for paths, patios and paving in the garden? Do they fit in well with the overall design, and do they suit the house? Is any garden furniture used in the garden, and, if so, is it safe, attractive, functional and in good condition?

4 MAINTENANCE

Is the garden well maintained and tidy? Are the beds kept free of weeds? Of course, on occasions specific weeds may be encouraged and enjoyed.

A lawn full of beautiful daisies is generally preferable to one that is completely weed-free and without a blade of grass out of place. Weed-free lawns generally require substantial inputs of herbicides and fertilisers if they are to remain without daisies! Some weeds may also be useful. Several common weeds, such as dandelions and shepherd's purse, are useful additions to spring salads. Chickweed is an excellent and therapeutic feed for caged birds. Different weeds act as food plants for wildlife by providing nectar, pollen and seeds for insects and birds.

Maintenance should include meeting the needs of specific plants, too. Are shrubs appropriately pruned and managed? I have seen gardens where all the shrubs are butchered and trimmed tightly – like topiary – several times of the year, making the garden resemble a green chessboard, and where the flowering shrubs lose most of the shoots on which new flowers and berries will grow the following year. Well-maintained roses will be regularly dead-headed and benefit from annual pruning to remove weak growth and dead shoots. If the garden is used as an exercise area for pets, is it kept clean and sweet-smelling?

5   ENVIRONMENTALLY FRIENDLY

Is the garden managed in an environmentally friendly way? That might include, for example, setting aside an area for wildlife or specifically planting species that attract and support wildlife, such as *Buddleja* (butterfly bush), whose flowers are rich in nectar and attract butterflies in summer. Is there a bird table where birds may be fed in winter? Or bird boxes?

Does the garden include its own composting facility, and is home-made compost used to nourish the plants? Is there a high degree of chemical use, such as herbicides and pesticides? If so, how is the gardener making efforts to reduce this usage?

WHAT PLANTS ARE GROWN BY BALLYMUN GARDENERS?

One of the greatest pleasures of visiting different gardens is to see what plants have been chosen for inclusion, and hearing the stories about where they came from and why they are being grown. While most of the species included are 'common or garden', occasional treasures occur, such as the beautiful blue-flowered climbing potato vine, *Solanum crispum* 'Glasnevin' – a variety originally raised at and named in honour of the National Botanic

Gardens. Its flower is included in the logo of the Gardens. Another unusual small tree I found was *Salix matsudana* 'Tortuosa' – a willow of Chinese origin with remarkable twisted branches and sometimes called the corkscrew willow. This variety was a chance mutation on the wild type, and is distinguished as having provided an eccentric walking stick for the Scottish comedian Harry Lauder. One garden was growing *Miscanthus* – so-called elephant grass. This is now becoming popular in Ireland as a biomass crop to provide an alternative source of fuel for electricity power stations. One of the rarest garden plants I saw was a fine specimen of the Chile lantern tree, *Crinodendron hookerianum*, which was growing in a front garden in Balcurris. In spring, it is covered in hanging, scarlet, bell-like flowers. Although, sadly, in Ireland we cannot provide it with the humming birds it needs for pollination, it nevertheless grows quickly and easily despite being so far away from its South American homeland.

Annual bedding plants are extremely popular in Ballymun gardens, and provide stunningly colourful displays in a number of gardens, borders, window boxes and hanging baskets. As well as the usual petunias, lobelia, pelargoniums, antirrhinums, marigolds and other common bedding plants, some unusual annuals are occasionally grown, such as opium poppies (*Papaver somniferum*; the decorative double-flowered non-productive form!), cosmos and arctosis. Several gardens have attractive herbaceous borders well stocked with perennial plants such as dahlias, lilies, daylilies, oxalis and sedums. Borders with roses are also popular, of course.

Growing fruit and vegetables in Ballymun could also be promoted very actively in the future, though there are still relatively few gardeners in Ballymun who grow them. It is certainly one of the most enjoyable aspects of gardening, and can be extremely rewarding. Home-grown crops of the ever-popular vegetables – such as tomatoes, runner beans, courgettes and lettuces – and herbs – such as parsley, mint, basil and others – can take up little room and are easily accommodated in small gardens, and can even be grown in containers and grow-bags on apartment balconies. Vegetable growing is also a wonderful way to encourage children to become interested in gardening. The flavour of home-grown garden produce is so much more intense than that bought in the shops.

I have no doubt that as the confidence and interest of Ballymun gardeners grow, they will become more adventurous in their planting, and will choose less usual plants. Visiting the National Botanic Gardens down the road in Glasnevin may give them ideas and inspiration, too.

GARDENING AND SUSTAINABILITY

In recent years, we have become much more aware of the need to live sustainably in our environment. Issues such as climate change, pollution, loss of natural habitats and biodiversity are now high-profile concerns. We are increasingly aware that care for the environment and development must go hand in hand if we are to enjoy a sustainable future. Sustainability issues, such as recycling and reducing waste, have come to the fore and nowhere more than in the garden. At the National Botanic Gardens in Glasnevin, we decided in recent years that sustainability had to be at the heart of our mission, and work has gone forward since then to do all we can to ensure that the Gardens becomes as close to a model of sustainability as we are able. Sustainability is also at the heart of the Ballymun regeneration mission, and it is good to see that this is a central component of so many different aspects of its programmes.

At its most basic level, sustainability means ensuring that we use the planet's resources in a wise way to guarantee that we pass on a healthy environment rich in the biological diversity, natural habitats and the natural resources that future generations will need. In Ireland and worldwide, there is increasing realisation of the urgent need to care for our environment, to sustain it and nurture it for the future. This includes all the efforts made to reduce, recycle and reuse waste, to conserve energy, and to conserve threatened plants, animals and their habitats. Our underlying philosophy should be that sustainability is everyone's responsibility.

In the garden, sustainability can be assisted by ensuring that our gardening efforts are as environmentally friendly as possible. Sustainable gardens can include:

- Composting: recycling organic waste from the garden and house;
- Growing plants for wildlife: planting species that provide habitats and food for animals such as birds and insects;
- Reducing the use of peat: boglands worldwide are under threat, and our efforts can help to preserve those that are left in Ireland for the future, as well as to keep the carbon dioxide they contain locked up

and not released into the atmosphere to contribute to climate change;
- Reducing the need for watering and irrigation: planting drought-tolerant species and mulching the soil to keep in moisture;
- Reducing the use of herbicides and pesticides;
- Going organic: feeding the garden with inorganic composts and fertilisers, preferably homemade in the garden;
- Growing more fruit and vegetables: the transportation of fruit and vegetables over long distances to our supermarkets contributes very significantly to climate change. Home-grown product is much more environmentally friendly, and it tastes better, too.

There are at least eight sustainability principles applicable to all urban landscapes, public and private:[4]

- Design for local environmental conditions;
- Plant selections that require little supplementary water;
- Non-invasive plant selections;
- Minimal chemical use;
- Provision of habitat for local native fauna;
- Water conservation measures;
- Minimal non-renewable energy consumption;
- Use of sustainably and locally sourced products and materials.

At the National Botanic Gardens, it is accepted that the institution should make strenuous efforts to ensure that its activities are fully in line with these principles, and are not detrimental or damaging to the environment. However, that is not going far enough. We also believe that we have a considerable responsibility and duty to promote sustainability among our visitors. The intention and hope is that over the coming years, we can develop the National Botanic Gardens as a model of sustainability, leading by example and playing a real and significant role in ensuring that we sustain our planet for future generations.

A project related to sustainability in the garden has been undertaken by the National Botanic Gardens and our collaborators in Ballymun in recent years. This collaboration includes the Gardens working with Ballymun Regeneration Ltd, and is funded by the Environmental Protection Agency

Environmental Research Technological Development and Innovation Programme. This project has involved the implementation of a community composting programme in the urban environment of Ballymun for the production of quality compost. The compost is being used in growth trials of horticultural plants with the aim of promoting the beneficial qualities of compost, and to help develop markets and local outlets for its distribution. In Ireland, only a very small number of similar initiatives have been undertaken, and there exists huge potential for further development.

The community composting project has been operating successfully over the past few years. The scheme involves local residents and the civic offices using a central composting system to convert kitchen waste into compost. A comprehensive quality management system was established to ensure consistency in methodology and compost quality, including:

- A procedure for checking composition of waste for contamination;
- A method of quantitatively logging data relating to organic waste collected and processed;
- A procedure for compost sampling and recording of time/ temperature profiles;
- An analysis of chemical–compost quality to consist of at least monthly testing to current national standards;
- Additional nutrient analysis necessary for effective pot-trial applications;
- Health and safety procedures for community composting.

The involvement of the National Botanic Gardens in the project was in hosting and supporting the compost trials. Following initial compost analysis, pot trials were carried out to determine the potential benefits of biowaste-produced compost in horticultural applications. Compost was used at varying rates as a substitute for potting mix. Growth rates (shoot length and root length) were monitored for a variety of species. The results were used to identify the possible use of compost as a potting-mix replacement and for reducing fertilising rates.

The Ballymun Composting Project is just one of the elements of the National Botanic Gardens programme in supporting sustainability. Our institutional efforts in sustainability can be broadly divided into four key components:

1   DEVELOPING ENVIRONMENTALLY FRIENDLY PRACTICES IN
    HORTICULTURE AND GARDEN MANAGEMENT

This includes the reduction and eventual elimination of the use of herbicides and pesticides that are potentially damaging to wildlife and the environment. For example, in the tropical glasshouses, cockroach infestation is being addressed very effectively using simple pitfall traps baited with solutions rich in sugar (such as Mi Wadi orange drink), rather than resorting to potentially dangerous chemicals. Integrated pest-management solutions to pest infestations are used as much as possible, and involve the release of predator insects that prey on, for example, greenfly, whitefly and red spider mite.

New composting programmes are also being developed that include composting all garden waste and making our own composts, leaf mould and mulches. As part of our regular programmes of events, demonstrations and lectures on compost making are included, and plans are in place to provide a public viewing area for the Gardens' own composting operations, including appropriate interpretation. The use of peat in the Gardens is being reduced significantly, recognising that in Ireland many important peat-land habitats continue to disappear through their exploitation for milled peat for horticulture. The replanting of the Great Palm House – restored and reopened in 2004 – was undertaken entirely without the use of peat in soils and composts.

In June 2008 the Gardens opened its own new Fruit and Vegetable Garden. Managed on organic principles, this new facility already includes over two hundred different fruit and vegetable crops and varieties, and is designed to act as a demonstration garden for visitors, and to inspire them to grow their own fruit and vegetables at home.

The Gardens also has an active policy and programme to encourage wildlife. In recent years, this has included the placing of bird-breeding nest boxes throughout the Gardens and reducing the number of feral cats, which prey on the wild bird populations.

2   PROMOTING AND SUPPORTING BIODIVERSITY CONSERVATION

Biodiversity is a relatively new word, and is not fully understood by many people. It is a combination of the words 'biological' and 'diversity'. It refers to the variety of all life on earth, including species and their habitats, as well as the genetic differences that occur within species, and the infinite variety of ecosystems made up of the plants, animals and other organisms. It also includes the complex interactions between species, such as pollinator mechanisms, competition and food chains.

Biodiversity conservation is an important part of the Gardens' mission, objectives and programmes, including conservation of national flora and supporting international efforts. The Gardens is particularly committed to the achievement of the Global Strategy for Plant Conservation developed and adopted by the United Nations Convention on Biological Diversity in 2002. Botanic gardens worldwide have become leaders in plant conservation, not only growing rare and endangered plants but also working to restore rare plants in the wild. Botanic gardens are also helping to raise public awareness of the importance of plants, and of the plight of so many that face extinction. The Gardens is a member of the Global Partnership for Plant Conservation – a network of some of the world's major thirty-five organisations working for plant conservation.

In the Gardens itself, a series of native plant habitats are maintained to demonstrate the diversity of Irish native flora and ecosystems, which is being significantly expanded between 2007–10. To support public awareness and the appreciation of Ireland's native flora, an annual course for the general public on Irish botany is offered, including night classes, field excursions and guided tours of the native plant collections. A comprehensive pot-grown collection of native plants is being created, too, and is used for educational purposes. In addition, the Gardens contains probably the largest remaining population of another native Irish endangered plant: the meadow saxifrage (*Saxifraga granulata*), which is being conserved, researched and monitored closely. The institution is also playing a part in a number of all-Ireland threatened species action plans: for the rare Irish orchid, *Spiranthes romanzoffiana*, and a filmy fern (the Killarney fern), *Trichomanes speciosum*. Our experience in recreating natural habitats may be helpful in the future, when local nature reserves are being developed or planned in Ballymun, elsewhere in Dublin and throughout Ireland.

3 EDUCATION FOR AND ABOUT THE ENVIRONMENT

Sustainability is included as a key element of the Gardens' education programmes, which feature interpretation and other projects developed by horticultural, scientific and educational staff. For example, in the Great Palm House, the horticultural team has since 2005 created an extensive ecological and educational-interpreted display of tropical plants demonstrating the complex structure of a tropical rainforest. The display includes a wide range of plants from Central America, particularly from Belize, with which the National Botanic Gardens has close links. A diversity of tropical economic plants is also on show, surrounding a traditional Mayan house constructed by staff of the Belize Botanic Garden who visited Glasnevin in 2005.

Educational visits and tours for children and others to learn about our biodiversity conservation efforts are offered by the staff of the Gardens' Visitor Centre. Classes of children from several Ballymun schools have already participated in these programmes. In addition, special workshops on sustainability are offered to children, and are particularly geared towards primary schools. Themed guided tours are also available for primary and secondary school groups on various subjects related to plants and sustainability. In 2006 the first of a series of special workshops for second-level school students was offered on the subject of sustainability. These were free of charge and consisted of a two-hour workshop on the theme of sustainability. The workshop explores forests, fuels, foods, and our reliance on plants and the natural environment, and features presentations, tours, role-play, and so on. The aim of the programme is to be cross-curricular in emphasis, covering aspects of geography, science and other subjects.

For the last three years, a Sustainability Week has been held at the Gardens. Stimulated by Ballymun's status as a Fairtrade town, Sustainability Week in 2006 saw Fairtrade coffee and tea introduced to the Gardens' restaurant. Since then, only such products are offered to visitors. This policy is being extended to include organic foods wherever possible. During the week, efforts made by the National Botanic Gardens and its entire staff to promote environmental care, recycling and biodiversity conservation are showcased for visitors. Sustainability Week also provides an opportunity for the institution to examine its own practices: what we are currently doing to promote sustainability, how we explain to visitors why we believe this is so important, and, most importantly, how we can become more effective in the future. In 2008 the traders at the Ballymun farmers' market were invited to participate in an environment fair that promoted a wide range of environmental organisations as well as organic and home-produced products.

In 2005 – and for the first time – gardening classes suitable for beginners were offered to the general public. These have become a regular and popular feature of the Gardens' operations, and have included participants from Ballymun. Subjects included in the gardening classes include an introduction to gardening, propagation, pests and diseases, soils and composting, choosing plants for your garden, design, managing a small greenhouse, indoor plants, planting trees and shrubs, perennials and grasses, roses, herbs, fruit and vegetables, and basic botany for gardeners. In the first year, the winner of the Ballymun Garden Competition, Ronnie McConnell, was invited to join the class as part of his prize. Going on from that success, in 2007 he became a judge in the Ballymun Gardens Competition itself, providing leadership and advice to the growing gardening community in Ballymun.

As a component of the Gardens' educational programmes, an innovative science education project for schools was launched in 2006. The project makes available to schools, via mini weather stations connected to the Internet, educational information and live environmental data about the collections and displays of tropical and desert plants at the National Botanic Gardens. Researchers from the National Centre for Sensor Research of Dublin City University developed mini weather stations to monitor environmental factors in the Great Palm House, the Succulent House and the Orchid House at the National Botanic Gardens. The mini weather stations – called motes – have sensors to monitor temperature, humidity, light levels, atmospheric pressure and oxygen levels in the air in each of the different houses. The network of sensors sends real-time environmental data via wireless connections to an interactive website called eco-sensor web (www.ecosensorweb.dcu.ie).

Environmental sensors also record the outdoor ambient environmental conditions, so that students can contrast the environmental conditions outdoors with those necessary for tropical plants such as banana, sugarcane, vanilla orchid, cacti and other succulent plants to thrive. A future priority will be to enhance the Gardens' website to include new web-based educational materials to promote environmental awareness, sustainability and understanding about the importance of plants and the threats they face.

4   RECYCLING AND REDUCING WASTE AND ENERGY CONSUMPTION

Efforts are made to reduce rubbish left by visitors to the Gardens, and increasingly we aim to manage and recycle waste on-site. At the moment, rubbish is transported to a nearby commercially operated recycling centre. Nevertheless, we also hope to reduce the quantity of waste produced and left by visitors in the Gardens by ensuring that products sold in the restaurant lack packaging or wrappers, and by encouraging visitors to take their rubbish home with them for recycling.

In 2005 an experiment was undertaken during Sustainability Week whereby all the rubbish left by visitors was collected for a one-week period and displayed the following week, while, at the same time, all rubbish bins in the Gardens were sealed. The experiment was a success, and little increase in litter left by visitors was detected. In 2008 new bins were introduced in which visitors could leave dry recyclable materials such as paper, drink cans, packaging and recyclable plastics.

Recycling paper and office waste is now a well-established feature of the Gardens' operations. For example, much waste paper is shredded and forms a useful component of our composting programme. Nevertheless, the greatest challenge will be to achieve significant energy savings in the large gas-heated tropical greenhouses, and to reduce our carbon emissions. However, new measures are being investigated, such as the installation of wood-pellet boilers, solar panels and the generation of hydro-electric power using the river. The first electric-powered vehicles were acquired by the Gardens in 2007. Many of the buildings and administrative offices are of historic importance, and energy conservation in such older buildings is problematic. Nevertheless, over the coming years, as restoration of several of these buildings goes ahead, efforts will be made to upgrade their insulation and energy efficiency. Energy-saving measures such as reducing electricity consumption are also being planned throughout the institution.

GARDENING BEYOND THE GARDEN

Gardening beyond private gardens in Ballymun is a valuable way of enhancing the quality of the environment, and making natural and green areas available for everyone in the community. This is particularly needed by those living in dwellings that are without their own gardens. Much good work has already been done: the planting of thousands of trees and the laying out of areas where amenity grasslands, hedgerows and designed parks can be maintained or created.

Gardening beyond the garden is also a valuable way of enhancing and managing biodiversity. The *Biodiversity Action Plan* provides valuable guidance and priorities on how this can be achieved over the coming years. The National Botanic Gardens is keen to assist in its implementation in any way it can.

The richest areas for biodiversity are in private gardens, public green spaces and hedgerows in Ballymun. Expanding the acreage of trees and woodlands in Ballymun is outlined as a priority in the plan. Some thoughts on these are given below. The special role of school gardens for promoting gardening, biodiversity and a love of nature among children is also considered briefly.

TREES AND WOODLANDS

Trees are or should be at the core of all urban environmental renewal programmes. Urban trees are vitally important and valuable because:

- They provide shelter from wind, rain and bright sun;
- They provide privacy;
- They help to screen unsightly views, and reduce noise and pollution;
- They provide homes and food for wildlife;
- They absorb carbon dioxide and other pollutants such as ozone, sulphur dioxide and carbon monoxide, and release oxygen;
- They can boost the value of the homes they surround;
- They can help to cool nearby houses in summer.

In Ireland, the natural 'climax' vegetation over much of the landscape would be woodlands had they not been largely removed for agriculture and settlement. It is not surprising, therefore, that a diverse range of species occur in the tree, shrub and herb layers of our woodland ecosystems. Of course, a wide range of native tree species is already widely grown and finds appropriate homes in many Irish gardens, and also forms an important component of the streetscape and parkland planting in all Irish cities and towns.

Trees are already an important component of the ecology of Ballymun. The *Biodiversity Action Plan* records 2.38 kilometres of tree lines,

4.19 kilometres of old and new hedgerows and 1.8 hectares of planted broad-leaved woodland. The plan also states that a thirty-year-old woodland is found in Poppintree, and a ten-year-old woodland in Balcurris Park, although both will need management if their wildlife value is to be enhanced. Common trees include ash (*Fraxinus excelsior*), alder (*Alnus glutinosa*), willow (sally; *Salix cinerea*), oak (*Quercus*) and Scot's pine (*Pinus sylvestris*), as well as a number of non-native trees such as maple (*Acer*), sycamore (*Acer pseudoplatanus*) and beech (*Fagus sylvatica*). Each of these could be enhanced by allowing or managing the under-storey to develop a natural vegetation of shrubs and herbs, and with enhancement planting of other native trees and shrubs such as holly (*Ilex aquifolium*), rowan or mountain ash (*Sorbus aucuparia*), elder (*Sambucus nigra*), hawthorn (*Crataegus monogyna*), birch (*Betula pendula* and *B. pubescens*), alder (*Alnus glutinosa*), hazel (*Corylus avellana*), yew (*Taxus baccata*) and the two native oaks (*Quercus petraea* and *Quercus robur*). Less common species might also be considered for planting, including spindle tree (*Euonymus europaeus*), crab apple (*Malus sylvestris*), dogwood (*Cornus sanguinea*) and guelder-rose (*Viburnus opulus*), several species of willow (*Salix*) and the cherry species, bird cherry (*Prunus padus*), wild cherry (*Prunus avium*) and sloe or blackthorn (*Prunus spinosa*).

HEDGEROWS
Although there are relatively few old hedgerows in Ballymun, good efforts are being made to establish more. In the past, they were the primary method for identifying and delineating boundaries. In some areas of Ireland, hedgerows have survived for hundreds of years, and include a wide diversity of tree, shrub and herb species. They are also important wildlife refuges, providing homes for birds, animals such as mice, bats and others, as well as for insects. The old remnant hedgerows in Ballymun include ash (*Fraxinus excelsior*), blackthorn (*Prunus spinosa*) and hawthorn (*Crataegus monogyna*), the classic and most typical hedgerow trees in Ireland. Other hedgerow species in the area include elder (*Sambucus nigra*) – a species associated with phosphate-rich soils – ivy (*Hedera helix*), dog rose (*Rosa canina*), bramble (*Rubus fruticosus*) and white willow (*Salix alba*).

Hedgerows can be regarded as one of the most typical elements of the Irish countryside – in effect, linear woodlands. They provide shelter, screening and privacy, act as windbreaks, provide wildlife refuges and corridors, and provide food for humans (such as wild blackberries, sloes, haws, rowan and elderberries) and for animals. As well as that, they also help to make an area more aesthetically pleasing.

SCHOOL GARDENS

School gardens are of great importance, and this is an area that may be developed further in Ballymun over the coming years. The development of ecological gardens as part of school facilities is a growing trend worldwide. Their importance is well recognised today, not only in building knowledge and awareness of the natural world, but also in fostering and renewing an appreciation of the environment. Sadly, most children in Ireland are much better able to identify the logos of major commercial corporations and Japanese cartoon characters than their own native trees and wildflowers. School gardens can help to redress this balance and promote greater understanding, knowledge and appreciation of wildlife and its importance. The famous Victorian children's book, *The Secret Garden* by Francis Hodgson Burnett – about three children who discover a garden and gently coax it back to life – presents well the healing power and security that can be a garden's greatest attributes. School gardens can help to develop a love of gardens among children, and that could become a lifetime interest and occupation for so many of them.

THE FUTURE

But what of the future? Despite the huge challenges we face in conserving, nurturing and protecting our environment, it is not difficult to be optimistic about the future of gardening and environmental protection in Ballymun. Nevertheless, the growth of an interest in gardening and the environment in Ballymun will need to be cherished and encouraged, and I hope that the National Botanic Gardens can play an ongoing part in this in the years ahead. The establishment and development of a vibrant Ballymun horticultural club could be helpful, so as to provide a forum for the exchange of ideas, enthusiasm, experience and to share plants. Such a club could also provide a means of encouraging young people to become more interested in plants and gardening.

Nature clubs – such as the Dublin Naturalists' Field Club – also provide a way for people to learn about, and become involved in, environmental and biodiversity protection. The club runs almost weekly excursions throughout the Dublin region, introducing members to the wide diversity of plants, animals, ecosystems and landscapes. In Ballymun, such local interest and expertise is badly needed, and will be invaluable to help implement the *Biodiversity Action Plan for Ballymun* over the coming years.

For too long, the environment was seen as a luxury to be considered after other aspects of development and human endeavour had been addressed. Today, we see that this is not the case, and that if development is to be sustainable, environmental concerns must be an essential component. Gardens and green spaces in Ballymun are, and will continue to be, among the most important elements of its regeneration, helping to strengthen a sustainable, secure and contented community. St Thomas Aquinas, the thirteenth-century mystic, said, 'You change people by delight. You change people by pleasure.' Gardening can provide that pleasure to change people, and can help to build the stable, happy and contented urban society that Ballymun needs so much.

NOTES AND REFERENCES

1   Simon Cocking (ed.), *The Ballymun EcoBook* (Dublin, Global Action Plan, 2004), p. 50.

2   John Prest, *The Garden of Eden: The Botanic Garden and the Re-creation of Paradise* (New Haven and London, Yale University Press, 1981), p. 122.

3   Mary Tubridy and Associates, *Biodiversity Action Plan for Ballymun* (BRL Image Project, 2008), p. 34.

4   Sheryn Pitman, 'Educating for Sustainable Urban Landscapes', *Roots: Botanic Gardens Conservation International Education Review*, vol. 4, no. 2 (October 2007), pp. 5–8.

Providing Effective Access to Legal Services

The Experience of the Ballymun Community Law Centre

GERRY WHYTE

In October 2002, Ballymun Community Law Centre (BCLC) became the second community law centre to open its doors in the Republic, taking its place alongside the Coolock Community Law Centre (now called the Northside Community Law Centre), which had commenced operations on 1 April 1975. In contrast to the state-run law centres operated by the Legal Aid Board, both the BCLC and the Northside Community Law Centre are controlled by management bodies, some of whose members are drawn from the local community. This is a defining characteristic of community law centres, and the establishment of BCLC represents an important entrenchment of this model of legal aid in this jurisdiction.

In this essay, I will put the establishment of BCLC in context by examining the various factors that prevent people in marginalised communities from availing of legal services, by listing the various approaches towards the provision of legal aid that have emerged during the past hundred years, and by providing, in particular, an account of the law centre movement.[1] I will then attempt to provide an account of the activities of BCLC from its inception to date.[2]

FACTORS IMPEDING ACCESS TO LEGAL SERVICES

In 1977 the Committee on Civil Legal Aid and Advice (hereafter, the Pringle Committee) concluded that four factors appeared to deter disadvantaged people from availing of legal services:

1. The belief that the cost will be beyond their reach;
2. Lack of knowledge of the types of service and doubt about the relevance to their problems of the services of solicitors: it is suggested, for example, that solicitors are trained only to handle legal difficulties which are of concern to the better-off (property rights as distinct from social welfare rights, expertise in handling court proceedings but not tribunal proceedings);
3. Socially underprivileged persons are reluctant to approach solicitors because they often find the atmosphere of a solicitor's office 'intimidating' – there is what the Incorporated Law Society describes as a 'psychological barrier' between socially deprived clients and solicitors, which presents both with immediate communication difficulties;
4. Difficulty in reaching solicitors' offices, particularly in Dublin, where they are generally situated in the central business area.[3]

In research carried out in 2002–3, Gogan identified the following factors as impeding access to legal services for residents of Ballymun: the fact that legal services were not provided in the locality, the intimidating nature of the legal culture, the difficulty in arranging child-minding to enable the client to meet with a legal advisor, transport difficulties, difficulty in understanding legal language, unsuitable hours of business during which legal services could be accessed, the cost of such services, hearing difficulties, intimidation and a feeling of being excluded.[4]

MODELS OF LEGAL AID

The different models used for delivering legal services to the socially disadvantaged over the last hundred years or so can be classified broadly into four categories over a spectrum of models ranging from those concerned solely with the servicing of individual cases to those 'strategic' models that attempt to tackle the social problems confronting their client communities. Describing the differences between service and strategic models, Frederick Zemans comments,

> The service model is the traditional and the most common form of legal services. An outgrowth of the juridical and charitable approach, service models confine their attention to

discrete claims and problems brought to a programme by an individual with a readily categorised legal problem. This approach grows directly out of the traditional approach to protecting rights which [is essentially legalistic and individual] – inevitably over-loaded, service models can expend little time or energy in educating the community or on outreach programmes. Since service models accept the norms of the legal system and provide a service for poor people which, in the opinion of the administrators (inevitably lawyers), is the same for the poor as for the rich, poor people using service schemes face many of the same obstacles that they would encounter within the traditional setting. Such service models offer little recognition of the uniqueness of the poor person's lifestyle. They neither make the service psychologically more accessible, nor do they attempt to handle problems which have not been on the traditional agenda of legal services (e.g. eviction). The service model reinforces the distance between the 'recipient' and the 'deliverer' of the service by encouraging clients to assume passive and dependent roles in their relations with the legal aid scheme. Lawyers write briefs; interview witnesses; negotiate settlements and go to court. The client's perspective is generally of an over-worked, under-paid lawyer who is dealing with the immediate problem and ignoring the fundamental cancer of poverty and poverty-related problems that continue to affect the client.[5]

Strategic models, in contrast, are

orientated to identifying the significant social problems facing the community it is serving. While dealing with the inevitable daily problems, a strategic legal-services programme attempts to develop a long-term approach of research, reform and education to deal with the more fundamental issues. Rather than handling cases which are relevant to the lawyer's experience, a strategic programme sets priorities in one or several areas of concern to a particular community such as the environment, housing, land-ownership, occupational health, or immigration. In concert with the geographic community or the community of interest, the professional will consider collective issues or the complaints of a class of individuals – a significant distinction between the service and strategic models is in methodology. While the service model perceives itself as bound to the court and to litigation, the strategic model views advocacy as only one potential strategy. Other strategies might include tenant-organising, lobbying the legislature, television and media coverage, or community picketing of a particularly abhorrent landlord.[6]

The earliest of these models, and one firmly located at the 'service model' end of the spectrum, is the charitable model that appeared in England, the US, Germany, France and Italy towards the end of the nineteenth century. Charitable legal aid schemes were controlled by the profession, and did not challenge in any fundamental way the biases of the legal system. Moreover, assistance tended to be provided only to 'the deserving poor', and the schemes reinforced prevailing beliefs that poverty was primarily attributable to the perceived character defects of the poor.

The latter half of the twentieth century witnessed a move from the charitable model to state provision of legal aid, with the growth of what is called the 'judicare model' of legal aid in many Western countries, and which, again, is to be found closer to the 'service model' end of our spectrum of models. Under this model, the state pays the legal profession to provide legal services to needy individuals, and one of the strengths of this model is that it sees legal aid as an entitlement, however limited, of the needy client, rather than as a matter of charity. Moreover, it provides greater coverage than the charitable model, and a very wide choice of lawyer for the client. As against that, this type of model relies on the client taking the initiative to seek help, and, even then, private practitioners tend not to be conversant with those areas of the law of most relevance to poor people, such as welfare law, housing law and consumer law.

The third model of legal aid is the 'salaried model', whereby lawyers are employed on a full-time basis either by the state or by NGOs (non-governmental organisations) to provide legal services to the poor. This model is available in both 'service' and 'strategic' versions. According to

Paterson, both versions normally share certain characteristics.[7] They are publicly funded, independent (in that the management of the schemes is intended to be independent of the legal profession and of the state), limited in scope, means-tested, free, and the services are provided by a closed panel of full-time salaried lawyers (as opposed to private practitioners). The strategic version of the model has four additional characteristics: it is proactive (i.e. it pursues 'a proactive strategy of targeting the local problems which [it wishes] to focus on, collecting data and making submissions to relevant bodies and attempting to reach potential clients by advertising, circulars and public meetings'[8]), controlled (it only takes on certain types of case, and in limited numbers), community orientated (its focus is on the problems faced by the community and on community organisation) and, finally, committed to law reform through litigation strategy or lobbying.

The fourth and final model is the 'mixed delivery' model, which combines elements of the judicare and salaried models, particularly the strategic version of the latter model. In some jurisdictions, such as Sweden, the Netherlands and some Canadian provinces such as Quebec and Ontario, this integration was planned, but in other jurisdictions this development came about in an *ad hoc* fashion, with the two models existing side by side but operating independently of one another.

Where does the Irish experience fit into this categorisation of legal aid schemes? In fact, there are elements of the first three models present in the Irish legal landscape, though in relation to civil law, it is the service version of the salaried model which predominates. The charitable model is represented by the tradition within the legal profession of pro bono work, though this is not at all as systematically organised as in the US, where law firms allocate a designated proportion of their time to pro bono work.[9] In the Irish context, personal injuries claims are often taken by lawyers on a 'no foal, no fee' basis. However, more speculative claims involving worthy causes are sometimes also taken on this basis, and at a time during the 1980s when the Free Legal Advice Centres (FLAC) could not afford to employ a solicitor, it had little difficulty arranging for its clients to be represented in court by sympathetic solicitors and barristers.

There are two examples of the judicare model in the Irish legal system. The statutory criminal legal aid scheme operates on this basis. In addition, while the civil legal aid scheme run by the Legal Aid Board relies predominantly on full-time salaried staff, there is some limited involvement of private practitioners.

Finally, as just mentioned, the state's civil legal aid scheme is predominantly a service version of the salaried model, while a number of NGOs – including BCLC, the Northside Community Law Centre and FLAC – provide a strategic version of the salaried model of legal aid.

Of these NGOs, both BCLC and Northside Community Law Centre belong to the law centre movement, to which I now turn.

ORIGINS OF LAW CENTRE MOVEMENT

As we have noted, the salaried model of legal aid – whereby lawyers are employed on a full-time basis either by the state or by NGOs to provide legal services to the poor – was the third model of legal aid to emerge in modern times. This model originated in the US during the 1960s as part of President Johnson's War on Poverty, pursuant to which the Federal Office of Economic Opportunity established its Legal Services Program. Debate over whether the Legal Services Program should focus on law and social reform, or instead concentrate on servicing individual cases, was initially resolved in favour of the former, strategic approach, and, as a result, a number of law centres were established in various disadvantaged neighbourhoods throughout the country. These centres were designed to redress substantive inequalities through the use of test cases and class actions, by organising clients around common poverty issues and educating them as to their legal rights, and through political lobbying. Furthermore, the centres sought to achieve meaningful representation of community interests on their management committees. Using these tactics, the law centre movement hoped to assist marginalised communities in tackling structural causes of poverty and exclusion.

CLASSIFICATION OF LAW CENTRES

Following the US example, neighbourhood law centres were also established in Australia, Canada, Finland, New Zealand, the Netherlands and the UK. However, they did not necessarily imitate the US model in all respects, and, in particular, many law centres tended to concentrate on the servicing of individual cases, to the detriment of strategic work.

So law centres range from purely service models to exclusively strategic models, with many centres trying to combine elements of both models. Law centres that veer towards the service model end of the spectrum are reactive in that they have to devote most, if not all, of their energies to coping with the flood of individual cases coming through the door. In support of this approach, it can be argued that it meets a need for legal services, that it can enhance a centre's reputation in the community, and that, in ideal circumstances, it can usefully inform the centre's strategic work. However, this approach to legal aid work does carry with it a number of disadvantages, of which the greatest is that the pressure of work it creates can seriously impair the centre's ability to engage in strategic action, thereby minimising the centre's impact on the problems facing the community. There is also some evidence that the quality of service devoted to individual cases can decline as, under the pressure of a heavy caseload, law centre employees tend to deal with those cases in a routine manner. Moreover, the pressure of casework can often lead to a high level of staff turnover. Finally, reliance on the service model tends to blind law centres to the potential of tactics not normally employed by lawyers for resolving community problems, such as lobbying, picketing and so on.

Law centres committed to both the servicing of individual cases and the pursuit of more long-term strategies frequently impose limitations on the cases they take on in order to create room for strategic action. Thus, a centre may restrict itself to representing people living within a defined catchment area, and may also refuse to take on certain types of case. In very difficult circumstances, such a centre may also close its doors temporarily to new cases in order to clear a backlog of work.

CHARACTERISTICS OF LAW CENTRES

Notwithstanding variations in structure and functions, law centres tend to have certain shared characteristics. In particular, law centres invariably provide their services free of charge, while the staff providing the service are salaried and therefore not hidebound by considerations of profitability when deciding what type of work to pursue. Moreover, recognising the limitations of conventional legal practice in meeting the needs of their clients, law centres often employ lay advisers, community workers and social workers alongside legal practitioners.

A commitment on the part of some law centres to empowering their clients, their staff and the local community results in some of the more striking features of the law centre movement. This commitment reflects the view that one of the more insidious consequences of poverty is the powerlessness of its victims, and that the abolition of poverty entails giving marginalised individuals and communities control over their own destinies. In addition, community involvement in determining the policy of law centres arguably results in the most effective deployment of scarce resources, as community representatives are best placed to identify the community's greatest needs. Related to this is the argument that public-interest advocacy has the greatest chance of securing change if it is grounded in a popular mood, and that community involvement in the running of a law centre greatly facilitates the centre in tapping into such a mood.

The goal of empowering the local community can be pursued in a number of different ways. One can vest control of the law centre itself in a management committee containing a built-in majority of community representatives, and in that way seek to ensure that the centre remains responsive to local wishes. However, as Stephens observes,

> [This] is not an easy concept to operationalise for it depends both on the willingness of local people to come forward for election to a management committee and on their abilities to function within that structure and not to be intimidated by any professional members of the committee.[10]

Another strategy here is to support and encourage (and sometimes initiate) local community groups who will campaign directly on behalf of their own members, and who may also instruct the law centre to take legal action on their behalf. Thus, law centres may assist a local group with the process of incorporation or with drafting a constitution. Law centres may also help to organise clients with a common grievance into mutual self-support groups.

Having provided a context for the activities of BCLC, I turn now to consider its activities since it commenced operations in 2002.

ESTABLISHMENT OF BALLYMUN COMMUNITY LAW CENTRE LTD

The immediate origins of BCLC may be found in the response of the Free Legal Advice Centres Ltd to a letter sent in March 1998 by Ballymun

Regeneration Ltd (BRL)[11] to a number of NGOs inviting them to locate their services in Ballymun. At a meeting with BRL in May 1998, FLAC suggested that a community law centre be established in Ballymun. Since its establishment in 1969, FLAC has campaigned for effective access to legal services for marginalised individuals and communities.[12] Committed to the strategic model of legal aid, FLAC had set up the Coolock Community Law Centre in 1975, and had subsequently campaigned, unsuccessfully, for the establishment of community law centres in Tallaght and Clondalkin. The proposal to establish a community law centre in Ballymun, therefore, fitted in well with FLAC's vision of how the legal system could be made to work to the benefit of disadvantaged communities.

Few communities were more disadvantaged than Ballymun.[13] In 1998, for example, Ballymun had the highest percentage (44 per cent) of households headed by lone parents in the country; 71 per cent of local authority tenants in the area were solely dependent on social welfare; and 53 per cent of the children in Ballymun left school at the age of fifteen. A further measure of disadvantage, viewed simply from a legal perspective, is that prior to 2007, there was no solicitor's practice in this community, and that prior to the establishment of BCLC, the only legal service available to the residents of Ballymun was an advice clinic operated by FLAC two evenings a week. According to a report commissioned by the Ballymun Area Partnership Company in 1995,

> Ballymun occupies one extreme of the spectrum of disadvantage covered by all of the Area Partnerships. The problems which arise from this are therefore more severe and interrelated than is the case in other areas and people residing in Ballymun are clearly subjected to the highest level of cumulative deprivation.[14]

Yet there were also a number of positive factors that worked in favour of FLAC's proposal. One was the fact that a number of community organisations had developed in direct response to the adversity faced by the residents of Ballymun since the 1960s,[15] and so, by targeting these groups, it was relatively easy to enlist community support for the proposal. This support was crucially important, particularly in light of the recommendation from the Craig Gardner Report in 1993 that the local authority should involve the tenants in all future planning and redevelopment of the estate. The proposal also benefitted from the fact that, in early 1997, the government with Dublin Corporation (now Dublin City Council) had officially designated Ballymun as an area for renewal, establishing BRL later in the year for the purpose of developing and implementing a blueprint for the regeneration of the area. The idea of a community law centre fitted in with the belief of key personnel within BRL that the residents of Ballymun needed to be empowered in the context of the overall regeneration of Ballymun, and this support from BRL was a key factor in leading to the establishment of BCLC.

The first public step in the campaign to establish BCLC took place on 25 January 1999, when a meeting was convened by the Community Action Programme, a local community resource centre, to consider FLAC's proposal. Arising out of this meeting, BCLC Campaign was set up, and this eventually included representatives from the various Ballymun area forums, Ballymun Citizens' Information Centre, Ballymun Credit Union, Ballymun Housing Task Force, Ballymun Partnership, BRL, Coolock Community Law Centre, Dublin City University, Dublin Corporation, the Eastern Health Board, FLAC, An Garda Síochána, the Legal Aid Board, Lifestart, the Men's Network, the Money Advice and Budgeting Service, the National College of Ireland, Scoil an tSeachtar Laoch, SIPTU, Threshold, Urrus, Welfare Rights Group, the Women's Resource Centre and the Youth Action Programme. The campaign was formally launched on 23 July 1999, and Dave Ellis – who had more than twenty years' experience working as the community law officer with the Coolock Community Law Centre – was retained as a consultant.

BCLC Campaign initially devoted a significant amount of energy to fundraising, and using monies provided by various public and private bodies, the campaign was able to commission a feasibility study and an action plan during 2000. Published in January 2000, the feasibility study essentially called for a community-based law centre engaged in both service and strategic legal aid work. Thus, it recommended that BCLC should engage in casework for residents of a defined catchment area centred on Ballymun and the immediate surrounding areas;[16] that priority should be given to family law, housing, employment law, social welfare, equality issues and debt; and that, where appropriate, BCLC should work in conjunction with such bodies as the Legal Aid Board, local welfare rights groups and Ballymun MABS (Money Advice and Budgeting Service). The study also suggested that BCLC should support local community groups by providing legal advice and by taking referrals, and that it should also provide training for such groups to assist them in developing their services. It was also envisaged that BCLC would disseminate information to the general public on legal rights, and that it would, in conjunction with local groups, identify law reform issues that promote justice and equality for the community. The study further recommended that the law centre should be based in a central location, develop outreach services, and be part of an integrated approach to the delivery of information and advice services in the area. In relation to management of the centre, the study recommended that this be community based, with facilities to involve persons with particular skills through co-options or sub-groups.

BCLC Campaign followed up the feasibility study with the publication, in November 2000, of its action plan, which again argued the case for a strategic, community-based model of legal aid working in partnership with the statutory sector and NGOs, and engaged in casework, community support work, training, educational programmes, law reform and social policy work, and research. The following April, sufficient funding had been secured to enable the campaign to employ a project development manager, Patricia Scanlon, based in premises provided by BRL.

In the meantime, and following the publication of the feasibility study in January 2000, BCLC Campaign had held meetings with a number of public bodies, including the Legal Aid Board. Because of the regeneration programme, the Board saw Ballymun as a special case, distinct from other communities, and so, during 2000, it joined the campaign committee. In September 2001 the campaign entered into negotiations with the Board as to how the latter might be able to support the services to be provided by BCLC, and in February 2002 the Legal Aid Board agreed to a joint venture partnership with BCLC whereby the Board would provide paralegal support to BCLC to enable the latter to refer appropriate cases to the Board. The Board also agreed to facilitate any of its own solicitors who wished to apply for employment with BCLC by offering a secondment. This public/private relationship between the Legal Aid Board and BCLC marked an important step in the development of the partnership approach to the delivery of legal aid as advocated in the campaign's feasibility study.

February 2002 was significant in another respect because it was during this month that BCLC, working in conjunction with the National College of Ireland, offered a training course for community activists to enable them to sit on management committees in the area. This would appear to be the first service of any type provided by BCLC to the local community.

The following month, BCLC employed an administrator, Christina Beresford, and in November 2002 the centre recruited a solicitor, Frank Murphy, on an initial two-year contract funded by grants from the Joseph Rowntree Charitable Trust and from FLAC. Frank Murphy was seconded from the Legal Aid Board for this purpose, and the Board also provided the centre with a law clerk, Nina Maher, whose function was to process family-law applications from Ballymun residents seeking legal aid from the Legal Aid Board through their private practitioner scheme.

Less than four years after the initial public meeting in January 1999, BCLC was now fully open for business.

SERVICES PROVIDED

BCLC provides legal advice and legal aid[17] to individual residents in Ballymun, and also engages in more strategic work designed to assist the community as a whole. Its activities may be listed under three headings.

1   CASEWORK

In 2000 BCLC's Action Plan cautioned that,

> [S]uch is the need for legal services in the area that it is unlikely Ballymun Community Law Centre will be in a position to meet all of that demand [relating to casework], and certainly not in its initial stage of development.[18]

Accordingly, it recommended that BCLC should prioritise certain types of casework, and that it should work in partnership with such organisations as the Legal Aid Board, Threshold and MABS.

The experience of other law centres certainly supports the view that law centres wishing to pursue strategic work cannot afford to operate an open-door policy in relation to casework, as otherwise they will be swamped.[19] BCLC has, therefore, prudently placed some restrictions on the type of case it will take on. Clients must reside within a defined geographical area, and the centre will not act in criminal cases, neighbour disputes (though these may be referred to BCLC's mediation service) and conveyancing matters. Moreover, BCLC will not provide legal services where they could be obtained from another body unless the centre's solicitor considers that it would be appropriate for BCLC to take on the case.

Legal aid and advice are provided by BCLC's solicitor operating from the centre's premises provided by Dublin City Council in Shangan Road, or through BCLC's outreach clinics in Ballymun Library, Ballymun Employment Centre, Balcurris/Balbutcher Forum office and Poppintree Community Centre. Where cases have to go to court, BCLC invariably benefits from the tradition within the Bar of taking on worthy cases on a *pro bono* basis. In addition, both Threshold and Dublin North West Citizens' Information Service operate advice clinics through the law centre, while, as already mentioned, the centre also provides a referral service to the Legal Aid Board. As the 2003 Ballymun Evaluation Report points out,

> Having the various agencies under the one roof enables appointments to be made with the agency best placed to handle the query. Where a seemingly non-legal query to one of these agencies turns out to have legal implications, the Centre's structure enables an appropriate referral to be made 'in-house'.[20]

The report also noted that having the other agencies operate under the umbrella of BCLC helps to maintain confidentiality, in that a client could be visiting any of the organisations in the centre.[21] Where a person consults one of the other agencies, that agency remains the file holder, and the services of BCLC are used only to complement the services of the agency. Thus, BCLC will only take on cases raising legal issues that are beyond the capability of the relevant agency.

Two aspects of BCLC's casework worth noting are its use of mediation in appropriate cases, and its readiness to pursue a litigation strategy whereby important issues are brought to court in the hope of achieving an outcome that will promote social reform.

Alternative dispute resolution (ADR) has been identified as an important element in securing access to justice,[22] and in 2000 BCLC's action plan recommended that the centre should develop a range of alternative dispute-resolution methods, including a comprehensive community mediation service.[23] Three different mediation programmes are currently offered through BCLC. In 2002 BCLC launched Mediation Ballymun, a project with ten volunteers overseen by a steering group, and designed to develop community mediation as an alternative method of dispute resolution for civil cases – other than family disputes – involving residents of Ballymun. BCLC faced a challenge in raising the profile of this service, but now the point has been reached where, for example, community organisations, including An Garda Síochána, are referring some neighbour disputes to Mediation Ballymun. In 2006 the Family Support Agency, a statutory body, started a pilot programme in family mediation through the law centre, and more recently, BCLC has pioneered peer mediation for children aged between eight and twelve by providing training for children in fifth class in primary school so that they can use mediation for resolving future disputes.

At the same time, one should strike a cautionary note about the use of ADR by those who are economically and socially disadvantaged. Aron argues that ADR is only effective where a number of conditions are satisfied:

1. The controversy involves negotiable issues, as opposed to non-negotiable issues of principle;
2. The number of people involved is relatively small;
3. The interests of the principals have been defined and accepted as legitimate;
4. The critical facts are known or knowable within reasonable cost and time constraints;
5. There is rough parity of power among parties;
6. There is some pressure, such as a statutory deadline, on everyone to reach agreement in a timely fashion.[24]

Aron's fifth condition, in particular, raises the question of whether ADR is suitable for resolving employment disputes.

BCLC has pursued a litigation strategy on at least one occasion. In *Dublin City Council v. Fennell*,[25] the centre acted for the defendant, a tenant of Dublin City Council, who sought to resist her eviction by invoking the provisions of the European Convention on Human Rights. In the event, the Supreme Court held that the European Convention on Human Rights Act 2003 – which enables Irish courts to apply the European Convention on Human Rights – did not apply retrospectively to events occurring before the Act came into operation on 31 December 2003, and so did not apply to tenants, such as the defendant, who were served with a notice to quit prior to that date. The use of litigation strategy is a feature of law centres operating a strategic version of legal aid, though, as the *Fennell* case illustrates, this strategy does have some significant drawbacks and, as such, is a strategy that should be used cautiously.[26]

Unlike other activities engaged in by law centres, casework is essentially reactive in that a law centre is dependent on potential clients realising that their particular difficulty may have a legal solution, and that the centre is a relevant source of help.[27] Between January 2003 and December 2006,[28] BCLC's solicitor has provided legal advice in 513 cases and legal representation in forty-nine, covering such areas of the law as housing law, consumer law, family law,[29] debt, social welfare, equality, tort and employment law. As residents of Ballymun become more familiar with BCLC's work, demand for this aspect of its services is likely to grow significantly, and the centre may eventually have to take steps to ensure that individual casework does not overwhelm its more long-term, strategic work.

2 EDUCATION AND TRAINING

One of the factors identified in the Pringle Report as impeding access to the law is the fact that many people are unaware of their legal rights, and may therefore not appreciate that lawyers could be of assistance to them. The remedy here, of course, is to provide the public with information as to their legal rights, and since 2002 BCLC has devoted a considerable amount of its time and energy to community legal education. As already noted, the first service provided by BCLC was a training course in organisational management offered in conjunction with the National College of Ireland (NCI) to community activists in February 2002. Working in conjunction with NCI and other organisations – such as FLAC, Northside Community Law Centre, Amnesty International (Irish Section), Dublin City University and National University of Ireland, Galway[30] – BCLC subsequently organised a series of legal talks on family, consumer, welfare, equality, property, housing, company and criminal law, and courses on active citizenship, family law, housing advocacy and advice, employment law, criminal law, Travellers and the law, human rights law, and primary health care and the law. A number of these courses obtained FETAC (Further Education and Training Awards Council) approval, thereby providing participants with recognition for their achievements, and facilitating their ongoing adult education. In 2005, working in collaboration with the Irish section of Amnesty International, BCLC produced *Fight for Your Rights*, a very readable guide written for non-lawyers to the European Convention on Human Rights, and between 2004–7, BCLC was one of the organisers of the Legal Education for All Project which was designed to provide participants drawn from the Traveller community and from Ballymun with a basic legal education, thereby enabling them, if they wished, to pursue further legal studies and a career in law. BCLC also engaged with local schools as part of its community legal education programme, arranging placements in legal offices for transition-year students, running a legal essay competition and supporting local students participating in a national Mock Trial Competition.

Involvement in this type of work by BCLC is of crucial importance for a number of reasons. Most obviously, it empowers members of the local community, as rights are more effective if people are aware that they have such rights. Second, attendance at talks or courses run by BCLC helps to demystify the law and reduces the possibility of local residents being deterred from availing of legal services because they are intimidated by the legal process. Finally, this proactive work also raises the profile of BCLC within the community, and will inevitably lead to an increasing number of residents availing of the centre's other services, in particular, its legal aid and advice services.

3   LAW AND SOCIAL REFORM

The third prong of BCLC's activities – the promotion of law reform and social reform – has been the slowest to develop, reflecting BCLC's concentration of efforts initially on community legal education and casework. BCLC organised two public meetings in Ballymun with representatives of the Law Reform Commission in 2004 and 2005 to discuss the Commission's proposals for reform of the law relating to co-habitees and vulnerable adults, respectively; working with the Spent Convictions Group, the centre helped to draw up proposals for a Rehabilitation of Offenders Bill in 2007; and it is anticipated that the centre will shortly start drafting proposals for the reform of public housing law. However, as BCLC's caseload increases, the likelihood is that this increase will enable the centre to identify further areas of the law in need of reform.

EMPOWERING THE COMMUNITY

One of the key characteristics of a community law centre is that it is committed to empowering the local community, and two aspects of BCLC's operation demonstrate this commitment. We have already noted the extensive community legal education programme mounted by BCLC since it commenced operations in 2002. This contributes significantly to the empowerment of the Ballymun community by making residents aware of their legal entitlements. In addition, BCLC's management committee includes representatives of a number of community organisations, in addition to representatives of other important stakeholders.[31] The inclusion of community representatives on the management committee should ensure that the most effective use is made of scarce resources, as community representatives are best placed to identify the community's priority needs. It also implicitly recognises that disadvantage is as much about disempowerment as it is about lack of resources.

However, one should not underestimate the difficulty of ensuring effective community representation on the governing bodies of law centres, as experience elsewhere has shown. Typically, such community representatives are already active in at least one other community organisation, and are being asked to take on an additional commitment when appointed to the law centre. In addition, non-lawyers may find the law and the legal process intimidating, with the result that there is often a tendency to defer to the views of the lawyers on the management committee. BCLC, however, benefits from the fact that Ballymun has a tradition of strong community activism dating back to the 1960s, borne out of the adversity that confronted the community since its early days.

CONCLUSION

Interest in the law as a means of tackling social exclusion arguably stems from the failure of politics to protect adequately the interests of marginalised groups. However, the promotion of social inclusion is ultimately a political matter, though the legal system can make a useful contribution in highlighting injustice and, occasionally, in securing change. For lawyers to be most effective in tackling social exclusion, they need to be prepared to engage with the political system. They need to look beyond the individual client and to be prepared to work for the group of which their client is a representative. In my opinion, this is best achieved using the strategic model of legal aid, which seeks to address the social problems faced by particular communities, be they geographical communities, such as Ballymun, or communities of interest, such as, for example, Travellers or people with disabilities. The strategic approach, moreover, is not hidebound by the conventional tactic of litigation, but will also engage in political activity such as lobbying and community activism.

The establishment of BCLC in 2002 constituted an important strengthening of the strategic model of legal aid in this country, and raises the hope that similar community law centres might be set up in other disadvantaged communities, especially those targeted for regeneration. Should this happen, then it is arguable that we will have come close to realising the basic proposal of the Pringle Committee back in 1977. That committee had called for the introduction of a mixed-delivery model of legal aid, combining both service and strategic elements. In the aftermath of significant improvements made during the 1990s to the state scheme of civil legal aid administered by the Legal Aid Board, we now have a reasonably comprehensive service model of legal aid in this jurisdiction. The experience of BCLC shows the way forward for the future development of the complementary strategic model.

NOTES AND REFERENCES

1   For this section, I have drawn heavily on chapter 9 of my book: Gerry Whyte, *Social Inclusion and the Legal System: Public Interest Law in Ireland* (Dublin, Institute of Public Administration, 2002).

2   I am most grateful to the following individuals for their assistance with this section of

my paper: Frank Brady, Evelyn Hanlon, Catherine Hickey, Sonya Keniry, Paula McCann and Áine Rooney. However, responsibility for any views or opinions, together with any errors or omissions, is solely mine.

3   Whyte, *Social Inclusion and the Legal System*, op. cit. pp. 38–9.

4   Sue Gogan, *Law from a Community Perspective: Unmet Legal Need in Ballymun* (Dublin, 2005), p. 15. This research, carried out during 2002–3, was commissioned by BCLC and initially published in May 2004. A subsequent updated version was published in December 2005.

5   Frederick Zemans, 'Recent Trends in the Organization of Legal Services', *Anglo-American Law Review*, no. 283 (1985), pp. 291–2.

6   Ibid. pp. 292–3.

7   Alan Paterson, 'Legal Aid at the Crossroads', *Civil Justice Quarterly*, no. 124 (1991), pp. 132–4.

8   Ibid. p. 133.

9   Note, however, that the Bar Council now operates a Voluntary Assistance Scheme whereby barristers provide services directly to NGOs working with members of the community who cannot afford legal services. All areas of the law, other than family law (which is adequately provided for by the state scheme of civil legal aid), are covered by this scheme. The scheme makes available every service that barristers ordinarily provide to clients, and that may include acting for a particular individual whose case is supported by an NGO, and also providing advice in relation to law reform.

10 Mike Stephens, 'The Law Centre Movement: Professionalism and Community Control' in Zenon Bankowski and Geoff Mungham (eds), *Essays in Law and Society* (London, 1980), p. 128.

11 BRL was a company set up by the then Dublin Corporation in 1997 in order to develop and implement a blueprint for the regeneration of Ballymun,

12 For an account of FLAC's history and activities, see Whyte, *Social Inclusion and the Legal System*, op. cit. pp. 302–22.

13 For an excellent account of the history of Ballymun, see Robert Somerville-Woodward, 'Ballymun: A History, *c*.1600–1997', vols 1–2, synopsis (unpublished report for BRL, Dublin, 2002). Volume 2, in particular – covering the period from 1960 to 1997 – details the background to the decision in 1964 to relocate tenants from city-centre tenements to Ballymun, and the many challenges subsequently faced by this new community because of the failure to provide adequate facilities.

14 Gamma Report, cited in BCLC, Feasibility Study Report (2000), p. 7.

15 Thus the Craig Gardner Report, published in 1993, noted that 'Ballymun is an estate with a very strong sense of community identity, and a level of community activity which is very high … [this] level of activity is a symptom of the difficulties faced by the community because residents find so many matters about which they feel the need to organise in order to negotiate with those in authority', quoted in Somerville-Woodward, op. cit. p. 58.

16 Though this only covered a population of approximately twenty thousand people,

this limited catchment area was justified on the grounds of the scale of the
deprivation experienced by Ballymun residents.

17 Legal aid goes beyond the provision of legal advice to include the representation of
the client before a court or tribunal.

18 BCLC Action Plan 2000, p. 11.

19 I discuss this point further in Whyte, *Social Inclusion and the Legal System*, op. cit. pp.
323–4, 328–9.

20 BCLC Evaluation Report (2003), p. 12

21 Ibid.

22 See Mauro Cappelletti and Bryant Garth, *Access to Justice: Volume 1 – A World Survey*
(Milan, 1978), p. 49.

23 BCLC Action Plan 2000, p. 16.

24 Nan Aron, *Liberty and Justice for All: Public Interest Law in the 1980s and Beyond*
(Boulder, Westview Press, 1989), p. 111.

25 [2005] IESC 33, Supreme Court, 12 May 2005.

26 I analyse the advantages and disadvantages of litigation strategy in more detail in
chapter 8, Whyte, *Social Inclusion and the Legal System*, op. cit.

27 Article 5 of the Solicitors (Advertising) Regulations 1996 [S.I. no. 351 of 1996]
precludes solicitors from making unsolicited approaches to any person with a view to
being instructed in any legal matter.

28 Figures for 2007 were not available at the time of writing.

29 Towards the end of 2004, the Legal Aid Board had to redeploy its law clerk from
BCLC in order to meet the demand generated by its Private Practitioners Scheme, but
this service was restored in 2006.

30 The use of video-link facilities enabled Ballymun residents to participate in
Dr Pádraic Kenna's course at National University of Ireland, Galway, on housing
law in 2007.

31 The current management committee consists of three community representatives, a
staff representative and representatives from Dublin City Council, BRL, FLAC, the
Legal Aid Board and the National College of Ireland, together with one co-opted
member, a solicitor with extensive experience of legal aid work.

When All is Said and Done

A Reflection on the Role of Education in Building Active Citizenship and Social Capital in Ballymun

MICHELE RYAN

When I was first approached to contribute a reflection on ten years of regeneration in Ballymun, I wondered how best to describe a journey that has been dynamic, exciting, vibrant, and full of possibility.

I then considered how best to do justice to those many people with whom I have worked, and who I have watched give reality to a vision despite countless challenges to progress, most notably difficulty in maintaining conviction that what individuals and institutions can do can really make a difference.

But so much has been learned over this period.

On a personal level, I have become experienced in an area and an arena I knew very little about. The National College of Ireland (NCI), for its part, has defined and refined its provision of learning and skills for regeneration – its 'roadmap' for building active citizenship and social capital. And throughout these years, I have become deeply committed to seeing the promise of regeneration realised for those who have been most affected by its potential.

After all, it is the people of Ballymun who keep faith with the vision on a daily basis, and the people of Ballymun who will sustain it in the years to come – when all is said and done.

NCI has long been promoting education as vital to the creation of vibrant local communities, and making meaningful connection with programmes of regeneration to achieve that end. We are a relatively small provider in terms of the national third-level university and IT sector – although unique in being a not-for-profit third-level college – located in Dublin's docklands but with an outreach mission.

The educational vision which inspires us is two-dimensional: we believe individuals whose potential is nurtured can be enterprising in their own interests, and we believe those individuals can use their knowledge and competencies in the interests of their community and the wider society.

This vision – of personal fulfilment alongside social contribution – has been clearly articulated and documented by the college as having its intellectual roots in John Henry Newman's educational philosophy.[1] According to Newman, a university education is not professional or vocational. Rather, it expands individual outlook and capacity for social and civic interaction. Speaking in the context of Catholic ideology, Newman stressed that students should pursue excellence, yet remain loyal to higher religious pursuits of contributing to society. NCI's dedication to social contribution is expressed in its attempts to address social integration, social inclusion and social regeneration. The training of contributors to society, Newman argued, was a function of developing their intellects.

In contemporary terms, NCI interprets the training of contributors to society as the development of active citizens, and we adhere to the view that active citizenship is critical to enabling education contribute to social progress. And so the personal and social dimensions of NCI's educational philosophy are dynamically interrelated. The nurturing of individual potential cannot take place effectively without considering the influence on the individuals of their surrounding socio-cultural environment. And the personal enrichment needs of the individual cannot be considered in isolation from the social issues and needs of the community from which they come.

Consequently, NCI's assessment of, and response to, educational need is carried out at both individual and community levels, and our work involves not only direct involvement with learners on campus but also active engagement with the external community outside the walls of the institution.

NCI recognises that empowered and enterprising individuals are the greatest asset in social regeneration. Accordingly, we channel our efforts into the provision of (a) educational opportunities for all learners, and (b) active outreach to cohorts of learners traditionally under-represented in third-level education, such as second-chance learners, learners from disadvantaged environments, and learners in the workplace.

In particular, we contribute to building community and social cohesion by:

- Encouraging local people to learn from and with each other;
- Facilitating individuals to build on what they already know;
- Promoting neighbourliness, and 'grounding' the principles of inclusivity, equality and mutual regard;
- Setting personal experience in the wider context of regeneration;
- Enhancing the quality of information and advice on local issues available locally;
- Imparting skills to gain employment.

In this way, and in creating educational opportunities and responding in innovative ways to educational need, NCI works in close partnership with business and the local community. As part of this partnership process, our faculty includes practitioners from outside the institution who bring direct experience of the needs of workplace and community, thereby linking learners with 'real world' issues, and enabling them to be more fully engaged with society.

This approach resonates with the educational philosophy of Ernest Boyer,[2] who conceived of excellence in higher education as commitment to improving in a very intentional way the human condition through community partnerships that would enrich the campus, renew the community, and give dignity and status to the scholarship of service. However, we have sought to go one step further: in making the community a supportive learning environment for the individual learner, we have sought to create, in turn, 'learning communities'.

This effort has required active engagement with parents, schools, community groups, voluntary organisations, businesses and statutory agencies in the learner's community. And through the processes of engagement and partnership with the wider community, we have achieved a better understanding of the factors involved in releasing individual potential, and thereby are better able to fulfil the educational mission with which we have been charged.

By being thus grounded in a social context, and acting from a value base of service, NCI has avoided becoming an 'ivory tower' of traditional academic life, and has instead become a significant contributor to the implementation of lasting solutions to long-standing social issues.

And so we came to Ballymun.

At NCI, we believe community regeneration is about creating and sustaining communities in which people of all kinds can live together safely, happily and with a sense of belonging. We understand how instances of serious neighbourhood deprivation are all too real and clearly experienced by residents as having a damaging effect on their lives. Regeneration projects that catalyse a process of change and development aimed at revitalising such communities by improving living conditions and quality of life in them therefore have our active support.

Research in this field has now become a respected focus of academic scholarship. Successful community regeneration projects require much more than investment in physical infrastructure. A range of social factors needs to be fully integrated into all projects, programmes and initiatives. In fact, it has been shown that when community members take part in the process of redevelopment, they report a community spirit and a positive commitment to making regeneration work.[3] However, when the focus of regeneration is based solely on physical factors (i.e. refurbishment projects), there is little reported improvement in quality of life or socio–economic factors.

It is no longer acceptable, then, to consider providing opportunities for people to develop educational and life skills as marginal extras, although budgetary allocation often implies that it is. Investment in people demonstrates as big a return as any other – in fact, bigger, if we are looking into the future and talking sustainability.

For this reason, NCI has firmly embedded what it does within the ambit of social regeneration. We see our mandate as being not only to help people acquire the kinds of personal, social and vocational constructs required for active participation in community, but equally to work with them directly in situations where they can learn and practise skills for sustainable community living.

In this way, we see ourselves engaging with the large body of literature that has emerged regarding the contextualised nature of learning – in particular, on the role of the learner as a practitioner, whose situated learning activity occurs within a community of practice – i.e. the social organisation of the communities within which people learn, and through which they shape how and what they learn. And in this way, we see ourselves engaging with our Jesuit heritage of preparing students to apply their ultimate personal good for the common good. For this reason we believe that what we do is at the forefront of complementing programmes of social change.

NCI receives only 35 per cent of its funding from the state, and operates on a not-for-profit basis. Notwithstanding, we leverage what resources we have at our disposal and seek to provide a wide range of learning opportunities in as many different places as learning can occur, both formally and informally.

Over the last ten years, undoubtedly one of our biggest undertakings in this regard has been concurrent with the regeneration of Ballymun, where we have grounded and based our involvement in the reality of people's shared experiences of the transformative change that has been taking place there. Working either directly or indirectly through our community partners, we have encouraged local people to situate themselves within the story of regeneration, to gain skills, negotiate pathways, and to develop an interest in taking part in a process of lifelong learning for personal and community gain.

We originally coordinated our activities from an office 'borrowed' in Stormanstown House, and focused on the following:

- Creating positive change in attitudes, expectations and lifestyles;
- Improving communication and social interaction skills;
- Establishing forums for community 'voice' and engagement in neighbourhood planning;
- Facilitating community development, teamwork and the achievement of collective goals.

These activities were gradually enhanced to include:

- Fostering local leadership with targeted 'skills upgrades';
- Developing active citizens and socially vibrant neighbourhoods;
- Developing and implementing skills for social innovation;
- Adopting a people-based approach to socially inclusive research activities.

This work has found a willing and supportive partner in the regeneration company itself, for whom the educational philosophy of NCI seemed to resonate with the tenor of the masterplan, most notably:

- Increasing retention and completion rates in primary and second-level education;
- Providing a continuum of education for adult and community groups;
- Improving access to third-level education;
- Providing access and bridging mechanisms for mature students to gain IT and business administration skills;
- Increasing flexibility in educational delivery;
- Enhancing the advice, support and placement infrastructure for those seeking employment;
- Accessing approachable careers guidance services, especially for young people;
- Ensuring that basic skills support, numeracy and literacy initiatives are delivered as an integral part of other training programmes;
- Providing 'taster' opportunities for work placements within existing operations.

Down through the years, personal, professional and financial support from Ballymun Regeneration Ltd (BRL) has allowed us implement a range of innovative capacity-building, training, and community empowerment programmes to local people in local venues.

Initially through its Centre for Educational Opportunity, subsequently through the Educational Opportunity Programmes unit with the School of Business, and most recently through its School of Community Studies, NCI has provided over one thousand one hundred local people with a varied menu of options and opportunities to meet, reflect, learn, organise for change and develop capacity for action. Probably the best-known example of this has been the Transition (or housing support) Programme (1999–2008). Developed and delivered in association with the Community and Family Training Agency (CAFTA), the purpose of this programme was to support local people through a major transition in their lives – the move from living in the well-known tower blocks to new, purpose-built low-rise homes. In particular, the programme sought to:

- Provide a forum whereby BRL and Dublin City Council could provide accurate and relevant information on all aspects of regeneration to residents;
- Give participants voice and opportunity for offering feedback and suggestions;
- Develop relationships between participants, statutory bodies and community groups;
- Support participants through the change process, building a bond of understanding and neighbourhood spirit, and providing a platform for people to share their hopes and concerns;
- Develop awareness, hope and pride in the new Ballymun;
- Increase the self-esteem and confidence of participants, promoting appropriate ways of sustaining long-term quality community ownership and leadership.

The programme is divided into different modules as a way of linking in with residents throughout the process of construction, with the content of each module specifically designed to give relevant support at each of the critical stages.

Module	Objective vis-à-vis BRL community-sustainability strategy	Level 1 outcome	Level 2 outcome	Level 3 outcome
1 Regeneration	To acquire understanding of regeneration programme (micro and macro)	Awareness of masterplan	Understand the *process* of regeneration	Obtain broader perspective on regeneration programme
2 Transition	To develop practical skills in basic home-management techniques	Acquisition of new skills not previously required in high rise	Maintain the 'new' homes and environment	Sustain the physical environment
3 Change	To become aware of the impact of transition, and know how to adapt to change	Increased receptivity to change	Manage change within own lifeworld	Sustain selves within new environment
4 Capacity building	To develop understanding of the concept of community sustainability	Development of community spirit	Understand community development principles	Creation of potential social capital

In particular, it was always intended that the programme would be linked to the ongoing allocations (when possible), maintenance and estate management policies in Ballymun; be run before, during and after people move home; encourage individuals moving together to learn together; allow flexibility around content and timing; and be structured so that the learning is facilitated rather than taught.

The Transition (or housing support) Programme was subsequently extended to include the following modules post-transition, i.e. after participants had moved home.

5 Communication and community	To equip participants with the skills they need to live independently and to maintain themselves in their new homes	Awareness of ways of communicating mutual regard and neighbourliness in everyday discourse	Willingness to dialogue with a variety of different stakeholders in the community	Skills to build consensus and active citizenship
6 Home management		Awareness of the basics of home management, including credit and budget management	Some basic knowledge of interior design and DIY	Understanding of some of the difficulties facing family cohesion in housing developments, including behaviour management and anti-social behaviour
7 Housing management	To equip participants with the skills they need to build collaborative community	Awareness of the different responsibilities of landlords and tenants in relation to improvement works, property maintenance and upkeep	Understanding of the relationship between responsible citizenship and the maintenance of neighbourhood facilities	Resident participation and involvement in estates management
8 Community capacity-building		Awareness of the role of residents' associations in creating coalitions of interest	Understanding of local decision-making processes	Active participation in local community groups

An important part of the success of this programme has been its ability to help people rebuild and renew themselves in the midst of major change. This has been in no small part due to the calibre and commitment of the facilitators leading the programme down through the years. When people feel that the reality of their situation is understood, felt and acknowledged by other people, self-esteem is raised and self-determination enhanced. A sense of being part of something larger and connected to others happens, and people become enabled to form and sustain a vision of a different world.

Throughout this programme – and those others briefly described in the paragraphs below – NCI acknowledges the powerful influence on the learners of their community's attitudes, values, expectations and experiences with regard to education, and of the web of alliances and interactions that exist within any community.

We recognise that the critical actors in the creation of the right environment for the release of potential include not just the educational provider but also the family, the school – pre-school, primary, second-level – and the community – community groups, voluntary organisations, businesses and other providers of further and higher education. Accordingly, we perceive that a key dimension to our work is the development of strong and effective partnerships between the college and these other powerful actors in the educational arena.

This has been highlighted in our work with CAFTA on the Transition Programme, with Ballymun's Community Law Centre, and with those other organisations included below:

- Neighbourhood Renewal Programme (1999) – *in association with Ballymun Women's Resource Centre* – designed to prepare local people for community representative and leadership roles within the new local neighbourhoods – sought to enhance self-esteem, encourage solidarity and strengthen confidence – encouraged individuals to build on what they already knew;
- Active Citizenship for Local Development Programme (2000–3) – *in association with Ballymun Neighbourhood Council* (formerly Housing Taskforce) – designed to stimulate learning and understanding regarding the ways and means of active citizenship – sought to

promote neighbourliness and 'ground' the principles of inclusivity, equality and mutual regard;

- Discovering University (2001–4) – *in association with Ballymun Initiative for Third-level Education* (BITE) – developed with the intention of giving young people a hands-on experience of university life, introduce them to a variety of subjects in a range of disciplines, and give them opportunities to explore which options they prefer;
- Oral History Projects and Practice (2004–5) – *in association with Enneclann* – designed to train local people to record and document life stories and local histories as community memories – sought to set personal experience in the wider context of regeneration – encouraged greater understanding of other people's viewpoints;
- Housing Advice and Advocacy (2005–8), Family Law Matters (2005–8), Employment Law (2006–8) – *in association with Ballymun Community Law Centre* – designed for people working in community organisations – each seeks to enhance the quality of information and advice on local issues available locally;
- Family and Community Support (2007–8) – *in association with the Community and Family Training Agency* – explores the common ground shared by family and community development – seeks to impart skills necessary to gain employment in community building and/or family support roles;
- Parents in Education (2003–8) – *in association with local Home School Community Liaison Coordinators* – builds the self-confidence of parents so as to take on role as active learners and educational role models for their children.

Through these partnerships, we seek to create an effective learning community that presents education as an exciting opportunity, and that creates a supportive culture in which learners are encouraged and motivated to develop to their highest potential, and to build relationships, networks and norms that facilitate collective action. This, we believe, provides a firm foundation for the creation of social capital.

There is growing evidence that social capital within a community has important implications for educational development, that education is crucial to the creation of an active citizenry, and that active citizenship is vital for communities to regenerate.

Yet, although it has been recognised that education plays a key role in the promotion of active citizenship, it is the formal (learning that takes place within a formal learning system) and non-formal (organised learning outside the formal learning system) learning contexts that are typically emphasised. In particular, there is an emerging trend of incorporating teaching about civics and citizenship into formal educational curricula, while outside the formal system, public information programmes (such as that coordinated by the Taskforce on Active Citizenship), together with community development and community education, provides a means of learning for active citizenship.

What seems to have been forgotten is the informal and incidental learning of the attitudes, skills and values associated with active citizenship – the lifelong process by which every person acquires and accumulates knowledge, skills and attitudes from everyday experiences and exposures to the environment.

For this reason, we have determined that the common theme running through our portfolio of offerings will be a focus on social learning, i.e. on collective, innovative, problem-solving processes of action, reflection, communication and cooperation. Each discrete offering has been designed to encourage local people to reflect critically on their learning and the relevance of that learning to their everyday lives.

In defining and delivering this model, we have sought to be responsive to the personal, social, economic and environmental issues identified by local people as being important in terms of regeneration. And as our portfolio has grown, each programme has been structured in such a way as to introduce local people to an array of concepts and skills in a manner that builds upon existing experience and knowledge, and raises confidence in terms of participating both within their own communities and in wider society.

The significance of this for sustaining the outcomes of the regeneration programme in Ballymun is evident. The pedagogy itself has helped create the preconditions by stimulating motivation for participation, cooperation and exchange of information and knowledge. But employing pedagogical devices alone has not created the conditions for learning active citizenship. Rather, if there is one important lesson my involvement in Ballymun has taught me, it is that education for regeneration, if it is to be successful, must employ strategies to enable local people to (a) engage active agency so that the dynamic and social natures of active citizenship can be embedded firmly within activities within the community, and (b) apply their own experience, history, prejudices, assumptions and beliefs inside every teaching situation.

In addition, as people learn in different ways, we must also ensure that a variety of different ways of learning are offered to them. Besides classroom learning, we need to recognise the effectiveness of learning by doing and learning by observing others. We need to acknowledge the wisdom in the saying that 'Learning cannot be separated from use', and we must create opportunities to increase social contact, interaction and opportunities for mutual aid so that this can happen.

Over the last ten years in Ballymun, NCI has formulated a way and a style of working that we believe is responsive, flexible and democratic. We have gained an understanding of how best to link our activities to the regeneration programme and to the local community organisations that service it. In turn, the Ballymun experience has informed our practice and philosophy as an educational provider. We are now firmly convinced that when people are given an opportunity to develop skills of participation and responsible action, and to reflect upon, review and apply their learning within the framework of flexible yet structured educational processes, their individual social capital increases, and thereby increases their confidence and ability to contribute as active citizens to the development and sustainability of the communities with which they identify.

The OECD (Organisation for Economic Cooperation and Development) in 2007 determined that learning could foster civic and social engagement in the following three ways:

- By shaping what people know – the content of education provides knowledge and experience that facilitate engagement;
- By developing competencies – helping people apply, contribute and develop their capacity to engage;
- By cultivating values, attitudes, beliefs – motivating individuals to engage.

With this in mind – even knowing that the regeneration programme is now halfway through its project life cycle – NCI intends to:

- Continue to develop avenues for learning active citizenship and creating social capital for the remainder of the programme;
- Adopt a holistic approach and link all elements of our work together;
- Work in partnership and make use of all of the skills and knowledge available to us in order to build momentum in the regeneration activity;
- Ensure actions are evidence-based using primary research and consultation where appropriate, as well as making full use of the expertise of our partners, the experience of frontline staff, of academic research, and of work of other third-level providers;
- Be innovative in our approach; we will take risks and try new things in our attempts to conquer the challenges that social regeneration brings.

This is in keeping with our revitalised mission to 'widen participation in higher education and offer students the opportunity to acquire the skills and self-confidence to change their lives, contribute to a knowledge-based economy and become responsible, active citizens'. If we have got it right, success will be evident through:

- Reduced fear of crime: reduction in anti-social behaviour, juvenile nuisance, criminal damage, burglary and vehicle theft;
- Improved socio-economic activity: acquisition of job or better job, career change or self-employment;
- Increased social capital: the number of residents assisted and supported into voluntary work or taking up active membership of a voluntary organisation or local group;
- Improved associational linkages: individuals and groups organised and involved in structured grassroots community activity;
- Improved skills of local residents in decision-making: development of a sense of ownership and responsibility for community;
- Increased satisfaction with the local neighbourhood.

In this, we are holding true to our original intention and design: to ensure that education makes a positive contribution not only to the regeneration of the town of Ballymun but, equally, to the rejuvenation of the place and its people.

Stormanstown House is no longer standing, and the changing landscape of Ballymun becomes ever more evident. We believe that as the programme of regeneration moves into the next phase, more and more local people will be found in further and higher education, not only as young CAO (Central Applications Office) entrants, but also as workers and mature students studying both full- and part-time. The challenge is to ensure that the programmes and courses with which they engage deliver the understanding and skills needed to enable them become decision makers about their own futures and in their own right.

This requires much more than off-the-peg courses. We must continue to develop opportunities for learning in non-formal settings in ways that directly relate to people's everyday lives and to the different concerns facing the different cohorts and age groups. The focus of activity must be at community level, coordinated through local strategic partnerships; schools, adult-training centres, advice and information centres, and law centres must all be seen as part of those partnerships. There is already a richness of practice in many of these areas, developed by individuals, teachers, youth workers and community groups; in recent years, progress has accelerated. The time for local people to acquire the skills, knowledge and value base to become active citizens and champions of the vision of a new Ballymun has never been more opportune.

When all is said and done, the build-up of social capital will be a valuable legacy.

NOTES AND REFERENCES

1   Helen Ruddle, *Learning and Teaching Journal*, vol. 1, no. 1 (2004).
2   Ernest Boyer, 'Creating the New American College' in *Chronicle of Higher Education*, A48 (1994).
3   M. Wood and C. Vamplew, *Neighbourhood Images in Teesside: Regeneration or Decline?* (York, The Policy Press, Joseph Rowntree Foundation, 1999).

Bridging the 'Town and Gown' Divide

Ballymun's Regeneration and the Role of Dublin City University

RONNIE MUNCK AND DEIRIC Ó BROIN

The purpose of this chapter is, first, to situate the relationship between Dublin City University (DCU) and Ballymun Regeneration Ltd (BRL) in the broader discussion about the role of universities in economic and social development in Ireland and globally, and, second, to examine the nature of the deepening relationship between DCU and Ballymun in the context of Ballymun's regeneration, in particular the introduction and evolution of the university's civic engagement strategy.

UNIVERSITIES AND DEVELOPMENT STRATEGY

Increasingly, governments are reviewing the role of universities as key stakeholders in the development and implementation of locally based development strategies, and in some cases in the promotion of foreign and non-local investment. International evidence shows that the shift in orientation of regional strategies since the 1980s towards supply-side initiatives, regional institutional capacity and endogenous development-led governments 'to look to universities as providers of a number of inputs to the development process, whether it be scarce resources of skilled labour, technology, or management development'.[1] In addition, the wider involvement of universities in the civic life of their localities has been perhaps undervalued, both by the universities and local civic institutions.[2] Concurrently, the changing nature of the governance of the development interests of localities is producing more opportunities for universities to become involved in the planning and governance of their surroundings.[3]

From the perspective of Irish universities, there has been a number of developments that have implications for the way universities link to their local communities and which help situate Dublin City University's relationship with North Dublin and, in particular, the regeneration of Ballymun. These include:

- A change in the way government views the role of the university as being no longer a production line for teachers, doctors and lawyers, but for delivering higher education to a mass, or at least a much larger audience than heretofore;[4]
- A massively increased demand for skills and knowledge arising from the competitive nature of the global economy – the new 'knowledge economy';[5]
- Increasing rates of technological change and new ways of organising production and distribution of goods and services;[6]
- The move from government to governance, and the increased number of agencies having an input into the delivery of public services, including higher education;[7]
- New patterns of urban and regional development arising from the greater mobility of capital and labour, the decline of industrial sectors, and the emergence of new sectors.[8]

D.R. Charles notes that while all of these developments 'have a national and international character', each has different implications for particular parts of the university and how it interacts with 'specific local circumstance'.[9] For example, the increasingly competitive nature of the global economy, and Ireland's place in it as a very open economy, can mean very different things for a school of computing and for a school of music within a university.

Interestingly, it is often at a local level that the interactions of these new developments can become most visible. Universities themselves are also changing as they evolve from what they were traditionally perceived to be, but rarely were in practice – i.e. self-governing collections of individual scholars – to public institutions following directions, or at the very least heeding the strong suggestions, from a mix of central government departments and specialist public agencies. This is new territory for many universities and their staff. Many senior staff never had to deal with the IDA (Industrial Development Authority), Enterprise Ireland, Science Foundation Ireland or the Higher Education Authority in the earlier parts of their career. That era is probably irrevocably lost.

At the same time, universities are being requested to work closely with local communities and local public agencies to build capacity, support innovation and enterprise, to address access issues and to support or participate in networks. Irish universities have increasingly become part of the new processes of governance, their representatives sit on local government sub-committees and task forces, they participate in a variety of local development initiatives and, in DCU's case, they are engaging, in a variety of ways, with BRL in the regeneration of Ballymun.

A number of challenges face universities as they attempt to address these new demands. For example, there is pressure to ignore the local as (a) universities become more 'internationalised' in an effort to attract more students from outside Ireland, (b) devise new partnerships, alliances and cooperative ventures with other universities, both in Ireland and abroad, and (c) develop relationships with private enterprise, both indigenous and transnational. It is important to bear in mind that globalisation has not made and is unlikely to make all urban places alike. Where you live and work matters more than ever when it comes to 'accessing jobs, income, public amenities, schools and green space'.[10]

A response, though not the only one, is for universities to work with other local agencies and groups – for example, local governments and chambers of commerce – to promote local concerns and discoveries internationally so that the wider world becomes aware of 'our' institution and 'our' locality. The aim is that the 'global' and the 'local' should be complementary, and that linkages and dialogical relationships should be established with other universities and their localities. This process is often referred to, rather inelegantly, as 'glocalisation'. It is this unusual blend of global challenge and local response that confronts universities and their localities.

BEYOND THE 'TOWN AND GOWN' CONFLICT

Gaffikin et al. observe that the university, in addition to being 'a significant source of received knowledge or wisdom' and a centre for 'culture, aesthetic direction and the moral force shaping the "civilised" society', also contributes to the economic health and physical landscape of localities.[11] This latter simple fact has often been overlooked. Indeed, for localities, the university is perceived as an island or 'enclave'.[12] As universities across Europe and the US have developed new ways of breaking down barriers between the academic 'enclave' and the local community, they have sought new ways to perceive themselves. From DCU's perspective, it views itself as an increasingly 'engaged' university. In this way, it seeks to 'reinforce the role of the university as a key urban institution, not an enclave of learning that happens to find itself in a city but a key element of the city'.[13] This development is a crucial part of the process whereby universities help localities engage with the myriad of globalising processes facing them. For example, DCU is represented on the board of a large number of local agencies and organisations, including the board of BRL, three area partnerships, a citizens' information centre, a regional think-and-do tank (NorDubCo), and an environmental NGO (non-governmental organisation) in its immediate area.

IRISH UNIVERSITIES AND URBAN DEVELOPMENT

Having examined the international trends in the evolving relationship between universities and economic and social development, it is important to note that Ireland is a relative newcomer to the scene. In Ireland – where an increasingly large proportion of our population lives in towns and cities – virtually all aspects of public policy could be claimed to have links to the 'urban'. This is a relatively recent development. While Ireland has become an increasingly urban country, the public policy perspective often appears to be focused on our rural issues. It is as if the public imagination has yet to make the leap from our rural and agriculturally focused recent past to our urban and services-based future.

Parallel to this failure to make this leap of imagination is the public's failure to understand the growing and changing role of universities – in particular, their importance to the country's economic development. It is now possible to state that Ireland's universities are likely to be the engine for economic development for the next generation. Not only will they educate young and not-so-young men and women to contribute to Ireland's civic, social and economic development, but their role as the producers of both basic and applied research is also growing and will continue to do so. In addition, universities are increasingly creating new commercial ventures and working in partnership with indigenous and transnational corporations to create employment and new products and services. These new roles have yet to be fully embedded in public policy, but that process has started, and will create many new challenges for both Irish universities and public policy makers.

In terms of understanding the public policies underpinning urban policies in Ireland – in particular, the background to urban regeneration projects like Ballymun and the role a university might play – it is necessary to clearly understand the socio-economic factors that caused the need for urban regeneration projects in the first place. These include the problems of physical dereliction, economic decline and social exclusion, and the accompanying issues of crime, anti-social behaviour and environmental degradation. We also need to address the increasingly problematic interactions between different ethnic and racial groups in a number of urban and periurban communities in Dublin. Hill calls these the 'wicked issues' because they are multifaceted in nature, they cross public service delivery and agency boundaries, and because they have no obvious solutions.[14] Tackling these 'wicked issues' and working to raise standards in education (including retention and attainment rates), health, the quality of urban design and of housing can often dominate the short-term political agenda, but are very difficult to address meaningfully in the immediate. As a result, both central and local government are often criticised for the fragmented, ad hoc and uncoordinated attempts to solve these issues.[15]

At the present time, these issues have a new urgency. The nature of the economic growth Ireland has experienced during the Celtic Tiger era has created increasingly segregated communities and extremes of wealth and poverty.[16] A reinvigorated approach to urban policy is required because of the magnitude and complexity of the issues outlined above, and because of changes in employment practices, industrial restructuring, and the move from manufacturing to services; for example, many European and US cities now have 'dual, segmented labour markets with increased unemployment and growing inequality'[17], i.e. once a worker is locked into the secondary labour market, such as casual and/or part-time employment, there is only a limited opportunity to move to the primary segment. As a result, putting the unemployed under pressure to find employment without providing them with realistic job opportunities on the demand side does not improve their chances of finding employment. In this context, many thinkers on urban development note that while industry may succeed by redeploying operations offshore to take advantage of lower labour costs, the consequences of disinvestment can be traumatic for specific cities and for particular areas within cities. The social implications are no less important. The marginalisation of vulnerable groups within the labour market and the resultant exclusion is not merely from the world of work, but also from access to housing, public services and even the right of citizen participation.[18] The contribution universities can play in addressing these obstacles is significant, but the necessary policy support and appropriate funding mechanisms are often lacking. While this may sometimes encourage the development of innovative solutions, it can result in problems of sustainability.

Public policy has often exacerbated this situation with poor housing design and allocation policies. Over the past twenty-five years, public policy has increasingly moved from a planning-led urban development approach to one oriented by the market. In Britain, this involved a move from a 'public sector dominated' policy process to 'mixed public-private systems of service delivery, and from bureaucratic pluralism to consumer choice and quality standards'.[19] While Ireland has, arguably, yet to experience the full extent of the neo-liberal policy agenda, it is clear that the parameters that framed the debate in other countries are in place here. Broadly speaking, neo-liberalism refers to the doctrine that market exchange is an ethic in itself, capable of acting as a guide for all human action. It has become dominant in both thought and practice throughout much of the world since the early 1970s. Its spread has depended upon a reconstitution of state powers such that privatisation, finance and market processes are emphasised. State interventions in the economy are minimised, while the obligations of the state to provide for the welfare of its citizens are diminished.

In some ways, this is what makes the regeneration of Ballymun so exciting: it represents a publicly managed and accountable effort to redevelop a locality without resorting to the vagaries of Public-Private Partnerships – that is, an arrangement whereby a public service is delivered in cooperation with the private sector. Not only has the public sphere retained control of the regeneration process; it has also shown how public-public partnerships – that is, partnerships between different public agencies – have huge potential to address social needs. Furthermore, it has worked with private developers and businesses without incurring the costs associated with other regeneration projects.

DCU IN THE COMMUNITY

We no longer hear so much about universities as 'ivory towers' divorced from the real world. Today, the complaint is more about the 'corporate university' dancing to the tune of the big pharmaceuticals and other corporate players. Many commentators now refer to the phenomenon of 'academic capitalism', as learning for learning's sake gives way to the business agenda. While not wishing to deny that the contemporary university is affected by the market in many ways, we must note that it is also part of the community.

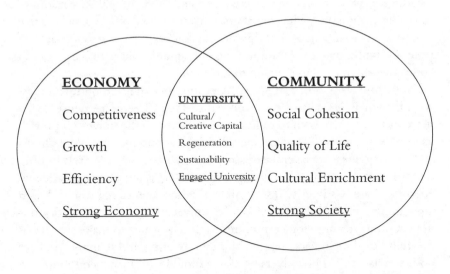

We see in this diagram how the engaged university is both impacted by, and contributes to, a strong economy and a strong, vibrant society. Certainly, both domains pull the university in sometimes conflicting directions. But we can also envisage – and maybe should seek out – the ways in which economic and social factors may act in unison, and even create synergies and a win–win situation.

The engaged university recognises that it is part of the community around it. The success of a university is very often completely intertwined with the prospects of the civic community of which it forms a part. A thriving university boosts the town or city in which it is situated. Likewise, a dynamic city is good news for any university trying to make its mark in a global knowledge system. The productive interaction and mutual engagement between the university and the wider community are beneficial to both in so many ways.

It is now increasingly acknowledged that universities can play an important role in community development, in support of civil society, in a knowledge-based global economy and in a socially challenged world. It can lead to enhanced human and social capital development, improved professional infrastructure and capacity-building and, more broadly, to benefits for the socio-economic, environmental and cultural dimensions of the wider community. The contribution towards the development of active citizenship is an intangible but significant addition. To generate debates on issues of significance to communities is also an area where universities can contribute directly to the quality of life.

If the university is not an ivory tower, nor an extension of the business world, then it needs to be socially embedded. There are dense social networks some may wish to call 'social capital' tying the university in with its local community. These can include social, economic, cultural, political and sporting links. Social embeddedness is a two-way street – a relationship that is sometimes fraught but always productive. As our close colleagues at Arizona State University (ASU) put it when describing their design aspiration to be socially embedded: 'A university can have an enormous impact on its surrounding community, and ASU wants to make sure it has the right kind of impact: sustainable, empowering and helping to effect positive change.'[20] The university is – or should be – firmly committed to social transformation and the pursuit of knowledge for the benefit of the community. A socially embedded university becomes anchored in a community, with its positive democratic and communal values. In its turn, the university can put its considerable intellectual resources to imaginative use to build thriving communities.

Some universities do not seem conscious of the place they inhabit but smart universities make use of their surroundings and create mutually beneficial linkages with local communities and neighbourhoods. DCU is a Dublin city university in a very real sense. We do not exist only in an anonymous international academic market. Local issues impinge on us in a direct manner; for example, in relation to Metro North or the siting of IKEA in Ballymun. For its part, DCU – as a sizeable public institution – has the ability to bring community issues to light with a certain degree of independence and moral legitimacy.

The global history of university–community engagement in pursuit of citizenship highlights its importance in terms of defining university identity, and in promoting sustainable cities and regions. For this citizenship strategy to be effective and durable, it requires deliberate and mutually determined collaboration between all sections of the university community (academic staff, administrative staff and students) and the wider community. Over and beyond this 'buy-in' with all sections of the university and the community, there is need for this strategy to be embedded in practice as well as principle. It is all very well for citizenship/community strategies to feature in strategic and mission statements, but these need to be embedded in academic and student culture for them to deliver. We now need to move towards a new stage where we will make time and resources available for staff and students, to build and maintain community partnerships, and to reward successful engagement strategies in practice.

Finally, we could say that an engaged university will seek to develop 'academic citizenship' among its staff and students. As a player with considerable weight in our local communities, the university needs to act in a socially responsible manner. The contemporary university should not conceive of community engagement as a luxury or a sideline. Rather, we need to understand citizenship as a vital third leg of what a university is about in addition to – and equal to – research and teaching. Student learning outcomes will be significantly enhanced through innovative curricula that are relevant to community issues and priorities. Increased opportunities for students experiential learning through community engagement will benefit them and the university. New research opportunities and funding sources can also be opened up for academics who engage creatively and openly with their wider community. There is an intangible but nonetheless real boost to a university's reputation when it is seen to act as a good citizen towards its wider community. Community engagement should therefore be seen as a core activity of the contemporary university. If this does not happen, the university will end up being a research-and-development adjunct to industry. If a university loses its social relevance and denies a commitment to academic citizenship, it is in danger of making itself irrelevant.

The above somewhat abstract though rather novel debate when set in an Irish context led DCU to promote a civic engagement strategy for the first time as part of the 2005–8 Leadership through Foresight strategy. The university agenda, according to the OECD (Organisation for Economic Cooperation and Development), 'has moved on from a desire to simply increase the general education of the population and the output of scientific research ... there is now a greater concern to harness University education and research to specific economic and social objectives'.[21] In particular, it is recognised that universities can and must play a role in the development of civil society and in building sustainable communities. The university is doing far more than preparing its students for employment: it is seeking to help create fully rounded citizens of their community. The Citizenship and Community Engagement Strategy is thus focused on enhancing citizenship and community sustainability, and on fostering lifelong learning. The potential benefits for the community and the university alike are considerable. It is the connection between the academy and the community that will produce synergies by putting forward new ideas and changing the way people work together. It is too late for the contemporary university to go back to the days of the ivory tower. DCU, fortunately, missed that phase; the option now is engage or risk social irrelevance.

In June 2008 DCU in the Community was opened in an approximately 130-square-metre educational facility in the heart of Ballymun. The planning for this exciting venture goes back to 2006, with Ballymun Regeneration Ltd acting as key promoter. It fitted in with the launching of DCU's own civic engagement strategy, and the synergy produced by this partnership was extremely productive. We were joined by the City of Dublin VEC (Vocational Educational Committee) in an innovative partnership to produce joined-up thinking in bridging the gap between the formal educational qualifications of local residents and university-entry requirements. The Shangan Road building has already begun to act as a real window between a severely disadvantaged neighbourhood and the world of higher education. Within DCU, this social and educational experiment is causing waves across the system. How to 'mainstream' it? How to resource it? Should we try to open other such centres? These are, of course, the problems of success, and we are proud to be making a tangible contribution to addressing the very serious deficit in terms of access to university in our direct community.

Another side of DCU's engagement with the community is its ongoing effort to establish the DCU Science Shop, whose subtitle, Community Knowledge Exchange, captures well what it is designed to accomplish. Aided by a European Union grant, we have already completed a pilot project in partnership with CAIRDE,[22] a local NGO that works with migrants around health issues within a capacity-building framework. This NGO-led research partnership addressed the vital and neglected issue of migrants' well-being from a mental-health perspective. Future projects with local partners are planned in the area of environmental issues. Within DCU, we are setting up structures and procedures so that community-based learning can prosper and be recognised as part of 'normal' teaching and learning. Our underlying objective is to move away from a 'knowledge transfer' model, where the university is seen as the font of all wisdom, to a more egalitarian 'knowledge development partnership', where experiential wisdom and learning is recognised as valuable and essential to the engaged university.

DCU, like all the other Irish universities, is at a crossroads. We can no longer do business as in the past – therein lies the path to obsolescence – but the pathways to the future are not yet clear. As part of our path-finding mission, we are engaging in an ambitious foresight exercise[23] designed to map out the scenarios now opening up, and also navigating a way into the future that is both imaginative and productive. One of the emerging priorities is precisely that we need to focus on the social relevance of our science and technology research. Universities are well placed – we would argue – to link the requirements of the economy with the demands of citizenship. The production of knowledge was once engaged in for its own sake; now we see the instrumentalisation of knowledge by market requirements, which has undermined the traditional elitist role of the university. The contemporary university can regain a positive role by prioritising social goals, by researching in socially relevant ways and by placing social inclusion at the heart of its mission.

DCU intends to play an increasing role with regard to the community around it. It is well placed to bridge the gap between science/technology and citizenship. Science needs to be relevant to people, and to engage with the day-to-day life of the citizen. Technology – not least, information and communication technology – permeates the world around us, but it needs to be humanised. DCU is also well placed to bridge the gap between the global and the local. We are constantly reminded that we live in a global knowledge economy, but we also live in particular places. In DCU's case, it is firmly embedded in Dublin's Northside – a hinterland characterised by acute deprivation, but also a great creative dynamism. For DCU, its civic engagement strategy is not an 'add-on' – something nice to do during the good times; rather, we are firmly committed to building our civic engagement role by promoting DCU in the community in all its aspects, and working alongside others to promote social, economic and cultural development in our part of the city.

NOTES AND REFERENCES

1   D.R. Charles, 'Universities and Territorial Development: Reshaping the Regional Role of UK Universities', *Local Economy*, vol. 18, no. 1 (2003), p. 7.

2   E. Shils, *The Order of Learning – Essays on the Contemporary University* (New Brunswick, Transaction Press, 1997), p. 166.

3   F. Moulaert, *Globalization and Integrated Area Development in European Cities* (Oxford, Oxford University Press, 2002), p. 13.

4   L. Downey, *Creating Ireland's Innovation Society: The Next Strategic Step* (Dublin, Forfás/Higher Education Authority, 2003).

5   M. Peters and T. May, 'Universities, Regional Policy and the Knowledge Economy', *Policy Futures in Education*, vol. 2, no. 2 (2004), p. 263.

6   Forfás, *The Report of the High Level Group on Manufacturing* (Dublin, Forfás, 2008).

7   P. Clancy and G. Murphy, *Outsourcing Government – Public Bodies and Accountability* (Dublin, New Island, 2005); A. McGauran, K. Verhoest and P.C. Humphreys, *The Corporate Governance of Agencies in Ireland* (Dublin, IPA, 2005), p. 9; D. Ó Broin and E. Waters, *Governing Below the Centre: Local Governance in Ireland* (Dublin, New Island, 2007).

8   D. Hill, *Urban Policy and Politics in Britain* (Basingstoke, Palgrave Macmillan, 2000); M. Boddy and M. Parkinson, *City Matters – Competitiveness, Cohesion and Urban Governance* (Bristol, Policy Press, 2004); N. Buck, I. Gordon, A. Harding and I. Turok,

Changing Cities – Rethinking Competitiveness, Cohesion and Governance (Bristol, Policy Press, 2005).

9   Charles, 'Universities and Territorial Development', op. cit. p. 8.

10 H.V. Savitch and P. Kantor, *Cities in the International Marketplace: The Political Economy of Urban Development in North America and Western Europe* (Princeton, Princeton University Press, 2002), p. 16.

11 F. Gaffikin, E. McEldowney, C. Menendez and D. Perry, *The Engaged University* (Belfast, Queens University Belfast, 2008), p. i.

12 Ibid.

13 Ibid. p ii.

14 Hill, *Urban Policy and Politics in Britain*, op. cit. p. 1.

15 OECD, *Ireland: Towards an Integrated Public Service* (Paris, OECD, 2008); O. Quinn, *Advisers or Advocates: The Impact of State Agencies on Social Policy* (Dublin, IPA, 2008); Ó Broin et al. *Governing Below the Centre*, op. cit.

16 D. Jacobson, P. Kirby and D. Ó Broin, *Taming the Tiger – Social Exclusion in a Globalised Ireland* (Dublin, New Island, 2006).

17 R. Hambleton, H.V. Savitch and M. Stewart, 'Globalism and Local Democracy' in Hambleton, Savitch and Stewart (eds), *Globalism and Local Democracy: Challenge and Change in Europe and North America* (Basingstoke, Palgrave Macmillan, 2002), p. 1.

18 D. Ó Broin, 'Participation at the Periphery: Community Participation in Reformed Local Government Structures' in *The Journal of Irish Urban Studies*, vol. 1, issue 1 (2002), pp. 47–59.

19 Hill, *Urban Policy and Politics in Britain*, op. cit. p. 2.

20 Arizona State University, *Five-year Strategic Plan Fiscal Years 2009–2013* (Phoenix, Arizona State University, 2008).

21 OECD, *University Research Management: Developing Research in New Institutions* (Paris, OECD, 2005).

22 www.cairde.ie

23 www.dcu.ie/themes

Fostering an Enterprise Culture in Ballymun

RONAN KING

If you think you can, or you think you can't – you are probably right.
Henry Ford

An té nach bhfuil láidir ní folar dó a bheith glic.
Whoever is not strong must be wily.
Irish proverb

Whatever their individual scope, all national and international experiences in urban regeneration agree on one point: successful renewal strategies are those that accommodate and integrate the physical, social and economic elements of regeneration as completely as possible. The urban tapestry is always a complex one, and urban planners – particularly in the context of regeneration – are attempting to weave strands together that, in normal circumstances, grow, support, colour and enhance one another over the course of generations. But whatever the speed or intensity of the operation, the final result must ultimately be judged by its ability to stand the test of time. As my fellow authors have dealt comprehensively with the physical and social dimensions of delivering the largest regeneration project ever undertaken in Europe, my focus in this essay is very deliberately on the third dimension – delivering a sustainable culture of job and wealth creation for all in Ballymun.

The quotations above have long informed my personal beliefs and approaches to both business and life. Like all great insights, they encapsulate immediately obvious truths while, at the same time, inviting us to question and review our conventional understanding of the world. They are, in fact, nothing less than a manifesto in miniature for an enterprise culture. Virtually every entrepreneur begins their career with the conviction – the inherent self-belief – that they can be quicker, smarter and more agile than the establishment figures they compete against. It is a philosophy, indeed, that underpinned the entire economic transformation of our island from the early 1990s onward. How a peripheral, basket-case economy of the 1980s became Europe's best performer a decade later is a story of investment, partnership and education, certainly; but the Irish word *glic*, or 'wily' – which is often somewhat imperfectly translated into 'clever' – is pointedly relevant here, too. With limited resources but unlimited ambition, Ireland generated an entirely new 'can do' culture virtually out of nothing. It developed a sense of self-belief and optimism that allowed our innate cunning and innovation to thrive – at home – for the first time in our modern history. Many have pointed to a confluence of successful achievements on the international sports fields and on the cultural stage as having set the backdrop for the new and urgent business dynamic that emerged in Ireland. What is certain is that it became a place where optimism supplanted the near fatalism of the past, and a new and vibrant dialogue was opened up with investors and multinationals seeking a foothold in the European Union (EU). This spontaneous new business culture was (and remains) prized for its ability to identify with, and meet the needs of those competing at the highest level, with the result that Ireland became the 'top of mind' location for multinationals seeking a serious foothold in the EU. Ireland, long under-performing and undervalued, moved from a post-colonial, dependency culture to a role model for emerging economies across the world. The challenge now – and it is as pertinent to Ballymun specifically as it is to Ireland generally – is to sustain that self-belief, to build on the hard-won achievements, and to look both outwards and inwards for the many lucrative opportunities still to be reaped.

INITIATING ENTERPRISE

To be enterprising is, intrinsically, to be fluid; to see the world not as others wish you to see it, fixed and immutable, but rather as something malleable and responsive to your influence. Enterprising people are not just those who transform financial capital, but those who influence social, environmental and cultural capital, too. In the pursuit and development of an enterprise culture in Ballymun, I am conscious that a viable interpretation of words such as 'enterprise' and 'entrepreneurial' must engage the broader *social* as well as the narrower *economic* meaning. The two, in fact, are inextricably linked. The business of creating and sustaining wealth and employment is only possible in a culture that supports it. An enterprise culture is, at its broadest, a place where opportunity exists and where people are comfortable with grasping it. It is, from a personal perspective, the recognition that our actions are materially linked to improvements in our life, and that the acquisition of skills and education as well as displays of resourcefulness, creativity and self-discipline – in all their forms – should be encouraged and rewarded.

What enterprise is not is the creation of a society of individuals, detached and distanced by an invisible caste system of privilege. Nor, even in its narrowest sense, is it expressed only in the desire and ability to establish and run a business. Clearly, there are enterprising employees as well as enterprising employers. Most succinctly, enterprise is a way of looking at the world that positions each individual contribution as part of a shared, positive and interconnected future.

There is a risk, when making such assertions, of speaking in a language that is abstract and seemingly vague. So it is important to stress the relatively simple litmus tests that establish whether an enterprise culture exists or not. Enterprise thrives in a community where:

- Creativity and ideas are valued;
- The impulse of an individual to start a business is supported by family and friends;
- Engagement with state agencies, the financial sector and information services is easy, positive and encouraging.

In short, it is a place where entrepreneurs are seen as playing their part in a functioning, viable community.

A SENSE OF EXCLUSION

The people of Ballymun have a long and blunt experience of being cut off from such opportunities, but it is worth remembering, as we address this exclusion in new and meaningful ways, that they were not unique in this. The sense of exclusion from economic opportunities was pervasive in Irish society only two decades ago. In the mid-1980s, Roddy Doyle wrote in *The Commitments* that 'The Irish are the blacks of Europe, and Dubliners are the blacks of Ireland.' He meant by this an emphatic correlation between the experiences of Irish people and African Americans – both subjugated economically, yet both vibrant and creative in their cultural output. It goes without saying that the perception of Ireland and Irishness has turned almost 360 degrees since the writing of *The Commitments*, but this advance, with economic growth its engine, has been, almost inevitably, uneven. Without the regeneration process initiated in the 1990s, Ballymun and its people would certainly have suffered even more from the prosperity gap that is perceived to have opened in our society. We are fortunate then that, whatever challenges we must address in economic regeneration, we have moved beyond a profound, even abject sense of being left behind and failed by economic progress.

There are many others well placed to talk about the specifics of transformation enacted over this momentous decade in the town's history, and though I will draw from these experiences, my intention in this essay is to focus on what I believe is the next step in Ballymun's journey. The role that I, as chairman, hope to play in this period has been made very much easier not just by the outstanding work of my predecessors, Danny O'Hare and Maureen Lynott, but by the ongoing contribution and commitment of a broad range of civil and public servants and all the stakeholders in Ballymun's regeneration. One of my key objectives going forward will be to link and coordinate the journey of Ballymun with that of the Greater Dublin city region. My aim, throughout, is to support – and if necessary, to fight for – the last and most critical element in Ballymun's regeneration jigsaw: the inculcation of a vibrant and sustainable business and enterprise culture that sets Ballymun apart, while at the same time allows Ballymun to be seen as an intrinsic element in the development of our capital city.

RETURN ON INVESTMENT

From its inception, Ballymun Regeneration Ltd (BRL), guided by a comprehensive masterplan, has made the most complete commitment possible to meeting the challenges of economic regeneration, being realistic at all times about the fundamental challenges the town faces in generating an economy where none existed before. BRL has promoted a cohesive partnership approach to economic regeneration, recognising that the evolution of both physical capital – in the form of new buildings, new neighbourhoods and new amenities – and social capital – in the form of an enthusiastic and skilled workforce – are the baseline to which significant economic capital will be attracted, and upon which economic activity will ultimately be generated. It has recognised, too, that, like any new base, this is one that needs to be set in place carefully before it can be built upon. An economy cannot be put in place without a significant infrastructure to support it; it is the final pillar of development and one that benefits fundamentally from the elements that precede it.

We are fortunate, then, to be at the point where the huge amount of financial and social capital invested in developing this base can finally be rewarded. In acceding to the demands of the long-suffering local community, the government recognised, in the mid-1990s, that there could be no short cuts or quick-fix solutions to rectifying the huge mistakes of Ballymun's past. The commitment to complete regeneration that was made from the start was critical to the successful outcome that we can now look forward to. This is not simply because of the scale of physical rebuilding required, but because significant investment represented the only tangible and meaningful way to demonstrate good faith with a beleaguered community well used to broken and empty promises. A half-hearted or niggardly approach at the beginning would have sent out a very obvious message to Ballymun that its needs and its future were not being taken seriously, and the necessary buy-in would have been much harder to achieve. This is a point worth stressing, particularly to those critics who seize on any opportunity to allege 'waste' and 'excess' in the regeneration process.

The investment by many other critical-service providers has been no less important, and the contribution and cooperation of Dublin City Council, the Health Service Executive, An Garda Síochána, Dublin Bus, the National Roads Authority and the Railway Procurement Agency, as well as community and housing services, educators and local development bodies, have been exceptional. All recognised in the regeneration process the opportunity for new thinking, and have developed new and interconnected strategies to engage with the needs of this emerging community.

By the time it is complete, over one billion euros in public funding will have been invested in Ballymun, an investment that is, first and foremost, an investment in people and community rather than bricks and mortar. It is, for all that, an investment on which the wider population has the right to expect a return. In this case, it is one that will be quantified in desirable social outcomes, in quality of life, prosperity and growth. These are the dividends that BRL is, in a sense, guardian of, and the board's intention is to secure and increase the yield long into the future.

We should, however, remember that the people of Ballymun are arguably the biggest investors of all. It is they who built and maintained a community spirit when conditions were at their most adverse. Their fortitude, their pride in being identified with Ballymun, and their heritage and culture are central to the wealth and value of the town, and represent an asset which we now bring forward and hope to develop in far more positive circumstances.

It would be well to add, at this point, that there is no better example of social investment than the level of commitment demonstrated by the one hundred-plus employees of BRL, many of whom have made this project not just their work, but the centre of their lives for the last decade. These are public servants who have put a sense of duty far above financial remuneration and far beyond the normal requirements of the nine-to-five. Over the years, they have confronted the challenges of regeneration in very real ways, facing down the threats and intimidation of drug dealers, gangsters and other peddlers in human misery, and putting themselves in real physical danger in the process. They did so because they believe fundamentally in this project. BRL is an organisation in which personal courage, principle, hope, aspiration and determination are all part of the everyday currency of business. As we move into the final phase in the lifespan of BRL, all of us who work with it continue to benefit and be inspired by these energies and convictions.

CRITICAL MASS

The logic of regeneration is, in some senses, inevitable. As infrastructure and social structures change, so the relationships they determine change also. Many new organisational, community and business supports have already been put in place to meet the needs of the emerging town of Ballymun, and there are excellent and inspirational success stories within it. But it would be a critical error to assume that a laissez-faire attitude could satisfy the community's greater objectives for a sustainable economic future. Indeed, the regeneration process, for all its successes, risks becoming a cosmetic exercise if economic activity does not receive the same priority and resources as the other elements of the masterplan.

We are at a stage, then, of 'critical mass' in Ballymun's history, when the sense of opportunity and challenge is heightened and sharpened to a particular degree. Ironically, as we celebrate a decade of achievement, the greatest risk for the entire process now becomes most apparent. A failure to establish sufficient mass in terms of economic sustainability would threaten the community not only with a regression into marginalisation but a regression doubled in intensity by the sense of disappointment and disenchantment. Despite a transformed physical environment, the footprint of Ballymun's marginalised past is not hard to find. The town has a higher than average unemployment rate, and significantly lower educational attainment than the national average. The majority of its workers must commute to other areas for employment. Though newly housed, Ballymun has significant clusters of people who still need to be newly resourced: encouraged, supported and assisted to extend their skills range and to seek gainful employment. Failure in the economic sphere would, along with marginalisation and exclusion, almost certainly lead to a return, with new virulence, of the social problems that blighted this community over many decades.

LEARNING FROM OTHERS

This is not, however, a scenario that I believe will prevail. Having had personal experience in planning such ambitious regeneration projects as the Dublin Docklands and Belfast's Titanic Quarter, I believe that there are important lessons to be applied to Ballymun, and grounds for optimism, as long as we 'believe that we can'.

Whereas the redevelopment of the Docklands area involved transforming a central brown-field site, and targeted investors specifically operating in financial services, Ballymun's regeneration has been preoccupied with recreating the living spaces of a pre-existing but marginalised and disadvantaged community. The Docklands project was a classic model of transforming a largely redundant waterfront site, putting high-value jobs, retail and living opportunities at its core. Ballymun, by contrast, is almost conventional town planning in reverse. Here, we have built the houses, amenities and infrastructure first, and now seek to find an economy that can animate and sustain them. Ballymun is not unique in facing this very postmodern challenge, but its scale makes it highly significant. We can be proud, then, that solutions pioneered here are providing lessons for similar redevelopment projects right across Europe.

In spite of these key structural differences, the Dublin Docklands and Ballymun benefit from having at least one thing in common: culturally, both seek to dissolve barriers between diverse communities, and to ensure that the process of urban regeneration tackles both the ghetto and the fortress mentality. As Ballymun advances and aspires to become a town that meets and satisfies many different social and cultural needs, the experience of the Docklands communities have particular relevance. Great care was taken, from the beginning, to support positive interaction between the new and traditional communities, and though it is an ongoing challenge, the Docklands have shown that integration can accumulate into a dynamic and valuable resource in its own right. The Docklands also offer a viable model for how business and the community can interact fruitfully. I make this point recognising that there remains in Ireland – particularly, though not uniquely, in disadvantaged areas – scepticism, if not downright distrust, as to the objectives and goals of business and its relationship with the broader community.

ALIGNMENT

Community aspirations can and should be aligned with the needs of business and commerce. There is, in fact, no conflict between the two. Having served as president of the Dublin Chamber of Commerce in 2007–8, I can say that while the Chamber is unashamedly supportive of harnessing the commercial potential of the city, it has many other areas of concern as well. The Chamber is one of the oldest public voluntary organisations in Ireland, and, fundamentally, is an organisation passionate about the city, its culture, its people and its future. It takes a great interest, therefore, in any infrastructural, social or economic issue that impacts on the city's development and affects the lives of the inhabitants. As a non-political advocacy group, it promotes Dublin as the only economic region in Ireland with the ability to compete against other major cities and economic hubs around the world, and in straitened economic circumstances, it believes that focus, alignment and strategy are necessary if this fact is to benefit not just the Greater Dublin Area, but the entire economy of Ireland.

The Chamber has identified a number of key strategic imperatives necessary for Dublin to maintain the competitive edge that transformed it in the last decade. In essence, the city must continue and intensify its drive towards becoming a hub of creativity; it must attract knowledge industries that benefit from and generate creativity; it must anticipate and invest in the infrastructure that supports such businesses; and it must brand and identify itself internationally, asserting vigorously the qualities that make it such an attractive place to live and work. In short, the Chamber believes that Dublin needs to trigger a new Enlightenment, where the city becomes a place of progress and agility, and specifically a place where:

· Creative solutions are envisaged as part of our business culture;
· Being a testing ground for new ideas is encouraged;
· We learn from and share our knowledge and creativity with others;
· Success is viewed as a positive that benefits our entire society;
· Our education system values enterprise and a 'let's do it' mentality;
· Our true competition is recognised as international, not national;
· Specialisation and niche services are seen as key to growth.

In a key 2007 report, *Developing a Knowledge City Region*, the Chamber highlighted concrete initiatives to support and develop this process. A number of these have particular relevance to Ballymun, among them:

· A targeted system for the purchase of PCs;
· A rapid increase in the use of information and communications technology within our education system;
· The piloting of WiFi across Dublin's public transport system;
· The encouragement of tailored and practical training of SME (small and medium enterprise) managers in information and communications technology;
· Ensuring every new home is fibre-ready;
· The up-skilling of workers in the early learning and childcare sector.

These are practical supports – some new and innovative, others already in place among our rivals – that will set the framework for the emergence of a culture in which knowledge capital and creativity can flourish.

How the Dublin city region manages the current national and international economic downturn will be a critical test of its enterprise capability and its ability to evolve. Growth is all about confidence, and in spite of its current problems, Dublin has every reason to be confident about its position as a competitive economic zone in Europe and beyond. If, as seems entirely likely, the Dublin city region grows to a population of two million by the end of the next decade, pressure and opportunity will be placed in equal amount on its housing stock and its infrastructure. Dublin will need to change, innovate and adapt rapidly, and the need for interconnectivity between its different regions will intensify. Of course, it is not alone in facing these challenges. The global trend towards urbanisation reached a tipping point in 2007 when, for the first time in the history of mankind, over 50 per cent of the world's population lived in urban environments. It is now recognised globally that planned city living is the only viable solution to providing quality of life for rapidly growing populations. There are major opportunities to interface the regeneration of Ballymun with the development needs of the Dublin city region. Ballymun has the potential not simply to respond to its own historic needs but to anticipate and evolve structures to become a centre for continued growth and prosperity for the broader region.

Ballymun, in this context, can create a quality of life not just for its own community but for the thousands of workers and their families who will come to live there in the coming decade.

PERCEPTIONS

It is critical that the invisible barriers that limit ownership of ideas, the entrepreneurial spirit and business confidence should not gain extra life because of our current economic concerns. In spite of the dramatic changes within Ballymun, it is fair to say that perceptions outside continue to experience a time lag. Some would argue that the name Ballymun will always conjure up negative images, particularly in the national context. But other parts of Ireland have suffered from severe social problems and negative stereotyping and have managed, in spite of this, to become dynamic hubs of business and enterprise. Ballymun will do the same, recognising that the most effective way to overcome prejudice is by witness. Bringing the business community to see what has been achieved here, and highlighting the suitability and attractiveness of the area for investment will be central to completing the stakeholder circle. Inward investment has been critical to the success of the entire Irish economy. Attractiveness to outside investment must be one of the cornerstones of the town's economic development strategy as well as a driver of a sustainable culture of enterprise within it. Ballymun has substantial lands available to it on the M50 corridor, and BRL is looking very actively at the infrastructural development necessary to open them fully to investment. The town will be promoted assertively and confidently in this process, both in conjunction with the state investment bodies, and on its own if necessary. When there are opportunities, we will go after them and establish in the minds of national and international investors the opportunity and rewards available to those first movers who take advantage of them.

RESOURCES

In spite of our island's economic success over the last fifteen years, some have argued over the extent to which an entrepreneurial spirit can truly be said to pervade here. While there are numerous individual success stories, it is a fact that, set against the European average, a disproportionate amount of our wealth and job generation is as a result of foreign direct investment. What is clear, as our economy moves into uncertain territory, is that both an enterprise culture and an indigenous corporate business sector become increasingly important in safeguarding our economic future. Building a local and indigenous business resource through creative linkages with inward investment will be a key element of BRL's strategy. 'Creating an enterprise culture' should ultimately become as familiar a refrain in Ballymun as in any other significant town in Ireland.

If Ballymun is to reach its potential in this process, education resources are critical. Young people – indeed, people of all ages – have the innate capacity and talent to do a great many things. If they are only allowed the opportunity to investigate their own skills, and given the tools to test and develop them, extraordinary things are possible. The word 'education' derives from the Latin *educare*, meaning 'to lead or draw out from within'.

The Irish education system is, in contrast, primarily driven by the need to inculcate information which, satisfactorily regurgitated, forms the basis for our points system. It is an environment where the resources and cultural context of each school are hugely influential in deciding the educational outcome of its students. It is not, for all that, entirely without the ability to encourage initiative. The Royal Dublin Society (RDS) Student Innovation Awards, aimed at transition-year students, is a fine example of an education process geared specifically to enterprise and to opening the minds of students to a future as entrepreneurs. But all too often, such projects depend on the resources of individual schools, and young people in disadvantaged areas are far less likely than others to be among those invited to think of the business world as a place they could have a stake in. They are also, of course, far less likely than students from more affluent areas to progress to third-level education, and so are denied the key resources necessary to enter and succeed in the business world.

Dublin City University (DCU) must count high among the resources that could help reverse this situation; a huge door-step advantage that Ballymun has only very recently begun to exploit. The location of a new 300-student residence on Ballymun Main Street was the first step in building meaningful and substantial linkages between the two. All of our third-level institutions have roles to play in positioning Dublin in the premier league of knowledge cities, and DCU easily ranks as one of our most ambitious and innovative. The strategic development of the town is already benefiting from educational outreach programmes, and the development of diverse and creative engagements between university and community could lead, ultimately, to the development of vibrant business incubation centres, the attraction of high-end jobs for highly educated workers, and the creation of many supporting downstream jobs.

BALLYMUN: SIM CITY?

The popular computer game *Sims* invites players to build and manage (among many other things) their own virtual town. Managed from the 'eye of God' perspective, they control the fortunes and destiny of their inhabitants, and as any experienced player knows, laying down the right infrastructure at the start is key to successful outcomes in the long term. There are a few essentials: putting your town close to a major traffic artery;

ensuring it has a port and airport; putting in a metro line or two; and adding a university so that its inhabitants have the resources to develop the town in the next generation.

Ballymun is probably no *Sims* player's idea of an ideal town, yet, extraordinarily, it has in place (or will, with the completion of Metro North) all these advantages. More amazingly still, it is only now, with a decade of regeneration completed, that we are in a position to engage in the first serious dialogue about how to take advantage of these resources. Envisaged in this way, Ballymun can no longer be seen as a marginalised, disadvantaged environment, but as a grossly undervalued asset. How often have we seen Irish investors sent this message about developing regions in Central and Eastern Europe, and watched as they scrambled to pick up properties in areas about which they knew next to nothing but had great expectations of rewards in the future? Soon, I hope, we will be able to talk about Dublin's prime investment opportunity as one sitting on its own doorstep, and be able to make a far more convincing case as to future returns.

Dublin Airport is the gateway for some twenty-five million people entering and exiting Ireland every year. Destination Ballymun is doing a great deal of work to establish the town as a place attractive to those who come for leisure and tourism. As a business and residential hub, its proximity must also be exploited. We live in an international commuting culture where people may choose to live in Dublin but work in London, Brussels or Geneva. Ballymun is in an ideal position to provide high-quality accommodation, and business and community services for people to whom proximity to the airport is important.

The Port Tunnel has, similarly, created a degree of access from Dublin's city centre to the north city that has yet to be fully exploited. There is no reason why Ballymun cannot be the first to take advantage of this major infrastructural asset in developing its attractiveness to business and logistics providers. Similarly, the development of the Dublin Metro will bring with it not just a new infrastructural solution to Dublin, but should create a major economic corridor that will have Ballymun at its centre. BRL will work to ensure that the town is ready to maximise its positioning and potential as this major investment project develops.

In terms of building a sense of destination, it is hard to overstate the value of the opening of the IKEA store in 2009. There is surely no other retailer in the world that could generate the level of excitement, employment, prestige and volume of visitors that the Swedish home furnishings giant will bring to Ballymun. As well as being a destination in its own right, IKEA brings with it a lot of downstream potential, and not just in the more obvious service areas. The opportunities for supply could ideally position Ballymun as a centre for manufacturing and logistics, taking advantage of its dual accessibility to port and airport. A visit to IKEA will be, for many, the first visit ever to Ballymun, and our intention is to use this as a chance to promote other retail and cultural opportunities within the town. We can conjecture the possibility of Ballymun becoming a major centre of retail facilities, satisfying not just its own community but others in the Dublin region and beyond.

The development of a new shopping centre is, of course, critical to completing the infrastructure circle for Ballymun. Though we can make many boasts in terms of the redevelopment of its Main Street, residents rightly question why their needs for a satisfactory modern retail centre have not yet been met. At the time of writing, the last regulatory hurdles of what has been a long and arduous process appear to have been leapt, and we look forward to work beginning in earnest in 2009. A modern, well-resourced shopping centre is a basic civic amenity in any town, and BRL will not consider its role complete until such a development is finished and operational.

THE 'NEXT GENERATION' CHALLENGE

As it enters its second, and certainly its final, decade of existence, the role of BRL will continue to be that of a development agency focused on providing leadership and support for the community it serves. As Ballymun sheds the legacy of deprivation and exclusion, the challenge of economic advance is implicitly tied to its future, and the aspiration of all who are involved in its regeneration is to see a region emerge that is autonomous, distinct, confident and, yet, fully integrated within the Dublin city region.

Ten years ago, Ballymun – having experienced forty years of marginalisation – emerged fragile and scarred but determined. Today, it is in a position, undreamed of back then, to stake its claim as Ireland's premier twenty-first-century town. It can only truly assume this mantle, however, if it manages to exploit the new opportunities at its disposal.

We are now ready to enter a period of acceleration and excitement in this process. Nothing can be taken for granted on this journey except that the decade-long determination of its stakeholders to succeed remains undimmed. The optimism released by the process of regeneration can, I believe, be transformed over the next few years into a new civic self-confidence as Ballymun fosters a 'can do' mentality across many different spheres of activity. We have no better role model than our country's recent history as to what can be achieved when self-belief and confidence surmount scepticism and doubt in the economic arena. Ballymun's 'next generation' challenge has already been set: it must ultimately determine the shape of its own future, generate and attract new business leaders and entrepreneurs, and execute a business culture that maximises its strengths and opportunities. I look forward to working with stakeholders and all the community as we support, drive and generate the next hugely exciting chapter in Ballymun's history.

Ballymun: Future-proofing with a Green Community

DUNCAN STEWART

Ballymun's high-rise housing complex was conceived in the 1960s as a single social sector, exclusively residential solution to a major social housing shortage nationally. Developed on green fields on the outskirts of North Dublin city, it embodied a state response to this housing crisis whereby contemporary global and European social housing concepts were transposed directly to Ireland without due consideration for the specific needs of the social sector it set out to house. Neither did it respond to the social and community-related implications of moving large numbers of inner-city families to this remote location – as it was perceived at the time – beyond the outskirts of North Dublin's suburbs.

This system-built, 'functionally designed' accommodation may have provided a much better and more modern standard of housing than was experienced in the congested old tenements of Dublin's north inner city, and when first unveiled the project was hyped as the symbol for the emerging new 'industrialised Ireland', and an example for other social housing projects to follow.

Its imposing high-rise accommodation quickly proved unsuitable to Dubliners, who were unprepared for this lifestyle change. The remoteness of the flats left many parents separated from their children, who roamed in unsupervised groups in search of adventure in the large open spaces bereft of sport or play facilities. The members of this social group – who had been brought up in a culture of closely knit communities and were often dependent on their relatives, who lived in close proximity – found it especially difficult. The lucky few who were employed at the time had difficulties in travelling to work in the inner city, where the only work opportunities that suited their skills existed. They often had large young families that were unable to cope with this changed circumstance.

These high-rise blocks, with a low-density layout, stretched out over a vast area, where they were set in a large, open, 'prairie' landscape, with insufficient public transport to local facilities, schools and shops.

Ballymun, like other new housing developments at the time – such as Ballyfermot and Finglas – developed as single-use and single social group areas, comprised of people rehoused from the inner city and who used to live and work around the old industries or the docks. Others were rural people migrating to Dublin in search of work opportunities, little prepared for this style of living. As these areas became stigmatised as ghettos, it made it even more difficult for the residents to get work. With growing unemployment and young people left idle, disadvantaged and frustrated, unsocial behaviour started slowly to infest the area. Despite all this, many of the younger generation growing up in the flats adapted well to this high-rise lifestyle, where friends and neighbours formed strong bonds. But with growing concerns in the 1990s, Dublin City Council set out a comprehensive new strategy for urban renewal and social regeneration for Ballymun, which commenced in 1998.

BALLYMUN'S URBAN REGENERATION AND THE DEVELOPMENT OF A NEW TOWN

Over the past ten years, we have seen the new town of Ballymun unfold. Its original residents moved from the older, now obsolete tower blocks and medium-rise, linear, social housing 'flat' complexes – comprised of a system-build of repetitive precast concrete wall panels – to new homes in neighbourhoods with their own architectural identities, integrated communities, attractive landscaped parks and play spaces, new schools and community facilities.

The first objective of Ballymun Regeneration Ltd (BRL) was to rehouse the existing tenants from each apartment block. As the old towers were systematically dismantled – and after close consultation and preparation – the residents were relocated to new housing units. A major difficulty was building a 'new' town where the existing community continued to live, and where disruption and nuisances from construction sites needed to be carefully managed. What has emerged from this well-planned urban design and implementation strategy is now shaping up to be Ireland's first comprehensively regenerated new town, with a population of about thirty thousand residents.

The new Ballymun town centre has started to take shape, and provides well-designed urban spaces enclosed by new public service, cultural, recreational and commercial buildings with contemporary architectural treatments, together with landscaped play facilities. The new town itself has prioritised sports and play facilities, with well-landscaped public parks.

As Dublin has grown and sprawled into the countryside well beyond Ballymun in recent years, this new town is now strategically located within easy reach of Dublin's city centre. It is directly adjacent to, and within, the ring of Dublin's M50 motorway, and is close to the airport, new industrial and office parks, Dublin City University and the M1 to Belfast.

The transformation from the old flat complexes has performed exceptionally well to date. It has dramatically improved the urban environment, and seems much appreciated by the local community, where a noticeable cultural change has unfolded. Residents of Ballymun now show a growing civic pride of place, a greater sense of identity and esteem, and appear to act more responsibly towards their new physical environs. Raising awareness has been a key factor in this: residents' meetings, public consultations, training workshops and so on have empowered residents to adapt to a changed urban landscape. It has motivated them to respect and manage their new homes, and to care for and protect their local environs.

A comprehensive waste collection and recycling culture has become mainstream for residents. This includes food waste digestion and green waste composting. Water conservation and rainwater-harvesting measures, together with home energy management, have permeated this changing community.

NEW CHALLENGES AND OPPORTUNITIES AHEAD

BRL has recently launched a new biodiversity plan that sets out a strategy for landscaping the new developments with extensive planting of indigenous broadleaf trees. It will create natural habitats for wildlife, help to filter the air and absorb carbon dioxide from the atmosphere. This new urban forestry programme will, in due course, soften, screen, enhance and mature the newly built urban environments.

A growing issue is energy. Fuel costs rise and daunting challenges loom concerning our future security of energy supply. There is also an urgent need to mitigate our growing greenhouse gas emissions, which will entail a paradigm shift in the way we generate and use energy, and will have a major effect on our lifestyles. With Ireland's growing vulnerability arising from a current 92 per cent dependence on imported fuel, and our carbon dioxide emissions way out of line with our mandatory requirements as specified by the European Union, there is an urgent need to respond in a sustainable way to this growing predicament. As energy costs rise, the number of people caught in the 'fuel poverty' net is growing. By tackling these problems and conceiving appropriate solutions, opportunities will be created for towns like Ballymun to lead the way towards a more sustainable future for Ireland.

Heating our buildings, powering our homes, industries and public infrastructure, and solving our transport needs is emerging as one of the greatest challenges facing us. Transforming Ballymun into a 'sustainable' new town, as many European towns are attempting, is, in my opinion, a new and exciting challenge for this community.

Ballymun is shortly commencing phase four: the next stage of its building development, comprising four hundred new housing units. These dwellings and apartments will be designed and constructed to an A2- or A3-rated standard of energy efficiency – at least 60 per cent better than was required by our previous building regulations, and 20 per cent better than the revised standards introduced in July 2008. There will be much higher standards of thermal insulation in roofs, external walls, ground floors and glazing, with an airtight building envelope and controlled ventilation. A unique condensing unit will ensure high-efficiency gas boilers, and this will dramatically reduce the heating demand and energy consumption of the new residential units, and – like most modern private apartments – make inefficient traditional fireplaces in living rooms obsolete.

The proposed Emerald Housing Co-op will demonstrate the future solutions for sustainable housing. As oil, gas and electricity prices rise, there will be a need to switch from these fuels to renewable sources such as solar energy, wind power and biomass (wood or energy crops) for space heating.

Rather than change all the existing boilers, it may be more practical and cost effective to pipe for 'district heating' to the older houses and apartments, leaving the existing heating systems undisturbed. 'District heating' could be fed from local combined heat and power plants, and from renewable energy sources.

There is huge potential for wind energy in Ballymun. Many of the large open spaces and public parks could accommodate wind turbines. Like the 850-megawatt embedded turbine at Dundalk Institute of Technology, they need to be of a sufficient height to avoid the wind turbulence caused by tall buildings, and at a reasonable distance from houses. These could contribute to the 'green' agenda of Ballymun by reducing electricity demand for street lighting and so on, and become a visual celebration of renewable energy. An ideal location for large wind generators would be in the open landscaped areas close to the M50. They would send a clear signal that Ballymun is going 'green'.

Large arrays of photovoltaic panels to generate electricity and thermal solar collectors could be positioned on many of the south-facing slopes of houses and public buildings, and on existing flat roofs inclined to the southern sun. All future buildings could be designed to include south-facing pitched roofs, thereby maximising the potential of integrating this clean, free, low-maintenance and zero-CO_2 solar energy.

As energy costs rise, so too will the price of food. Intensive food production and food miles from imports require substantial amounts of energy inputs. Over the next few years, I believe we will see a resurgence in local farm produce. Ballymun is fortunate to be located in a farming region with a strong tradition in horticulture. With this local back-up and knowledge in food production, more householders will start growing their own vegetables and fruit in their back gardens, and even on balconies and flat roofs of apartments, once they have been made safe for access. In most urban centres in Europe, where people live predominantly in apartments, allotments have been developed to satisfy this need. They are usually very neat and attractive, and besides offering a pleasant and convenient place for residents to grow their own vegetables, fruit and flowers, they create interaction in the community and a strong social bond. There are still many open spaces in Ballymun sufficiently close to the residences to develop this very desirable and sustainable activity. Clusters of small, shared garden plots like this would add greatly to Ballymun's natural resource and ambience, and encourage a culture of growing and self-sufficiency.

A culture of caring for the environment is also developing in Ballymun, where waste recycling, centralised food waste digestion and green waste composting is already well established in this regenerated new community. The positive environmental impact of the voluntary non-governmental organisation, Global Action Plan, has raised an awareness that has permeated the whole community. It has been fostered and strongly supported by BRL, with the necessary assistance of local volunteers and residents. Water conservation measures have been introduced in many of the dwellings, and rainwater harvesting with the use of water butts for landscaping has been very successful.

Regarding sustainable transport, mobility and accessibility, Ballymun is located within reasonable proximity of the city centre, and presently served by a Quality Bus Corridor (QBC). The proposed Metro line to the city centre is strategically critical for Ballymun's sustainable future. This will minimise the need for car use and petrol consumption, provide connections to Dublin's growing bus and train integrated network, and help reduce CO_2 emissions. Local transport within the new town is provided by a bus service connecting the various neighbourhoods to the town centre, and eventually to the proposed Metro line.

The further development of safe and convenient cycling lanes and secure bicycle parking is critical for the town's future, as are footpaths for walking to schools, shops and bus stops. This will encourage the use of more sustainable modes of transport, thereby helping to minimise the use of private cars and unsightly car parking lots. If the Metro line is introduced, it could facilitate the new town in transforming into a virtually car-free, sustainable urban centre.

I believe that the urban redevelopment has transformed Ballymun beyond belief. If ten years ago, I had tried to visualise its future, I could not have comprehended the holistic change that has now unfolded. It is one of Ireland's real housing success stories, despite the madness and greed of the building boom's insatiable 'Celtic Tiger' that has left its scars on the landscape in many other places around the country. Among Ballymun's positive attributes are its high quality urban design, social inclusion, community enhancement, neighbourhood identity and pedestrian permeability. Its well-thought-out, landscaped recreational spaces create a sense of place and positive public space. They are enclosed by the new apartments and houses, from where parents can keep in contact with and supervise their children as they play below.

The overall redevelopment has achieved the necessary sustainable densities, without overcrowding, and without reverting to anonymous high-rise blocks. Yet its new landmark towers act like gateways, accentuating the character of the town centre. The design and development facilitated mixed-use and diverse house types, suitable for families, single people, elderly residents and people with disabilities. The housing varies from medium-rise apartment buildings and own-door duplexes over single- and two-storey units, to conventional terraced two- and three-storey family houses with back gardens. The diverse architectural styles, varied forms and unique treatments clearly expressed in each neighbourhood create interest, surprise and identity as one moves from place to place – a consequence of BRL's efforts to research and address the specific needs of the residents it was rehousing.

Ballymun must now stand among other sustainable contemporary towns of Europe as a model to be followed. It is a wonderful and vibrant place to live and put down roots for a full life. I am confident that with the enthusiasm, commitment, synergy and professionalism of all those on the BRL and Dublin City Council teams who, working with the residents, have helped shape this town, that Ballymun will blossom as it matures and settles. Here's to all the BRL team, to Ballymun's sustainable future and to all its citizens!

Linking Urban Regeneration and Sustainable Development

The Rediscovery Centre, Ballymun

ANNA DAVIES

It is now commonly accepted that those who are poorest, most deprived, vulnerable and socially excluded also experience the greatest environmental inequalities. These inequalities are visible at a range of scales from the supranational to the local. While the international reach of the mass media frequently reminds us of the extensive gulf between experiences of people in the global North and South, stark inequalities also exist between rich and poor within nations and between localities. Indeed, it has been established that the poorest communities disproportionately experience local problems such as litter and fly-tipping, graffiti and uninviting public spaces.[1] Cumulatively, these indicators of poor-quality environments can be linked to wider socio-economic problems such as unemployment, drug abuse, crime and educational underachievement. Such problems impact negatively on people's quality of life, and affect their health and sense of well-being.[2]

Recognition of the links between deprivation and poor-quality environments has led to calls for a socially inclusive approach to sustainable community regeneration.[3] For, as Lucas et al. suggest, focusing on economic regeneration that provides skills and employment experience without attention to local environmental problems can result in a selective exodus whereby those who are able to will seek a better quality of life elsewhere.[4] At the same time, attending to the revitalisation of physical environments without addressing community needs may lead to the marginalisation of local residents as gentrification occurs and property prices increase.

However, encouraging attention to environmental issues in the context of urban regeneration has proved particularly frustrating for those concerned with sustainable development. It has been argued that focusing on environmental improvements can deter community participation in projects when concern for the environment is perceived to be an issue for the affluent or specialist professionals. While it may be true that those who live in deprived communities rarely invoke terms such as 'local environment' or 'sustainable development', research has shown that they do hold, and can articulate, a keen understanding of the interlaced nature of local environmental, social and economic issues.[5] It would seem likely, then, that to link sustainable development with urban regeneration successfully requires appropriate processes to bring together relevant actors and residents, allowing all to find a voice.

This chapter reflects on the practice of linking urban neighbourhood renewal and sustainable development through the case study of the Rediscovery Centre, Ballymun. The Rediscovery Centre is examined as a site of integrated grassroots enterprise that explicitly seeks sustainable community regeneration. A description of the centre and its activities, particularly focusing on the most developed initiative, a community-based furniture recycling project, is presented. The penultimate section reflects on the future for such schemes given the current national planning context in Ireland. Finally, key challenges and opportunities for sustainability enterprises are identified. First, however, consideration is given to the intersection of sustainable development, regeneration and grassroots enterprise.

SUSTAINABLE DEVELOPMENT, REGENERATION AND COMMUNITY ENTERPRISE

The link between urban regeneration and sustainability was tenuous for much of the last century.[6] In the UK, towards the end of the last millennium, researchers such as Couch and Dennemann,[7] Gibbs et al.[8] and Gibbs[9] wrote extensively about the contradictions between the push towards economic competitiveness – central to many urban regeneration programmes – and calls for more sustainable development. In particular, Gibbs identified the tensions between sustainable development's emphasis on participation and local democracy, and the privatisation that so often dominated economic rejuvenation initiatives.[10] However, in recent years rhetorical transformations among urban policy makers, particularly within the European Union, have begun to emerge.[11] Within these policy statements, it is argued that urban planning can and should give equal status to the environmental, social and economic consequences of every development, and that it is possible to revitalise depressed areas in ways that satisfy the wishes of both residents and businesses. What is clear from such statements is a sense that 'a key aspect of sustainable development is to regenerate neighbourhoods "from the inside"'.[12] What this means is that creating a sense of ownership, which can be fostered when local people are involved in decisions, may itself stimulate further improvement, thus developing a self-fulfilling sustainability to the regeneration agenda. As an additional benefit, such community-led projects are often seen as enabling significant environmental gains with a minimum of resources.[13]

One way of explicitly bringing together urban regeneration and sustainable development can be identified in the adoption of environmental concerns within some social economy initiatives. Such initiatives have been termed 'grassroots sustainability enterprises'[14] because they include economic activities (albeit operating on a not-for-profit basis) that support the social needs of local communities (geographical communities as well as communities in terms of need or interest), while also enabling a continued focus on environmental issues. Activities such as community gardening, fuel poverty alleviation schemes and environmental education projects may all qualify as grassroots sustainability enterprises,[15] providing there is a desire to generate self-help, counter social exclusion and build grassroots empowerment.[16]

Waste management is one arena of grassroots sustainability enterprise where initiatives have been identified across the globe – for example, in Africa,[17] Asia,[18] New Zealand,[19] the UK[20] and North America.[21] However, while there is now an emerging body of literature on broader waste management issues in Ireland,[22] grassroots sustainability enterprise in the field of waste has received little attention from policy makers. Documents such as the 1996 *Waste Management Act* (and its amendments),[23] the 1998 *Changing Our Ways* policy statement,[24] and the *Protection of the Environment Act,*[25] for example, do not mention this sphere of activity. This does not mean that waste-related sustainability enterprises do not exist in Ireland, but the extent of their activity is limited in comparison with many other countries.[26] Given this restricted development of waste-related grassroots sustainability enterprise, the Rediscovery Centre in Ballymun provides an innovative focal point both for the local community to reflect on the value of materials previously perceived as waste, and for the wider policy community to consider the benefits of such facilities for sustainable regeneration.

THE REDISCOVERY CENTRE

Importantly, from a sustainable development perspective, the regeneration programme established by Ballymun Regeneration Ltd (BRL) is characterised by a progressive approach to urban renewal. As the title of this volume suggests, the focus of BRL has been on innovation through regeneration. In particular, BRL has attempted to combine physical improvements to the area with economic and social regeneration. Initially, the integration of sustainability concerns was facilitated by environmental action plans. In 2000 Global Action Plan (GAP) Ireland – an environmental action group that forms part of an international network of organisations – was invited to work with the community in Ballymun, and in 2001 GAP Ballymun was established. In line with the aims of Local Agenda 21, GAP Ballymun works with communities to provide them with the practical tools that they need to make a difference to the sustainable development of the areas in which they live.

A key component of the vision for sustainable development in Ballymun is the Waste Management Strategy produced by BRL working with GAP and Dublin City Council. The Waste Management Strategy, which aims to become a model for waste minimisation strategies and recycling throughout Ireland, incorporates a hierarchy of facilities starting at the household level and including drop-off points and bring-centres and, finally, a Rediscovery Centre. The idea behind the Rediscovery Centre emerged from recognition of growing national and international concern in relation to the management of natural resources and waste. It is envisaged that the centre will encourage and support innovative recycling and reuse programmes within Ballymun and the surrounding areas; to 'rediscover' the fullest potential of materials commonly known as waste.[27] As well as dealing with the current and future waste needs in Ballymun, the objectives of the centre are to create local employment and employment training opportunities, to change the negative perception of second-hand products and materials, and to show Ballymun as a positive model for a holistic approach to waste management in Ireland. In this way, the Rediscovery Centre typifies the ethos of a grassroots sustainability enterprise, and fulfils demands for integrated and sustainable community development.

Although the Rediscovery Centre building – based on a low-environmental-impact design – will not be complete until 2009, there are a number of associated initiatives already under development: rediscover fashion, community re-paint, community composting and furniture recycling. Rediscover fashion is a programme that was launched at the Greener Ballymun conference in May 2008. It aims to use 100 per cent recycled clothing and materials to develop a designer clothing and accessories brand. Of the other three community recycling schemes, community re-paint – initiated by the Rediscovery Centre, working in partnership with GAP Ballymun, Silloge ECO (Environmental Community Organisation) and the Poppintree Environmental Project – collects, sorts and redistributes paint that is normally sent by households and traders to landfill. The community composting scheme – funded by the Environmental Research Technological Development and Innovation Programme – involves local residents and the civic offices using a central composting system to recycle kitchen waste. The compost is distributed to various community gardens through a gardening action programme operating in the area. The final initiative – furniture recycling – has multiple goals, and is a partnership initiative between a number of organisations in the public and community sectors, including BRL, Poppintree Environmental Project, FÁS (Foras Áiseanna Saothair, the training and employment authority), Sunflower Recycling and Dublin City Council. In addition to showing that furniture can be reused and restored rather than being sent for disposal in landfill or dumped illegally, the furniture recycling project provides employment and training opportunities for the local community. While the other activities of the Rediscovery Centre are very much in their infancy, the furniture recycling project was established in 2006, and a recent evaluation of it has been conducted.[28]

In line with calls emanating from the European Commission[29] and researchers, such as Gibbs,[30] Lucas and Fuller,[31] and Eames,[32] the furniture recycling project seeks to be a self-sustaining community enterprise. In essence, the project involves the training of community members to refurbish and redistribute donated furniture. According to Mullin,[33] the project has multiple goals including:

- Increasing awareness about waste and resource management within and beyond the local community (educational);
- Contributing to local, national and international targets to reduce waste sent to landfill (environmental);
- Providing affordable and high-quality materials for resale within local communities (social and economic capacity building);
- Offering training opportunities and employment opportunities to marginalised sections of the community (economic development);
- Developing a self-financing activity through sales, repairs, training allowances, donations, community funding opportunities and a not-for-profit ethos (financial sustainability).

The furniture recycling project operates within the Poppintree area of Ballymun. Trainees work a two-and-a-half-day week, with the manager employed for three and a half days to manage the training programme and administer the initiative. Space constraints mean that temporary storage facilities in two separate locations within the local area are currently being used for furniture that has yet to be refurbished, or is waiting for resale/redistribution. Donated furniture is predominantly collected by employees for a minimal collection fee, although low-income households are not charged for the service. The collected furniture is then stripped, repaired and repainted or French polished, and items are taken for resale to the monthly farmers' market held in Ballymun.

The project is predominantly funded by BRL and FÁS via the Poppintree Environmental Project. BRL provided start-up funding in 2006 along with the manager's salary and ongoing expenses, and continues to support the running of the project by covering insurance, rental and transport costs. The FÁS Community Employment Scheme pays for trainee wages, materials and training requirements, with the ultimate goal of facilitating the transition of participants into employment or further education. To ensure continuity of funding, any initiatives availing of Community Employment funds are required to demonstrate that their trainees are making such a progression into the workplace, and that all training is officially accredited. According to the research conducted by Mullin,[34] funding from BRL and FÁS ensures that the ongoing costs of the project are covered, while any profits made from sales, repairs and collection charges are reinvested in the scheme. While the project is too recently established for an accurate picture of progression to be identified, an ambitious target of 80 per cent has been set for the numbers of employees moving on to further employment or education.

From an environmental perspective, the project has made a contribution to removing waste from the landfill waste stream. Mullin reported that in 2007 6,500 kilograms of material were recovered, with 2,000 kilograms restored and sold, 1,200 kilograms passed on for direct reuse and 2,400 kilograms in storage.[35] Of the materials collected, 900 kilograms were disposed of to landfill, resulting in a recycling rate of 87 per cent. However, it is the combination of the self-financing not-for-profit environmental initiative with a social component that distinguishes a sustainability enterprise from other economic development or environmental initiatives. In contrast to kilograms of waste diverted from landfill or costs incurred, many of the social benefits of sustainability enterprises are hard to measure quantitatively. As reported in Davies, for example, the generation of greater self-esteem through workplace interactions within sustainability enterprises could lead to stronger community and family bonds, provide more positive role models for younger generations, and help reduce drug and alcohol abuse among participants, though providing concrete evidence of such contributions is difficult.[36] It is a serious problem for sustainability enterprises that traditional accounting techniques tend to identify the measurable rather than what is necessarily important, and a range of sustainability accounting mechanisms – sometimes referred to as green or social accounting – is being developed to try and rectify this situation.[37]

In the absence of an agreed mechanism for evaluating the social impact of sustainability enterprises, Mullin interviewed employees in an attempt to establish the impact that participation in the furniture recycling project has had on their quality of life.[38] In addition to the more obvious benefits of skills acquisition through training, the employees also commented on how the project provided an opportunity for them to change the structure and focus of their lives. In some cases, this was related to developing a disciplined approach to coming into work at a prescribed time every week; in others, it was overcoming the social isolation that often comes with unemployment.

At the same time, however, difficulties have been encountered by the furniture recycling initiative. In one instance, there were problems regarding the need for certification of training as required by the Community Employment Scheme. The necessary skills for furniture recycling – such as French polishing and reupholstering, which are taught at the project – have not traditionally been certified in a way that FÁS would normally recognise, and this has led to difficulties over funding. However, the major obstacle facing the project to date has been space constraints and the availability of only one room for all the activities of the operation. There is a lack of space for storing both donated furniture awaiting refurbishment and for restored furniture awaiting resale. In addition, the lack of office space means there is little privacy for one-to-one interactions between trainees and the manager, or for administration of the project. A knock-on effect of the limited availability of storage is that the project is unable to respond to potential donations of large items such as lounge suites, and this restricts the expansion of the operation. Another problem relates to the retail dimension of the project. Sales of refurbished furniture are limited to one public outlet – the monthly farmers' market in Ballymun – and this restricts the spectrum of potential buyers for the items. Although significant at present, these last two issues will be addressed once the Rediscovery Centre building is opened, with its larger facilities and the provision of the eco-shop as a permanent retail outlet for goods.

Despite these challenges, the furniture project has clearly provided economic opportunities for marginalised sections of the community, contributed to reducing the amount of waste going to landfill, and provided enhanced possibilities for greater social interaction. So what is the future for such grassroots sustainability enterprises?

THE FUTURE FOR GRASSROOTS SUSTAINABILITY ENTERPRISES

The Rediscovery Centre and its activities, particularly the furniture recycling component, appear to be successfully addressing the call of central government for increased sustainable development that is 'about getting the balance right between the economy, social issues and the environment ...

It's about getting these three elements working together.'[39] It is surprising, then, that such grassroots sustainability activities are not more visible in national sustainability agendas. Instead, Ireland's sustainable development strategy focuses primarily on the economy–environment interface. Such an approach is associated with the concept of ecological modernisation that is characterised by an optimistic win-win view of achieving economic development and environmental protection simultaneously.[40] Yet it is more than a decade since David Pepper took the ecological modernisation thrust of Ireland's sustainable development policy to task for allowing economic imperatives to dominate development while leaving more progressive environmental policies and, more specifically, innovative social initiatives on the margins. Over the years, his concerns have been echoed by others examining environmental policy,[41] agriculture[42] and natural resource exploitation.[43]

Of course, social concerns are receiving attention, and there have been seven social partnership agreements (SPAs) where issues of social and economic policy are agreed between the government and selected social partners. What does seem to be absent is a truly integrative approach to sustainable development that considers the economy, the environment and social issues simultaneously. Despite its title, *Sustaining Progress*, the sixth SPA (2003–5) still predominantly focused on issues of economic and social policy, with sustainable development only mentioned in relation to tax and agricultural policies. While the SPA suggested that '[s]pecific initiatives in support of entrepreneurship will be taken, including, in particular, to support entrepreneurship by women and in the social economy',[44] no link was made to the concept of sustainable development, and no further details were provided on the proposed initiatives. The current SPA, *Towards 2016,* takes a lifecycle approach to the social policy agenda, and again marginalises the concept of sustainable development. Although sustainable social and economic development is seen as central to Ireland's position in a dynamic world economy,[45] there is no mention of either the social economy or social enterprise as having a positive role to play in this. Rather, social finance is mooted as a means of combating social exclusion by providing repayable finance to community-focused activities.

Ireland's fourth National Development Plan, *Transforming Ireland – A Better Quality of Life for All,* marks some departure from the economic–

environment interpretation of sustainable development, stating that it 'rests on three *integrated* major pillars – economic, social and environmental' (emphasis added).[46] Yet there is little evidence of integration in the document itself. While the national policy agendas are preoccupied with parallel paths for environmental protection and social regeneration, it is up to innovative grassroots sustainability enterprises such as the Rediscovery Centre to demonstrate the benefits of truly integrating economic, environmental and social concerns.

CONCLUSION

What the Ballymun Rediscovery Centre initiative is demonstrating is that within a locality there is scope for basing a set of new and refocused economic development policies around sustainability. In addition to the focus on waste addressed in Ballymun, there are other ways in which urban regeneration and sustainability can be more closely linked. These could include developing local exchange trading systems (LETS), creating jobs through environmental improvement schemes and devising local indicators of sustainability. However, as Gibbs argues, such initiatives would need to be developed through an integrated holistic strategy rather than in isolation, and they would be challenging to implement in the face of enduring conditions of competitiveness in urban spaces and ongoing commitment to standard interpretations of an entrepreneurial state.[47] These conditions and commitments have been termed the 'third way' of urban regeneration because they appear to be attempting to tread a precarious line between welfare intervention and neoliberalism.[48] Although intuitively appealing, such approaches have already been criticised as being thinly veiled moral crusades that can be seen as merely a new way of disciplining local communities.[49] For as Burningham and Thrush rightly point out, 'it is important to remember that such places are not unequivocally poor environments – these places are "home" to those who live there, underpinned by close ties with friends and family. Casual descriptions of localities as "poor" or "polluted" offend residents, stigmatising their homes and by extension themselves.'[50]

Nonetheless, there is much to be learnt from the work of the Rediscovery Centre for policy makers, practitioners and researchers alike. In particular, the sensitive approach to the activities within the centre has, to date, ensured that it has aided revitalisation and identified the area as a site of innovation rather than reinforcing negative perceptions experienced by many communities facing multiple social and economic problems. Unfortunately, however inspiring isolated cases of good practice – such as the Rediscovery Centre – may be, they are unlikely to be sufficient for disseminating sustainable urban spaces across Ireland given the transboundary nature of many economic, environmental and social problems. The next challenge will be to expand and coordinate initiatives such as the centre beyond the locale to the city, the county and beyond. Crucial to meeting this upscaling challenge will be the development of evaluative frameworks for initiatives that can accommodate the more intangible qualities of social and community capacity building, and the impact of environmental quality on community self-esteem alongside the more quantitative measures of employment and certified training schemes. Given the current lack of acknowledgment for grassroots sustainability enterprises in national policy making circles, the onus for promoting such activities is very much on those who are already striving hard at the coalface to make livelihoods better for communities. As such, greater collaboration and communication between like-minded organisations and individuals can only help promote innovation and expansion in the sector.

NOTES AND REFERENCES

1   M. Eames, *Reconciling Environmental and Social Concerns: Findings from the JRF Research Programme* (York, Joseph Rowntree Foundation, 2006).
2   K. Burningham and D. Thrush, '*Rainforests are a Long Way From Here': The Environmental Concerns of Disadvantaged Groups* (York, Joseph Rowntree Foundation, 2001).
3   M. Eames, *Reconciling Environmental and Social Concerns*, op. cit.
4   K. Lucas, A. Ross and S. Fuller, *What's in a Name? Local Agenda 21, Community Planning and Neighbourhood Renewal* (York, Joseph Rowntree Foundation, 2003); K. Lucas, S. Fuller, A. Psaila and D. Thrush, *Prioritising Local Environmental Concerns: Where There's a Will There's a Way* (York, Joseph Rowntree Foundation, 2004).
5   Burningham and Thrush. '*Rainforests are a Long Way from Here*', op. cit.; Lucas et al., *What's in a Name?* op. cit.; A. Davies, 'Nature in Place: Public Visions of Nature-society Relationships in the UK' in R. van den Born, R. Lenders and W. de Groot (eds), *Visions of Nature* (Berlin, LIT-Verlag, 2006), pp. 87–105.
6   A. While, A. Jonas and D. Gibbs, 'The Environment and the Entrepreneurial City: Searching for the Urban "Sustainability-fix" in Manchester and Leeds', *International*

Journal of Urban and Regional Research, vol. 28, no. 3 (2004), pp. 549–69.

7   C. Couch and A. Dennemann, 'Urban Regeneration and Sustainable Development in Britain: The Example of the Liverpool Ropewalks Partnership', *Cities*, vol. 17, no. 2 (2000), pp. 137–47.

8   D. Gibbs, P. Deutz and A. Proctor, 'Industrial Ecology and Eco-industrial Development: A Potential Paradigm for Local and Regional Development', *Regional Studies*, vol. 39, no. 2 (2005), pp. 171–183.

9   D. Gibbs, 'Urban Sustainability and Economic Development in the United Kingdom: Exploring the Contradictions', *Cities*, vol. 14, no. 4 (1997), pp. 203–8.

10 Ibid.

11 European Commission, *Building the Future: EU Research for Sustainable Urban Development and Land Use: Sustainable Urban Environment* (Luxembourg, European Commission, 2004).

12 Ibid. p. 12.

13 S. Young, *Promoting Participation and Community-based Partnerships in the Context of Local Agenda 21: A Report for Practitioners* (Manchester, University of Manchester, 1996); R. Murray, *Creating Wealth from Waste* (Demos, London, 1999).

14 G. Seyfang and A. Smith, 'Grassroots Innovations for Sustainable Development: Towards a New Research and Policy Agenda', *Environmental Politics*, vol. 16, no. 4 (2007), pp. 584–603.

15 S. Young, 'Community-based Partnerships and Sustainable Development – A Third Force in the Social Economy' in S. Baker, M. Kousis, D. Richardson and S. Young (eds), *Politics of Sustainable Development: Theory, Policy and Practice Within the European Union* (London, Routledge, 1997), pp. 217–36; S. Young, 'Participation Strategies and Environmental Politics: Local Agenda 21' in G. Stoker (ed.), *The New Politics of British Local Governance* (London, Macmillan, 2000); L. Stocker and K. Barnett, 'The Significance and Praxis of Community-based Sustainability Projects: Community Gardens in Western Australia', *Local Environment*, vol. 3, no. 2 (1998), pp. 179–89; C. Vargas, 'Community Development and Micro-enterprises: Fostering Sustainable Development', *Sustainable Development*, vol. 8, no. 1 (2000), pp. 11–26; C. Church, *The Quiet Revolution: 10 Years Since Agenda 21: Measuring the Impact of Community-based Sustainable Development in the UK* (London, Shell Better Britain Campaign, 2002); C. Church and J. Elster, *Thinking Locally, Acting Nationally: Lessons for National Policy from Work on Local Sustainability* (York, Joseph Rowntree Foundation, 2002); P. Malhotra, 'Management of Community-based Energy Interventions in Rural Areas of India: Issues and Perspectives', *Sustainable Development*, vol. 14, no. 1 (2006), pp. 33–45.

16 J. Bucek and B. Smith, 'New Approaches to Local Democracy: Direct Democracy, Participation and the "Third Sector"', *Environment and Planning C: Government and Policy*, vol. 18, no. 1 (2000), pp. 3–16; A. Etzioni. *The Way to a Good Society* (London, Demos, 2000); G. Chanan, *Community Sector Anatomy* (London, Community Development Foundation, 2004).

17 G. Myers, *Disposable Cities: Garbage, Governance and Sustainable Development in Urban*

Africa (Aldershot, Ashgate, 2005).

18 T. Forsyth, 'Building Deliberative Public-Private Partnerships for Waste Management in Asia', *Geoforum*, vol. 36, no. 4 (2005), pp. 429–39.

19 L. White and L. du Preez, *Measuring the Community Sector's Contribution to New Zealand's Waste Strategy* (Kaikoura, Zero Waste Conference, 2005).

20 C. Robbins and J. Rowe, 'Unresolved Responsibilities: Exploring Local Democratisation and Sustainable Development Through a Community-based Waste Reduction Initiative', *Local Government Studies*, vol. 28, no. 1 (2002), pp. 37–58; D. Luckin and L. Sharp, *Sustainable Development in Practice: Community Waste Projects in the UK* (Bradford, University of Bradford, 2003); D. Luckin and L. Sharp, 'Exploring the Community Waste Sector: Are Sustainable Development and Social Capital Useful Concepts for Project-level Research?', *Community Development Journal*, no. 40 (2005), pp. 62–75.

21 A. Weinberg, D. Pellow and A. Schnaiberg, *Urban Recycling and the Search for Sustainable Community Development* (Princeton, NJ, Princeton University Press, 2000).

22 See M. Boyle, 'Cleaning up After the Celtic Tiger: Scalar "Fixes" in the Political Ecology of Tiger Economies', *Transactions of the Institute of British Geography NS*, vol. 27, no. 2 (2002), pp. 111–25; H. Fagan, 'Waste Management and its Contestation in the Republic of Ireland', *Capitalism, Nature, Socialism*, vol. 15, no. 1 (2004), pp. 83–102; S. Buckingham, D. Reeves and A. Batchelor, 'Wasting Women: The Environmental Justice of Including Women in Municipal Waste Management', *Local Environment*, vol. 10, no. 4 (2005), pp. 427–44; A. Davies, *The Geographies of Garbage Governance: Interventions, Interactions and Outcomes* (Aldershot, Ashgate, 2008).

23 Department of Environment and Local Government, *Waste Management Act* (Dublin, Government of Ireland, 1996).

24 Department of Environment and Local Government, *Changing Our Ways: A Policy Statement on Waste Management* (Dublin, Government of Ireland, 1999).

25 Department of Environment, Heritage and Local Government, *Protection of the Environment Act* (Dublin, Government of Ireland, 2003).

26 A. Davies, 'A Wasted Opportunity? Civil Society and Waste Management in Ireland', *Environmental Politics*, vol. 16, no. 1 (2007), pp. 52–72; Davies, *The Geographies of Garbage Governance: Interventions, Interactions and Outcomes*, op. cit.

27 BRL, *Ballymun Regeneration Progress Report 2005–6* (Dublin, BRL, 2007).

28 S. Mullin, 'Waste Not, Want Not: Furniture Recycling Project, Ballymun' (unpublished undergraduate dissertation, Trinity College Dublin, 2008).

29 European Commission, *Building the Future*, op. cit.

30 Gibbs, 'Urban Sustainability and Economic Development in the United Kingdom', op. cit.

31 K. Lucas and S. Fuller, 'Putting the "E" into LSPs: Representing the Environment Within Local Strategic Partnerships (LSPs) in the UK', *Local Environment*, vol. 10, no. 5 (2005), pp. 461–75.

32 Eames, *Reconciling Environmental and Social Concerns*, op. cit.

33 Mullin, 'Waste Not, Want Not', op. cit.

34 Ibid.

35 Ibid. p. 23

36 Davies, 'A Wasted Opportunity?', op. cit.

37 L. Darby and H. Jenkins, 'Applying Sustainability Indicators to the Social Enterprise Business Model: The Development and Application of an Indicator Set for Newport Wastesavers, Wales', *International Journal of Social Economics*, vol. 33, nos. 5–6 (2006), pp. 411–31; New Economics Foundation, *Proving and Improving: A Quality and Impact Toolkit for Social Enterprise* (London, New Economics Foundation, 2006).

38 Mullin, 'Waste Not, Want Not', op. cit.

39 Department of Environment, Heritage and Local Government, *Making Ireland's Development Sustainable* (Dublin, Government of Ireland, 2002).

40 See M. Hajer, *The Politics of Environmental Discourse, Ecological Modernisation and the Policy Process* (Oxford, Clarendon Press, 1995); R. Smith, 'Sustainability and the Rationalisation of the Environment', *Environmental Politics*, vol. 5, no. 3 (1996), pp. 476–500; J. Dryzek, *The Politics of the Earth: Environmental Discourses* (Oxford, Clarendon Press, 1997); P. Christoff, 'Ecological Modernisation: Ecological Modernities', *Environmental Politics*, vol. 5, no. 3 (1996), pp. 476–500.

41 G. Taylor, *Conserving the Emerald Tiger: The Politics of Environmental Regulation in Ireland* (Galway, Arlen House, 2001).

42 H. Tovey and P. Share, *A Sociology of Ireland* (Dublin, Gill and Macmillan, 2003).

43 L. Leonard, 'Environmentalism in Ireland: Ecological Modernisation Versus Populist Rural Sentiment', *Environmental Values*, vol. 16, no. 4 (2007), pp. 463–83.

44 Department of the Taoiseach, *Sustaining Progress: Social Partnership Agreement 2003–5* (Dublin, Government of Ireland, 2003), p. 52.

45 Department of the Taoiseach, *Towards 2016: Ten Year Framework Social Partnership Agreement 2006–15* (Dublin, Government of Ireland, 2006), p. 14.

46 Government of Ireland, *Transforming Ireland – A Better Quality of Life for All, National Development Plan 2007–2013* (Dublin, Government of Ireland, 2007), p. 117.

47 Gibbs, 'Urban Sustainability and Economic Development in the United Kingdom', op. cit.

48 M. Boyle, 'Sartre's Circular Dialectic and the Empires of Abstract Space: A History of Space and Place in Ballymun, Dublin', *Annals of the Association of American Geographers*, no. 95 (2005), pp. 181–201; M. Boyle and R. Rogerson, ' "Third Way" Urban Policy and the New Moral Politics of Community: A Comparative Analysis of Ballymun in Dublin and the Gorbals in Glasgow', *Urban Geography*, no. 27 (2006), pp. 201–27; R. Imrie and M. Raco, 'Community and the Changing Nature of Urban Policy' in Imrie and Raco (eds), *Urban Renaissance? New Labour, Community and Urban Policy* (London, Polity Press, 2003), pp. 2–36.

49 Boyle and Rogerson, ' "Third Way" Urban Policy', op. cit. p. 113.

50 Burningham and Thrush. *'Rainforests are a Long Way from Here'*, op. cit., p. 12.

Ballymun: A New Town Once Again

CIARÁN CUFFE

Ballymun was born out of crisis. In 1963 four people died when two tenement buildings collapsed in Dublin within ten days of one another. This led to the Minister for Local Government, Neil Blaney, proposing a new town of system-built dwellings on lands recently vacated by Albert Agricultural College in North Dublin.[1] A contract was signed in 1965, and the first tenants moved in a year later. However, problems quickly manifested themselves, and within four years the dream of a new town had faded into the harsh reality of state neglect, with cracked concrete panels and lifts that were forever breaking down. A shopping centre had failed to materialise, and concerns were raised about the lack of play facilities. A poignant Dáil exchange from 1970 saw Deputy Paddy Belton questioning the Minister for Local Government on the lack of toilet facilities for young children playing adjacent to the tower blocks that contained their homes on the twelfth floor.

Prior to Ballymun's construction, it was easy to have an unquestioning belief in modernity as the solution to Ireland's problems. Many felt that the white heat of technology would solve all our inherited Victorian ills. Anything that represented change had to be good. The fifties were characterised by emigration and stagnation, but now things would be different. The new Taoiseach, Seán Lemass, had adopted Whitaker's *First Programme for Economic Expansion*, and anything seemed possible. This was Ireland's opportunity to jump ahead of other countries, and to embrace the ideas of the future. A scale model of the Ballymun project held pride of place in the reception area of the new National Building Agency, and was seen as epitomising the spirit of the times.

The urban planning ideas of Swiss/French architect and planner Le Corbusier heavily influenced the design of Ballymun. A sketch for the Unité d'Habitation – his award-winning housing project built in 1945 – showed apartment blocks reminiscent of the blocks at Ballymun but brimming with amenities and surrounded by a sea of parkland. Le Corbusier's essay on the five points of a new architecture proposed that new buildings could be built of mass concrete on slender columns, thus raising them off the ground.[2] Old-fashioned pitched roofs would be replaced by roof gardens. Modern construction would no longer rely on heavy masonry walls, and would allow long ribbon windows and a free-flowing plan inside new buildings.

Not content with architecture, Le Corbusier set his sights on redesigning the city. In his eyes, the new city would consist of tall self-contained apartments surrounded by grass and trees. One of his sketches shows his vision of children playing in a paddling pond outside a modern kindergarten. He contrasts this with an older city scene of children playing on the footpath under the watchful eye of an onlooker at a window a floor above them. It was many years before adequate childcare facilities were provided in Ballymun, and in the meantime, it was quite a challenge to watch over your children from the eleventh or twelfth floor.

The seeds of discontent with modernity had already been sown five years before the tenants moved in to Ballymun. The American writer Jane Jacobs, in *The Death and Life of Great American Cities*[3] (published in 1961), questioned the urban renewal policies of the 1950s that had led to the bulldozing of neighbourhoods in older cities. She extolled the 'jumping, joyous urban jumble' of her adopted Greenwich Village in lower Manhattan. Whereas Le Corbusier extolled the new world of expressways, fast cars and cities in parkland settings, Jacobs celebrated the street and the subtle interactions between people that make communities. She wrote about defensible space; how traditional streets allowed people to supervise outside space in subtle but secure ways. Children could be seen and heard by their parents and neighbours when they played outside. Le Corbusier wished to replace this with his stark vision of modernity, and the Ballymun of the 1960s represents a watered-down version of his modernist dream.

Ballymun got the towers and the roads, but it took years for many basic amenities to be provided, and by the time that they were, the buildings themselves had developed significant defects. In 1970 a Dáil exchange revealed Deputy Justin Keating asking the Minister for Local Government, Bobby Molloy, whether he agreed that the situation in Ballymun represented 'a gross defect of planning of all the amenities of that satellite town of a culpable and scandalous nature.'[4] In his reply, Minister Molloy conceded that only five play spaces for young children and two all-weather play areas for football had been provided for a town with a juvenile population of eight thousand.

Regardless of the defects in Ballymun's planning and construction, it was a foolhardy experiment to move so many people from inner-city communities – where generations of families had lived – to a new town a world away from everything and everyone they knew. Basic amenities such as post offices and shopping facilities took years to arrive, and from the start Ballymun was characterised by a narrow demographic of housing tenure and income. In 1985 the introduction of a housing-surrender grant scheme led to many tenants surrendering their tenancies in order to receive a cash payment that could be used towards the purchase of a home. This increased social stratification and further ghettoised Ballymun.

Meanwhile, city officials struggled to learn from Ballymun's planning failures. Throughout the 1980s local authority managers still pushed their plans for new roads through the heart of Dublin city, destroying hundreds of historic buildings in the process. The institutional memory of the deaths that resulted from the collapse of a Georgian tenement in Fenian Street still held sway: Dublin Corporation officials preferred demolition over refurbishment for older buildings, with a soft spot for comprehensive redevelopment. The policy backlash against Ballymun was perhaps as damaging as the planning and layout of the new town itself. Dublin Corporation's housing schemes from this period placed two-storey housing units in the heart of the city, where they sat uncomfortably in the shadow of four- and five-storey Georgian buildings. Planning policies ricocheted from extolling high-rise to constructing low-rise housing a stone's throw from O'Connell Street. It was almost as if the existing city was of no consequence or relevance to their plans.

Dublin architect Gerry Cahill summed up what was required in the title of his seminal book, *Back to the Street*.[5] Cahill had worked extensively in the Liberties with the South Inner City Community Development Association, and he contended that the fabric of the city needed to be stitched back together so it could function better as a focus for human activity. His ideas backed up much of what had been written by Jacobs a generation earlier. The traditional urban forms of street and square worked well, and could be used as successfully today as in previous times. It took time for these ideas to permeate through to officialdom. However, the mood gradually changed within the City Council. The need to rebuild street frontages on the scorched earth sites left over from dual carriageway construction in the city led to higher-density development. Public housing schemes on Golden Lane in the Liberties and on North King Street in the north inner city were built four-storeys high, bringing back people and activity to sites that had lain derelict for decades. Tax incentives promoted private sector investment, and the inner city's population began to rise.

In the early nineties, one of the seven tower blocks in Ballymun was refurbished. Leaking joints in the aging system-built concrete tower were resealed, fencing was erected at the tower's base to create defensible space, and a concierge system was provided. In 1993 a detailed report was prepared by Craig Gardner Consultants on the future of Ballymun. The report advocated demolition of the taller blocks in preference to refurbishment. In 1997 a government decision was taken to demolish all of the tall blocks in Ballymun, and to set up a state-owned company, Ballymun Regeneration Ltd (BRL), to undertake the works. Within a year, a design competition for a masterplan for the new Ballymun was won by UK firm MacCormac Jamieson Prichard. A wide range of community groups and residents were involved in the detail of the masterplan, and regular newsletters kept residents updated on progress.

The decision to remove the roundabout from the centre of Ballymun and replace it with a main street would have made Le Corbusier turn in his grave. From now on, traffic would not be given pride of place in the town centre. No longer would pedestrians be forced underground, giving cars the right of way overhead. The counter revolution to modern architecture and planning had begun. Ballymun Road – a highway bounded by tower blocks and grass – would become Ballymun Main Street, traffic-calmed and flanked by shops. A thoroughfare was to become a destination.

Around that time, I met David Mackay, one of the 'three wise men' brought in by city architect, Jim Barrett, to advise on matters urban. Mackay said he hoped that one day a tram would glide down the Main Street, giving passengers front-row seats of the redeveloped town. This is one of the most glaring absences from the plan at its current stage of development, and it is hoped that the addition of a fixed-line rail link between Dublin city and Ballymun, and onwards to Dublin Airport and Swords, will reduce car traffic and further assist in the area's socio-economic and environmental improvements. Elsewhere in Dublin, the completion of LUAS light rail lines led to increases in housing prices and development along the two rail corridors, and the prospect of a LUAS or Metro through Ballymun could increase land values, and bring environmental and social benefits.

Early on in the regeneration process, I undertook work for the Ballymun Housing Task Force. My training as an architect and interest in how cities functioned – or did not, as the case may be – had led me to study planning at UCD (University College Dublin). The prospect of engaging directly with the residents of Ballymun appealed to me. A neighbourhood centre had been proposed for Poppintree, west of Ballymun Main Street, and I worked with nearby residents to determine what facilities it should contain. Together with my colleagues, we made a model of the neighbourhood that included the surrounding houses so that people could see where they lived relative to the new proposals. Photographs showing the front of peoples' homes were glued onto the cardboard model, and enabled residents to clearly identify where they lived relative to the new centre. Seeing one's own lace curtains on a model certainly allowed people to comprehend their place in the great scheme of things. We made a model of the proposed building in detachable blocks so that people could decide which parts of the centre they really wanted. Shops and overhead apartments were welcomed, as were workshops and terraced housing to the rear. However, residents baulked at the idea of a health centre at one end of the development, and a pub at the other; 'Fool me once, shame on you; fool me twice, shame on me' was the mood of those who gathered at a public meeting. A community that had borne the brunt of a social experiment thirty years previously did not want to experiment with our ideas of 'new urbanism'.[6] The cardboard models of the pub and health centre were left to one side.

Today, the neighbourhood centre is open for business, and though I believe it would have been better if it had contained additional facilities, there may be a stronger sense of community ownership through their decision-making in the planning process. Sherry Arnstein, the author of *A Ladder of Citizen Participation*,[7] might have been pleased with the outcome of the discussions about the Poppintree Centre. She identified eight rungs on the 'ladder of citizen participation', ranging from manipulation to citizen control. Allowing the community to determine the composition of a neighbourhood centre was a strong exercise in participatory democracy.

Concerns have been raised, however, about the degree of citizen involvement in the wider redevelopment process in Ballymun. Writing in 2003, Jenny Muir stated that significant concerns arose about the placing of new housing at Poppintree, and felt that, in overall terms, participation was closer to placation – located at the halfway point of Arnstein's 'ladder'.[8] Although Muir credits BRL for holding a 'Planning for Real' day and other initiatives, she suggests that the complexity of the redevelopment and poor record-keeping contributed to tensions in the redevelopment process. The redevelopment process is complex, and it has been challenging for local communities and for development companies to engage fully with the process.

Successful urban planning is often seen as resting on three pillars: economic, social and environmental. Halfway through the redevelopment process, there is room for debate as to how successfully the Ballymun project has tackled these three themes.

The regeneration of Ballymun has been an expensive and time-consuming project. Since it was announced in 1998, the project has more than doubled in cost from €442 million to €942 million, and the estimated completion date of 2008 has now stretched out to 2012. Although €290 million of the increase can be put down to inflation in the period up to 2006, it still represents a significant increase. In some respects, Ballymun has been a victim of the building boom of the last decade; it may have been difficult to retain staff at a time when the economy was expanding dramatically. Perhaps as growth slows down, it will be possible to move more quickly towards the completion of this flagship project. Some feel that too much emphasis has been placed on demolition as part of the redevelopment process. However, an example from Dublin's inner city illustrates how limited redevelopment can prove problematic. Fatima Mansions – a Dublin Corporation development of four hundred flats in fourteen separate four-storey blocks – was refurbished at a cost of €7 million in the early 1990s. Within a decade, social problems had re-emerged, and a decision was made to demolish and rebuild. It is noteworthy that the initial refurbishment was never completed, and tenants argued that no satisfactory management system had been put in place for the refurbished area. One of the arguments for rebuilding was that it will allow for a higher number of housing units to be built, and will allow for a greater social mix in the area. In Moyross in Limerick city, proposals have been put forward to demolish and rebuild 2,400 homes in a troubled neighbourhood at a cost of one billion euros.[9] The debate about building refurbishment versus demolition is ongoing.

There is a danger that the rush to demolish will shift attention away from the need to tackle underlying social issues, and that the softer side of renewal will fail to receive the attention that it deserves. However, there is growing evidence that inappropriate building forms, such as high-rise and isolated island blocks, are problematic for social housing regardless of the management structures put in place. The Craig Gardner Report from the early 1990s carefully evaluated the pilot refurbishment, and concluded that the life cycle costs of retaining substandard buildings would cost more than the costs of demolition and rebuilding.

Evaluating the social changes in Ballymun can be more challenging than assessing the physical changes. Perhaps the clearest means of doing so is to examine some of the performance indicators that were agreed by the monitoring committee of the Integrated Area Plan produced a decade ago. Unemployment fell by 25 per cent – from 2,173 to 1,201 – in the years from 1997–2001, but had risen to 1,542 by mid-2006. The committee stated that 'low levels of education attainment continue to be a serious barrier to economic and social regeneration'.[10] On a more positive note, the number of drug users presenting for treatment had diminished, and the report from a year previously stated that drug abuse had stabilised, and open drug dealing was no longer prevalent in Ballymun. A significant number of childcare places had been provided, and the report noted that property prices had increased at higher than market rates. These indicators were chosen by representatives on the monitoring group that include three employees of BRL, an estate agent and one community representative. The report concluded by stating that 'the goal of turning a failed area of the City into a vibrant place and contributor to physical, social and economic development is now achievable but needs ongoing support and nurture.'[11] A decade after the foundations for Ballymun's renewal were laid, it may be too early to fully evaluate the social changes that have taken place.

There has been success in recent years in attracting private housing to Ballymun. Prior to the adoption of the masterplan a decade ago, 80 per cent of all the housing provided was still owned and managed by the local authority. Significant diversity in housing tenure has emerged in recent years. Although the bulk of new housing units has been provided by the local authority through BRL, in order to replace demolished units, a substantial amount has been provided by other sectors. Hundreds of private housing units have been sold in Ballymun, and more than three thousand units are at planning or construction stage. In addition, hundreds of voluntary, cooperative and affordable housing units are occupied or under construction. This represents a significant shift, and the mix of housing tenure is bound to reduce the problems of ghettoisation that had previously existed.

There has always been a strong community spirit in Ballymun. A decade ago, the masterplan estimated that there were close on two hundred active community-based organisations in Ballymun. Many of these groups have now moved into new purpose-built premises. The new axis arts and cultural centre has provided a strong focus for many community and arts activities. It is crucial in future years that facilities and support structures ensure that opportunities for social interaction between all residents continue.

Perhaps a further change in housing policy is required, but one that would require government intervention. Many of the difficulties in Ballymun arose not only from poor planning and construction, but from housing policies that segregated people firmly by housing tenure. Despite attempts to blur the differences between private and public housing, there is still a wide social and economic divide between different forms of housing tenure. In addition, the myriad of housing supports available in recent years has increased options for beneficiaries, but added layers of complexity to the housing process. Ideally, a new model of housing that promotes community cohesion rather than division will emerge. Emer O'Siochru from Feasta – an environmental non-governmental organisation – has suggested that decoupling social supports from housing form and location would expand beneficiaries' freedom, boost sustainability and provide transparency for taxpayers. Existing social housing supports to delivery agents could be replaced with a housing benefit voucher that would be given directly to those seeking housing, and would be used for social, private or not-for-profit rentals, or for buying in the open market, in any location. Such a change would be radical, but could dramatically promote social integration. Even a more limited move that would allow local authority flats to be sold directly to the tenant could assist in allowing tenants to become stronger stakeholders in the community that they live in. It will take time to address public housing policies that, by their nature, promoted division rather than integration, but changes in the current system merit consideration.

In the late 1960s the new tenants of Ballymun moved into housing that was a world removed from Dublin tenements. Their spacious and airy new flats had central heating and overlooked the green fields of North Dublin. However, design defects and poor maintenance quickly led to deterioration in the quality of life for the inhabitants of Dublin's newest suburb. Forty years on, a new Ballymun is taking shape on what were once open fields. Some concerns have been raised about Ballymun's character changing from that of a suburb to an emergent town. Robert Guillemot of the Ballymun Environmental Group objected to several developments over fears regarding the loss of open space and playing grounds.[12] However, the UK Urban Task Force Report argues strongly for greater definition of open space:

> Public space should be conceived of as an outdoor room within a neighbourhood, somewhere to relax and enjoy the urban experience, a venue for different activities, from outdoor eating to street entertainment, from sport and play areas to a venue for civic or political functions; and most importantly of all as a place for walking or sitting out. Public spaces work best when they establish a direct relationship between the space and the people who live and work around it.[13]

The report recommends that a mixture of uses and households can contribute to successful renewal, and suggested that 'pyramids of intensity' should be provided with appropriate transport, social facilities and local amenities. Much of the recent construction in Ballymun is doing exactly this, and will lead to appropriate activity at the right locations. In Poppintree, what was once a scarred green space used by scrambler bikes and street drinkers is now a new neighbourhood centre. The new corner shop, pharmacy and beauty salon have brought a focus for an area once served only by a shop housed in a steel container.

The masterplan has changed on several occasions since it was produced ten years ago, but still represents a radical shift from the 1960s plan. It marks a retreat from the ideas of Le Corbusier and the New Towns movement in the UK. Instead, it refers back to the urban forms that characterised traditional Irish towns, both planned and unplanned. The basic building units of streets, squares, terraces and parks have been rediscovered, and are being used to great effect in establishing a sense of place and allowing people to take greater ownership of the neighbourhood in which they live.

A Main Street has emerged from the windswept open spaces that were the main feature of Ballymun. Most of the fifteen-storey towers have been demolished, and the tenants rehoused in two- and three-storey terraces. Gardening programmes have been put in place to assist a generation that grew up without a garden of their own. Although the Main Street is busy, most of the traffic is Ballymun related rather than passing through. Mixed-use neighbourhood centres have brought a focus to the individual quarters of Ballymun, and provide local services within a few minutes' walk of people's homes. The transformation of Ballymun from a second-rate modernist suburb to a twenty-first-century town is well underway.

However, in some respects the masterplan has been too cautious. Many existing institutional buildings in Ballymun – including schools, a church and a library – are low, one or two-storey buildings surrounded by a sea of grass or parking. The area around these buildings does little or nothing to promote community cohesion, and appears to suffer from a lack of maintenance. Perhaps a more radical approach would have been to replace these older structures with buildings that front onto the street, and contribute to the place-making qualities of the new town.

It is also notable that much of the new housing is lower in scale but achieves densities of fifty units per hectare in the neighbourhoods, which is higher than in the original Ballymun. This is understandable, as many residents see the surrounding semi-detached housing developments as an appropriate housing model to aspire to. However, if housing densities do not reach a critical mass, it will be difficult for local shops and services to survive unless they are subsidised.

The masterplan is less detailed in its treatment of the northern part of Ballymun. Here, the local authority changes from Dublin City Council to Fingal County Council, and a rationalisation of boundaries might be in order to ensure that all of Ballymun lies under one jurisdiction. The masterplan shows a large surface car park for a 'park and ride' location, and depicts 'possible' leisure complexes, retail stores and technology parks surrounded by roads. It appears as though planners retreated from contemporary planning back to the bad old days of the 1960s where the car was king. An IKEA furniture store is planned for this location, and BRL suggests that this will provide five hundred jobs, many of which could be filled by Ballymun residents. However, up to two thousand car-parking spaces will be provided, and this may cause traffic congestion in Ballymun and on the adjoining M50. A cap on the size of retail outlets was lifted in order to allow this development on the outskirts of the town. It will be of interest to see whether policies that rely on 'big box' multiples such as IKEA to pump prime job creation are successful.

The building programme is still only at a halfway stage, and there are many construction sites, surface car parks and empty shells of buildings awaiting demolition. One notable change over the ten years is the amount of greenery. There are trees almost everywhere you look, and small parks and clearly defined grassed areas have appeared. Instead of being SLOAP (Space Left Over After Planning), these are the reverse – spaces carefully designed to meet the needs of the community. Some residents are unhappy that playing fields have been moved to more remote locations, but there will be more types of outdoor space available than before. The emphasis is on quality, rather than quantity.

Ironically, elsewhere in Dublin, the modern movement is alive and well. A mixed-use development at Elmpark on the Rock Road close to Booterstown borrows heavily from the language of Le Corbusier's Unité.

The architecture critic, Ray Ryan, suggests that 'architecture aficionados may recall Le Corbusier's sinuous proposal for Algiers, or that megastructure's more relaxed siblings by Oscar Niemeyer'.[14] Although the housing blocks are set in an open landscape, and consist of tall, linear blocks with a central-heating plant, there are no broken lifts and nor do tenants suffer from the lack of amenities that characterised Ballymun in its early years. A key difference is the quality of finish and maintenance that will be provided. Its tenants and owners are mostly private, and pay for adequate maintenance – something that Dublin Corporation seemed unable or unwilling to do. True, the Elmpark development is at a forty-year remove from Ballymun, and expectations and building standards are now much higher. However, it is worth asking whether Ballymun's initial deficiencies were due more to the politics of social exclusion than a lack of finance and vision.

From the outset, the new Ballymun has sought to comply with best-practice standards or higher for the new homes that are replacing the older housing blocks. The new homes will be at least as generous as the existing homes in size, and be better insulated and thus cheaper to run. In practice, the new housing units have significantly exceeded the 1997 building regulations, and have been to the fore in raising the bar in thermal comfort. At a Greener Ballymun conference held in May 2008, an architect for BRL discussed the challenge of meeting the more difficult A-rating under the revised 2008 regulations, and emphasised the financial and environmental savings that can result from such a move. BRL has worked with the manufacturers of heat recovery systems to pioneer the 'energy catcher' – a type of heat recovery system that increases the efficiency of new condenser gas boilers. Innovations in building systems that can reduce energy use and lower greenhouse gas emissions have a crucial role to play in moving towards a low-carbon future.

Ballymun is midway through an incredible renaissance. Other communities in Dublin, Limerick and elsewhere are watching closely to see how the development succeeds. Students of planning are watching like an anxious parent on a child's first day at school to see how the regeneration unfolds. Both success or failure will be exaggerated and examined for lessons that may be applied to similar proposals elsewhere. In many respects, the state is trying to atone for past failures, and is acutely aware of the need to ensure that history does not repeat itself. This may be contributing to a certain cautiousness on behalf of those involved in the project.

If I were to give advice to those charged with delivering the new Ballymun, I would borrow from Daniel Burnham, the architect and planner of the city of Chicago in the nineteenth century, who stated:

> Make no little plans. They have no magic to stir men's blood and probably themselves will not be realized. Make big plans; aim high in hope and work, remembering that a noble, logical diagram once recorded will never die, but long after we are gone will be a living thing, asserting itself with ever-growing insistency ...[15]

After the difficulties encountered in Ballymun in its first phase of development, it would be easy to retreat towards prudence. However, the most successful periods of Dublin's development were marked by significant change from previous periods. The construction of the great Georgian squares, the public housing provided by the Iveagh Trust in the 1890s and the extensive Dublin Corporation housing schemes of the 1930s were radical in their day. Given the twin challenges of climate change and peak oil, it may be that increases in housing density in Ballymun will contribute towards sustainability. In the area of housing construction, BRL should maintain its impressive track record in surpassing existing building standards, and should aspire to an energy A-rating for every new home at the planning stage, with the aim of being an exemplar for Ireland of the 'passive home' standards. In addition, prioritising improvements in public transport, as well as stronger pedestrian and cycle priorities, could ensure that Ballymun leads the field as a role model for town planning in the new century.

In 2008 the physical regeneration of Ballymun is self-evident. In the distance, the spires and chimneys of Dublin city stand out against the backdrop of the mountains. Each day, there are more signs of terraced housing taking over from the grey precast-concrete panels that once dominated the skyline. There will be failure as well as success, but I sense that there is now a new-found confidence that will ensure the achievements will be greater than any setbacks along the way. People chat to each other on the Main Street, and there's a buzz of activity around the axis centre.

All is not rosy, but there is a sense of optimism about the changes that are occurring.

In Dublin's inner city, the Fatima Mansions area is also experiencing regeneration. Dublin City Council has stated: 'The success of the project will not be measured by whether the houses or shops work in 5 years time. The success of the neighbourhood will be whether people are happy there in 20 years time.'[16] The same could be said of Ballymun. The road ahead is not easy, but judging by the level of commitment from the community and those working on the project, the signs for the future are good.

NOTES AND REFERENCES

1 Sinéad Power, 'The Development of the Ballymun Housing Scheme, Dublin, 1965–1969', Department of Geography, University of Edinburgh, http://www.ucd.ie/gsi/pdf/33–2/ballymun.pdf (viewed 1 July 2008).
2 http://www.greatgridlock.net/Viipuri/archi.html (viewed 1 July 2008).
3 Jane Jacobs, *The Death and Life of Great American Cities* (New York, Random House, 1961).
4 http://historical–debates.oireachtas.ie/D/0247/D.0247.197006090017.html (viewed 1 July 2008).
5 Gerry Cahill, *Back to the Street* (Dublin, Housing Research Unit, UCD, Cement-Roadstone Holdings Ltd, 1980).
6 http://www.newurbanism.org (viewed 1 July 2008).
7 Sherry R. Arnstein, 'A Ladder of Citizen Participation', *Journal of the American Institute of Planners*, vol. 35, no. 4 (July 1969), pp. 216–24.
8 Jenny Muir, 'The Representation of Local Interests in Area-based Urban Regeneration Programmes', paper for the Housing Studies Association Conference, University of Bristol, 9–10 September 2003, https://www.york.ac.uk/inst/chp/hsa/papers/autumn03/Muir.pdf (viewed 1 July 2008).
9 Barry Duggan, 'Revamp of City Stalls, but Funds in Place', *Irish Independent*, 21 May 2008.
10 BRL, Monitoring Report 2005–6, http://brl.ie/pdf/Monitoring_Report_2005_2006_web.pdf (viewed 1 July 2008).
11 Ibid.
12 www.clubi.ie/aquarius–music/Ballymun/documents/objectionbuspark1–2final.rtf (viewed 1 July 2008).
13 Lord Rogers of Riverside (chair), 'Towards an Urban Renaissance', final report of the Urban Task Force (DETR, 1999).
14 Ray Ryan, 'Elmpark – An Urban Experiment', *Architecture – The Journal of the Royal Institute of Architects of Ireland*, no. 238, p. 49.

15 Daniel H. Burnham and Edward H. Bennett, 'Plan of Chicago', Commercial Club, Chicago, 1909.

16 Charles O'Neill (ed.), '11 Acres, 10 Steps', (Fatima Groups United, 2000).

A Horse of a Different Colour

ROBERT BALLAGH
in conversation with Declan Gorman

This is the abridged text of an interview with Robert Ballagh, conducted in Dublin in August 2008, in which he offers his personal recollections of the planning and early days of Ballymun in the 1960s, which coincided with his own developing political consciousness as a student and emerging artist. This political sensibility would inform aspects of his artistic work over the subsequent four decades, and would bring him into regular contact with marginalised communities – and the occasionally controversial area of public art – before returning two years ago to speak at the axis arts centre in a very changed Ballymun. For the sake of fluidity, I have edited out the questions that guided this conversation, which ranged from curiosity about his political journey to his reflections on community and public art, and his views about the current Ballymun regeneration.

I am, sadly, old enough to remember when there wasn't the Ballymun that people talk about now as Ballymun. I remember when it was countryside.

And then I remember the planning and development of Ballymun, because I happened to know one of the architects in the then Dublin Corporation who was working on it, and, of course, he was talking about a wonderfully exciting development. The scale and ambition of it was all very new in the Ireland of the early 1960s. And so, I was aware – maybe more than others – of the scale of the development, of the towers and all that.

I was an architectural student at the time, and we used to do an exchange trip with the architectural students of Belfast every year, and I remember going up for this visit to Belfast, and part of the programme was to go to a lecture by the chief architect of the GLC (Greater London Council). It was a fascinating lecture, because he was speaking of the experience of housing families – marginalised families, families with social problems – in high-rise developments. And it was terrifying, the statistics that the GLC had even then. He put up slides with graphs and so on (they didn't have Powerpoint in those days), and they conclusively proved that with that kind of tenancy, the higher you housed people, drug dependency increased, alcoholism increased, anti-social behaviour increased. They seemed to have concrete evidence of that reality.

So you had all these things going on in my head about Ballymun: the utopian architectural experiment; then the political 'strokery' of the government solving the Dublin housing crisis in one fell swoop by just building it all in one place and putting all the people there; and then the GLC saying it doesn't work.

And so it was built. I remember my brother-in-law was one of the first tenants. He was recently married with two children, and he got one of the flats in the lower-rise apartment blocks. I remember going out to visit him and being really impressed by the flats themselves. They were really spacious; very attractive, and they had balconies looking out. I remember that from his balcony, even though it was low-rise, you could see right over to the Dublin Mountains. But immediately, problems surfaced. I remember talking to his wife: nowhere for the kids to play, nowhere to shop. So, flats barely built, flats barely occupied, and already problems arising.

I think the real problem that developed with Ballymun was not an architectural problem, but a social and political problem; the neglect by the authorities, the failure to provide services, and then the perceived 'dumping' of difficult tenants – tenants with all sorts of social problems – all in the one area, leading to the anti-social issues which got the area such a bad name. And yet there were good people who liked living there.

I think that the decision to build Ballymun was made because of the political pressure to deal with the housing crisis. The way they did it was, 'Build these things, get the people in and that's it – that's the end of our responsibility', which I believe was short-sighted and so like stroke politics. 'Nobody can now say that we neglected the housing problem.' But they neglected the social problem!

The solution that they eventually came up with for the problem of Ballymun – and it is the kind of solution that politicians sometimes do come up with – was to knock the whole thing down and start again. But I think some of those Ballymun towers didn't need to be knocked down. I accept that there were problems and difficulties, but I still think the problems in Ballymun were social rather than architectural. I was in Belfast a few days ago, and I went down to the end of the Falls Road to the location of the Divis flats. There was a campaign to demolish Divis because they had had an identical problem to that of Ballymun, but there's one Divis block left that has been restored quite attractively. The British army are gone from the top of it, of course, and they've carefully chosen the tenants. It's all single couples or people without children or students or whatever. It has a good concierge system and it's a great success. I'm speaking after the horse has bolted: the Ballymun towers have gone now, but that's just a thought of mine.

To continue with the architectural theme, which, after all, is a part of the peoples' environment, I'm not mad about some of the new interventions in Ballymun. They don't seem to me to represent a brave march forward in terms of architecture from what they had before. What I do like about the regeneration project in Ballymun, however, is that there has been some attention paid this time around to the social and cultural needs of the people. I think that axis, the community resource and arts centre in Ballymun, is a fine example of that, and of course there's the Breaking Ground public art commissioning programme. There have been artistic interventions in various places, some successful and some not so successful. I had a brief involvement with a project in the Ballymun Health Care Centre working with some local artists on an artwork based on a local storytelling project. So, certainly this time around, there is an understanding that it's just not enough to provide a roof over somebody's family and think of that as the end of your responsibilities as a local authority.

This leads us into the question, what does civic responsibility entail: what should it entail? This time out, it's so different to the first time around. Ballymun opened in 1966. It was windswept … and then they built Ballymun shopping centre which always looked to me as if it was temporary, and then a pub which wasn't the most attractive place on the planet. It just seemed to me that the authorities – local politicians and national politicians – felt that once they had provided the housing, their obligations were over. There was the notion that a woman living with children on the tenth floor of a tower block could just leave the children to the lift and expect everything to be fine after that. There wasn't an extensive playground area with attendants and crèche facilities with supervision. To me, all of that should have been built into the project from the word go.

We can view the neglect of Ballymun against what was going on generally at the time. I lived in the north inner city, and when my kids were very small, there was a playground in Broadstone, with a building, and two women who were employed by the Corporation to play games with the kids. My kids were always over there and it was terrific, but then overnight the Corporation did away with all of those services. So it wasn't just Ballymun that suffered. We had a very unenlightened local authority in terms of how they saw their role – very minimal services: houses and roads. I simply couldn't understand it. I know, of course, it saved money, but who would have thought it was a good idea to get rid of children's playgrounds?

I think social and political attitudes were probably always part of my DNA. My background experience doesn't make too much sense. I ended up an artist but I never went to art college. I studied architecture. I gave up studying architecture to become a professional musician – so the path was certainly not a planned path and it certainly wasn't a straightforward path. Very often, things happened because I was open to suggestions from others.

One of the reasons I left college was despair at the failure of architecture to have a social responsibility even then. I went to college in 1960. I did it for three years, so I would have left around 1963. One of the big campaigns in Dublin at that time was the Dublin Housing Action Committee. There was a huge problem in Dublin with the provision of housing, homelessness, etc., and a shortage of housing. I looked around and, compared to now, very little was being built in Dublin. Very little housing was being built until Ballymun happened, and all the commercial building work – which was where most of the architects were earning their living – was office blocks. I found this almost immoral, that all the talent that was being produced by the architectural courses was actually failing to service a real social need, but instead building office blocks for developers.

The other reason I left college was I wanted to become a rock and roll musician, so the movement from studies to playing in a band wasn't that painful a decision! But I do remember that a concern about the social responsibility of the architect was part of that decision. So I always kind of thought like that.

I had my first exhibition in 1969. The kind of art I made then was very much influenced by pop art. It was a popular style, not in Ireland but internationally – Roy Liechtenstein, Andy Warhol, all of that kind of stuff. But the themes I chose were very different. All the pictures in my first exhibition were about the civil rights movement in America, the civil rights movement up North, the Vietnam War. I did an image of the black athletes in Mexico in 1968 at the Olympic Games, with their salute. It's got a lot of coverage recently because it's the fortieth anniversary of that event. So even then, the work had political and social concerns as part of its content.

When people came to me later on, when I had developed some kind of a profile, and said, 'Would you be interested in doing such and such a project with young people here?' or whatever, I was open to it. I was willing to try. I was very nervous about such work at the start, because even though it's not education, there is an educational role involved, and I have never been involved in education in any shape or form. I suppose I was a victim of it, like all of us going to school, but I never taught anyone, and so I was nervous. How do I deal with this? How do I deal with people? I decided I'd just let it flow and try to be honest in my dealings with people. And by and large, nearly all the projects I worked on were – well – very satisfying for me, and I think they were worthwhile for the people involved.

In the 1980s, I happened to know the architect, David Slattery, who was charged with the renovation and restoration of the Customs House, and he called to me one day and said, 'I'm going to be putting scaffolding all over the building – wouldn't it be a great idea to have some murals up there?'

I said, 'It's a great idea, but who's going to pay for it? Who's going to do it?' He came back and said that Sisk's, who were the contractors, were willing to put up some money. And then we contacted Crown Paints, who said they would supply the paint. We started looking at the design, and we suddenly realised that this was huge, and I said, 'I couldn't physically do this myself, it's just enormous! So what are we going to do?'

I met Mick Rafferty of NCCCAP (North City Centre Community Action Project). They had a training facility beside Liberty Hall at that time. And Mick said maybe we can do something here. They had some young people from the north inner city – Sheriff Street and Seán McDermott Street, particularly – working on a training course with ANCO [now defunct training and employment authority]. The solution took a little bit of time to work out. They couldn't just assign the young people to me. Instead, they made me an unpaid tutor. I was given these eighteen young people to work with on this mural project, along with their own regular tutor.

The next thing was to get a place to do it. The logistics of doing it on-site would have been impossible because it would have involved cranes and masses of extra scaffolding. I was put in touch with the Customs House Docks development organisation – Mark Kavanagh was the CEO – and they agreed to lend us Stack A, a wonderful building. So we were in Stack A for two or three months painting these murals, and I have to say, it was a terrific experience, and for a lot of the kids a really empowering experience. I know, for example, that in the Sheriff Street area, not many jobs would have come on-stream – because we're talking the eighties, a really grim time – and two of the girls got jobs afterwards with painting contractors!

I remember RTÉ came to do a little feature on it. This is what I am talking about: pride and empowerment and ownership. They were great kids, and, boy, could they talk, and yet the minute the mic was put in front of them, they all clammed up! They wouldn't speak, except this young one, she was great – Róisín was her name ... Róisín is probably forty now! I think it was the Six O'Clock News, and one of the RTÉ reporters asked, 'Now Róisín, how has this experience been?'

'Fuckin' brilliant!'

BEEP! Start again, please! Trying to get her to speak for a few seconds without expletives was difficult, but I always remember the final question: 'When this goes up in front of the Customs House, if anyone comes along and vandalises it, what will you think?'

'Wha'?'

'If anyone comes along and ...' And he suddenly realised she didn't know what he meant by vandalise. 'If somebody came along and painted on it or marked it what would you do?'

'I'd fuckin' kill them!'

It just illustrated the sense of ownership they had for this project. I thought that was a really successful project. They painted it all.

And you learn so much: these kids were so streetwise, so much smarter than me on that level, and yet so innocent in other ways. They knew all about drugs and all the social problems of the inner city, but one of them was talking to me, and he said, 'I suppose when this is over you'll be off to Benidorm?'

I said, 'Well, not Benidorm, anyway,' and I suddenly realised that not one of them had ever been outside Dublin, not even to Bray.

As part of the design, I incorporated a kind of a card – except the scale of the card was eight foot by six foot or thereabouts – and I got a big Magic Marker and they were all to sign their names. I gave it to them one by one, and one of the lads said, 'Nah, nah, I don't want to sign my name.' And I suddenly realised he couldn't write. You know, you learn a lot about yourself from these experiences – assumptions that you make are often wrong, etc. Afterwards, he came to me and said, 'Would you put my name on it?'

I think there is a very strong connection between civic responsibility, politics and art. My father would have been a big influence on me in this context. He was a real citizen. He used to say one thing which, as a kid, I'd think, What is he talking about? Say it was a nice summer's day, he'd go out, and I'd say, 'Where are you going?'

He'd say, 'I'm going to see my pictures in the National Gallery.'

And I'd say, 'They're not yours.'

And he'd say, 'They are mine.' My father had the attitude that the parks were his; the galleries were his; the museums were his. He was an Irish citizen and these were his. I inherited that from him – this belief in civic reality. If I'm a republican, I'm a civic republican. I believe that society is there for the benefit of us all. It's not for the benefit of a few, it's not for the benefit of the privileged, it's there for all of us, and this very definitely feeds into my art practice – that art should be at the service of society.

I was briefly on the Arts Council in the 1980s, for three years. The words 'community arts' were surfacing for the first time, and there were people who were distinctly uncomfortable with this idea. They very much had the notion or idea that there are only two kinds of art – good art and bad art – and that art made by non-professionals is bad art. They almost felt they had a duty to prevent it. I tried to champion the notion of art being an important part of a social project or whatever, even if it's not necessarily made by artists – whether it be through amateur drama or whatever. But I was pretty much a lone voice in that context at the time.

I would be the first to acknowledge that this kind of activity doesn't suit everybody. Some artists are very private people and that's fine. I don't criticise them for not getting involved. I just get a little weary with people criticising those who do get involved. It's not so much that the arts establishment feels threatened by it. I think they completely misunderstand or refuse to understand the significance of process over product. They always judge product. So they bring the wrong criteria to bear.

I'll give you an example. There was a marvellous show a couple of years ago in West Belfast called *Bin Lids*. Although there were some professional artists, including myself, involved, it was basically the local community telling their own story of the previous years of the Troubles. They went around the community and spoke to people; collected stories. People like Marie Jones and others were involved; I was involved on the design side, Conleth White was lighting designer. There were a handful of professional actors, but the rest were all locals. I recall one really poignant moment at rehearsals. They were doing a scene from the early seventies when there was an IRA ceasefire which broke down in Lenadoon. The British army were involved in an engagement, and I think certainly one, maybe two, priests were shot dead. And a little girl was shot dead who was just sent out for a bottle of milk and was caught in the crossfire or whatever. These scenes were being worked out, and there was a young girl acting the part of this child, and at rehearsals I noticed this couple sitting there, very emotional, and I said: 'Who are they?'

'The parents.'

It was their daughter's story being told for the very first time, twenty years after she'd been killed.

I thought it was a really important, significant cultural event, and I know that the establishment or elements of the establishment would sneer at something like that, because the critical judgement they would bring to bear would be that which they'd bring to a first night in the Abbey or the

Gate theatres, but this was a community hall in West Belfast! I just don't think you can make those kinds of comparisons at all. The important thing about that particular project and projects like that – whether they be in visual arts or in music or drama or whatever – is that it's about ordinary people finding a voice for themselves, telling their own story.

One of the big problems of modern society is that for so many people, their story is invisible. All the famous people, their stories are all over the place, whether it be a politician or pop star or whatever, but ordinary people, their story simply isn't told. And the thing about telling your own story is that it's an empowering experience. Any time I've observed people in this process of empowerment, I know that their lives will never be the same again. Again, you talk to the professionals about this and they've some notion in the back of their heads that if they give grants to this, will they become artists or will they become poets or will they become writers? No! And why should they? But they might become better people; more confident people; more enriched people; also, people who might go to the theatre once in a blue moon afterwards.

I fail to understand why many people involved in the arts don't see that. They don't see it as hugely valuable in terms of society. I have seen people flower, really flower: people who would have been written off by many previous to their experience in a project. I've seen people who were almost illiterate, and at the end of a project there's a confidence there that a whole period in traditional education couldn't give to them. It doesn't always work, but when it does work, one short experience in a cultural project can have that extraordinary empowering aspect to it.

As an artist, if you are honestly trying to facilitate creativity in others, I believe it's terribly important, for it to be successful, to leave your ego at the door. I think some artists might find this difficult, but if you are confident in yourself, in your own work and your own practice, it's no problem. Even though I would proudly have the Custom House murals illustrated as part of things I've done, I never think of it as '*my* work'. It's '*our* work'.

And I think it's terribly important that you don't try to impose your aesthetic ideas or concerns on to a project, whatever it is. Sometimes, that can be terribly challenging for the group of people you go to work with, because they're all saying, 'Robert Ballagh, he's coming in here and he'll show us and tell us what to do.'

But the first thing I say to them is, 'Right – what do you want to do?' And they say, 'We thought you'd tell us?'

'No, no!'

I did a mural with the KLEAR Project in Kilbarrack some years ago, and I met some women there – working on a literacy project – and I told them, 'You have to design this not me.' It was a mural within the school where they were based in Kilbarrack. I said, 'Don't worry about your designs being a bit sketchy or uneven or awkward because that's where I'll come in and "fix it up" and "straighten it up", but it's yours, not mine.'

In the case of murals, a lot of people would have little experience, particularly with the issue of scale, so they would definitely need some help. I did an anti-sectarianism mural with kids from a Gaelscoil in Belfast a couple of years ago. We all sat down with children's storybooks and illustrations, and the one they liked was an Oscar Wilde story. It had a secret garden in it, which was lovely inside and all ugly outside. We picked this as our theme. The lovely garden was locked with a big lock. This was our design. The lock had the word for sectarianism in Irish on it: *seicteachas*. In other words, sectarianism was preventing the children from getting into this beautiful place. The kids painting it were very good, and the idea was that when we had the walled garden finished, the kids would then draw loads of children clambering about outside. I said, 'This is where you can really enjoy yourselves. You can draw children with skateboards or whatever.' What I didn't realise was that they were working without any real understanding of scale. One person would draw a figure three inches high and another would do a figure twelve inches high. At this stage, I had to make a modest intervention. The artist may have a role to 'harmonise' but definitely not impose his own vision.

Some artists amaze me – and I'm being specific here. I'm sure it applies to all of the arts, but certainly in the visual arts, some artists are very, very cagey about letting other people see their techniques, to see what they do, because somehow or other they fear they might run off and copy them! That attitude amazes me. One thing amateurs in art are really obsessed with is technique – 'How do you do that?' I did a project earlier in the year with Bealtaine, working with arts groups in Meath, and they asked me about technique, so I actually brought in a load of stuff and showed them very simple techniques, and I remember them saying to me afterwards, 'That was amazing – I never knew how to do that!' That's also about leaving the ego at the door. You are there to help people, and this notion that you have some special way of doing something, that's all a load of bullshit! I find even if somebody tries to copy what you do exactly, they'll actually come up with something different because that's what we are as humans – we're all individuals.

I think one of the things you learn in life is that lazy minds love to pigeonhole and sometimes the headings we are given – 'public art', 'community art', etc. – are not helpful. But I'm delighted there's activity in the area of public art now, because I can remember the early years of my involvement in the arts, when public commissioning was very rare and there was very little money for it. When I was involved with the Artists' Association, one of the things we campaigned for, for years, was the Per Cent for Art Scheme, never in our wildest dreams believing that anyone would listen to us. And then, lo and behold, it happened. I don't know how you would legislate to make it work well every time, and I would certainly have some concerns about some of the things that have been funded through this scheme – where nobody is being consulted, nobody knowing what it is, where it's for, what function it performs, etc. – some of the objects fall into the category ... well, the Americans have a terrible phrase for it: the 'Turd on the Plaza'.

Recently, however, there have been some interesting projects funded by the Per Cent for Art Scheme that engage in more ephemeral areas. Musical compositions have been funded, poetry projects, drama projects, and that's interesting because previously it was always seen as 'this thing dumped down there', but ideas have loosened out, and the Per Cent Scheme is being seen as a vehicle for all sorts of artistic interventions, and I think that's by and large a good thing.

But we still come back all the time to the need to avoid patronising attitudes. I call it the 'doctor's prescription' – that art is inevitably good for you. Even if you don't like it, you have to get it into you, because it will make you a better person. And you have no say in the prescription: the doctor knows best. In our case, the Arts Council or somebody else knows best, and the recipient just has to take that medicine, and I think that's disastrous, absolutely disastrous. I think there must be consultation, there must be some sort of dialogue, and I would see that as the greatest problem in the whole process. After all, some public art works are forever! I am appalled, firstly, when there isn't transparency and, secondly, democracy in the whole process. I presume the intention of public art commissions is to enhance the lives of the people who live wherever this thing is happening. So why should they not have some say in this thing that's going to be in their midst? There is a terrible resistance to that, because there is a total lack of trust that ordinary people can make decisions about these things. Of course, they can get some guidance from professionals. I can tell you of a project involving the Fire Station Studios in Buckingham Street which represents a good example of where the professionals were there simply to give guidance, not to participate in the decision making. But that requires a lot of giving from the arts community, and I think this example is very rare.

In the Fire Station case, they commissioned a piece to commemorate all the heroin victims in the area. I was asked to serve on the commissioning committee. The local people picked the work in two stages, and our job on the committee was simply to shortlist artists, because we would never get started if we couldn't shortlist artists. And then our job was to explain to the local people the various works, because the local people wouldn't necessarily understand the practical implications of the difference between bronze or fibreglass or whatever – no aesthetic stuff, just how this would work! The shortlisted artists were given some money to go away and develop their ideas a bit more, and then there was a final selection which was made by the local people. So the sculpture was chosen not by the Arts Council or by some highfalutin committee. It was chosen by the local community, and as a consequence it has never been vandalised, so there are lessons to be learned.

I heard on the radio the other day that Anthony Gormley is going to give us a big man in the Liffey. While the art establishment would certainly be delighted that an artist of his significance was doing this, I was interested to hear the residents of City Quay talking about it. They weren't consulted, they weren't spoken to, and they don't want it. I don't know what could have been done, but certainly there's something terribly wrong when the people who live there and who are going to continue living there – the first thing they know about it is when they read about it in the newspaper. Or they see it on the news, and suddenly they realise they are going to have a man that's taller than Liberty Hall standing in the Liffey outside their houses. That just seems to me all wrong, and it boils down to this business of non-consultation and non-involvement.

I remember a classic example of this 'non-involvement'. It was way back in the seventies. There was a sculptural project called Oasis. The first year it happened, the venue was Merrion Square, and all the leading sculptors contributed. I even submitted a piece, but it was rejected by Dublin Corporation. My piece was commenting on internment, and used barbed wire. The Corporation found a by-law to say there could be no barbed wire used on Corporation property, so I failed to get my piece up! But all the leading sculptors of the day had their pieces up all over Merrion Square. Nobody realised at the time that the reason it had all gone so well was because in the daytime there was supervision and at night it was locked up.

Next year, they got very brave and decided to have it in St Anne's Park in Raheny. Nobody spoke to anyone about it other than to the park authorities, who gave permission – but otherwise, nobody spoke to anyone at all. Overnight, these sculptures appeared all over the place, and I remember Charlie Haughey opened it, but the next day, not one sculpture was standing. There were about forty pieces and they were destroyed, and of course the establishment reaction was 'Philistines!' and 'How dare they?' I remember thinking, Maybe if you had spoken to people and involved them in some shape or form, you might have had some hope.

I always think that in any kind of intervention, there must be transparency, there must be discussion, there must be debate. Eventually, the artist goes away and goes back to where he or she lives. He or she doesn't have to live with it. The people who are going to have to live with this intervention should have some involvement in the process.

But as regards the tendency to damage art works, I am fascinated by this, in that in other societies 'anti-social vandalism' isn't as evident, and I just wonder where does it come from? Some things mystify me. We have a bus shelter at the top of our street. The eejits break the glass in it practically every week. You feel like saying, 'It's yours! Why are you breaking the glass?' It just seems so irrational that it must be in our DNA or something. I know this isn't an adequate explanation but I think it's part of the 'us and them' sort of thing. There's a feeling, particularly among marginalised people, that 'it's not ours', and I think that somehow or another, there is a hangover from history – a failure to understand civic pride and civic responsibility.

For many centuries in this country, the ordinary Irish people were not part of the situation – the lovely buildings and so on. I know people will say, 'Oh God, you're going on about that again: "eight hundred years" and all that.' But I do think it plays a part. It seems to be more prevalent here, although, mind you, England has its own problems with anti-social behaviour.

On the wider issue of politics and civic responsibility, I think local democracy is tragically inefficient in Ireland. I think one of the main reasons is the stroke that was pulled by Fianna Fáil in the seventies with the abolition of rates as an election gimmick. It effectively impoverished the local authorities, and they've been impoverished ever since. There was a promise then that central government would pick up the tab, but this never really happened. I don't think if local authorities were adequately funded they would have ventured into some of the Public-Private Partnership regeneration deals that have collapsed recently. And the whole issue of privatisation of so many services would not be part of the agenda.

Because it is less powerful, local government seems less attractive for people wishing to become involved in politics, and as a consequence, in areas of planning and in so many crucial areas, it seems that the bureaucrats run it rather than the elected politicians. So many decisions nowadays seem to be made by the city manager or whoever, and I don't think that's right. Yes, there are the community activists – people who have been operating at the coalface for many years – people like Tony Gregory, Christy Burke, Mick Rafferty. There have been lots of them, but set against that, I saw a statistic a while ago, whereby the number of councillors on Dublin City Council who have resigned before their term of office is over is quite startling, which suggests that they find the whole thing very frustrating and have pulled out of it.

Also on the national scene, I think we are ill-served by the kind of parliamentary democracy we have. I like PR (proportional representation), but the single-transferable-vote system, where you end up with candidates in the one party vying with one another ... well, it seems to me to be a game that has less to do with serving the people than with getting elected. I think we need radical reform of national politics as well as local politics.

I haven't studied the background well enough to know what sort of consultation was involved in planning the current Ballymun regeneration, or whether they have looked at other situations in other countries. What they seem to have taken on board is what I would argue is a 'sentimental view'. As a democrat, we must always listen to the people, but there seems to be an acceptance of the desire of a lot of people who want a two-storey house with a front garden and a back garden. I'm not sure that that's the way for urban development to succeed. I think it must be a mix: undoubtedly, low-level housing, etc., but there must be medium level and high level, and a mix of tenancy, and so on. I think suburban sprawl is just so appalling. When you drive around the periphery of Dublin, you see these housing estates spreading and spreading with no cohesion, no sense to them at all. What was that famous song … 'Ticky Tacky Houses'. It would be a shame if Ballymun should succumb to that kind of approach to urban planning.

But I would be optimistic, and certainly the people in Ballymun that I've spoken to seem quite optimistic about things. They still have a lot of complaints, and I still think it needs some sort of grander vision in the grand scheme of things. When I go there, I just don't feel centred. Maybe that is to come with some of these artistic interventions – maybe John Byrne's horse will help – John Byrne's equestrian piece!

And I think something needs to be done maybe in the area of landscaping, because there has been very little landscaping so far. The space where that tower came down – the space in front of the axis centre – is just an open space at the moment. Maybe intervention is necessary. I love trees! There was a project with trees, a German artist, Joachim Gerz, was doing a project with trees. An artist doing things with trees might be interesting.

The project I was involved with at the Health Care Centre in Ballymun arose from a public art process whereby the Health Service Executive (HSE) invited submissions for an art work to go with the new health care building. I was asked to be part of a team along with local artist Paddy Kavanagh and Aideen McBride – a storyteller and a collector of stories, also from Ballymun. Our concept was that, rather than an alien work that would be just dropped in, we would seek a way to incorporate local stories. We were invited to outline the idea to the commissioning committee, which had representation from Breaking Ground and other interested parties. We didn't win the major commission, but they liked the idea, and they came back to us and asked if we might consider implementing part of the project on a scaled-down budget. Aideen and Paddy between them collected stories from the community – both native and foreign. These were produced in hard copy and also in CD format, and made available within the centre. I took the opening sentence from one of those stories and we created a carved wooden piece in elaborate lettering. The sentence referred to a ring and we incorporated a ring into the work. I took the piece away and painted it in my studio, and it was then hung on one of the walls of the waiting areas. So now people waiting to see a doctor or avail of services can access these local stories while they wait.

And, of course, there is the axis arts centre. I had a small exhibition there about two years ago, but my connection with axis Ballymun has mostly been through working with Ray Yeates in the theatre. You can have arts centres that talk about being part of the community and they're not that at all. I'm not going to name names, but we all know the sort of places that get Arts Council grants and local authority support but local people never go to them. I don't get that feeling in Ballymun. I think they do good work and it's a very valuable resource in Ballymun, and if they ask me, I'm there – and if I have the time, I'll row in.

You go there and there are people in the restaurant; there are people going to events. I give talks occasionally about art or about my art or whatever, and you're lucky to get twenty or thirty people, but when I gave a talk in Ballymun about two years ago about my work and my approach to my work, the theatre was full! So there is something going on there – people are interested. These weren't 'supporters' of mine who bussed in from somewhere else! These were local people. Local people are involved.

In the production of *Our National Games* by Gerard Humphries – which I worked on with Ray Yeates in axis Ballymun earlier this year – they had cast Warren Gifford, a local young fellow that Ray had found, and that was his acting debut – absolutely fantastic! This is what we have talked about, the absolute necessity for art not to be imposed – it doesn't matter how good it is, it can be wonderful, but if the people who are the audience for this art are not involved in some shape or form before the art arrives, it won't work. It's a hugely different dynamic when local people are involved.

Otherwise, I think it's doomed to fail because it would be seen as alien: 'It's not ours, it's not part of us.'

John Byrne's horse? I hadn't known that 'Lord Gough' survived after the IRA blew him up in the Phoenix Park. I was too young to carry an image of it, but apparently it was a fine equestrian statue and John obviously tracked it down and discovered it. It's in some big estate in England now. So Breaking Ground commissioned John, and he went over and got permission to cast the horse for this work for Ballymun, and then – because they are mad into ponies – he got different local kids to ride horses and photographed them. They had some sort of competition to pick the final one, and this girl was brought to London. With modern technology, you can be laser-shot in three dimensions and they can build a model out of that. Public art inevitably fails when there is not due consultation. But this piece references real community cultural attitudes – to horses and so on. Unlike some other public art, it doesn't feel like it's parachuted in; a case of some middle-class artists 'claiming' Ballymun or its spaces as somehow special, when local people have had to live there all their lives.

So, basically the sculpture is going to be a bronze with this Dublin working-class girl sitting on Lord Gough's horse in the middle of Ballymun. That works!

Heights and Consequences

Writing the Ballymun Trilogy

DERMOT BOLGER

Ballymun could always be a wary place for travellers, a lonely spot beyond the city's reach and remit. In 1773 Dublin newspapers carried accounts of highwaymen who held up mail coaches passing through the fields of Ballymun. The robbers were, according to the passengers, 'remarkably polite'. If they were local men, then the list of suspects would have been small. The 1851 census lists only five inhabited buildings in Ballymun. By 1900 this had grown to eight, housing a population of just thirty-four people. The population would have been bigger except for the Famine and cholera outbreaks that devastated nineteenth-century Ireland. Those unable to feed themselves were doomed to enter the North Dublin Workhouse. When Elizabeth Meade and her four-year-old son were forced in 1848 to lie down among the dying of that terrible establishment, I don't know if she looked back towards the Ballymun fields, where she is listed as being from. But if some vision of future tower blocks and teeming streets had suddenly arisen before her starving eyes, she would surely have dismissed this as so grotesque as to be a demonic hallucination.

Ballymun was still largely a latticed landscape of fields in 1959 when I was born in a back bedroom in Finglas Park, a mile from Ballymun. I include this autobiographic detail because, in being asked to address in this essay how I tried to imaginatively explore the past and present of Ballymun in the plays that comprise *The Ballymun Trilogy*, it is necessary to understand somewhere of where I was coming from and – most especially in *The Townlands of Brazil* – how the experiences of my own extended family helped to shape this work.

My parents were country people who met in Dublin in search of work in a war-becalmed Ireland. In 1949 they moved from a flat on the Grand Canal out to Finglas when it was still a small village. As well as my own parents buying a house in the first housing development to be built out in Finglas, two of my mother's siblings also purchased houses – one next door and one around the corner. The gardens were huge – more like allotments. It must have seemed like paradise gained. The theme of economic migration, which I explore in *The Townlands of Brazil,* has its origins in the fact that although my mother came from a family of eleven in Monaghan, and my father came from a family of seven in Wexford, all their siblings needed to emigrate to Britain for work, with the exception of the sons who got the respective houses in Monaghan and Wexford, and those three siblings who settled in Finglas.

But even among the trio who sought to build a life in Finglas, enforced economic migration would take its toll within a few years. My aunt and uncle, who lived next door, were forced to sell up and leave to seek work abroad, in the Vauxhall car plant in Luton. My other uncle managed to keep his family in Finglas, but to do so needed to emigrate alone to spend a period of his working life in English car plants, sending money home each week. Indeed, the only reason why I have an Irish accent – unlike many of my cousins – is that my father emigrated every week as a ship's cook for over forty years, while my mother waited every Friday for the registered letter with crisp English banknotes sent from whatever port he docked in.

I will describe *The Townlands of Brazil* in more detail later. But I have always seen both acts of that play – Act 1, which concerns a young Ballymun girl, living in what was then the countryside in 1963, being forced to seek a new life abroad just as the Ballymun towers are being erected, and Act 2, about a young Polish girl arriving out of economic necessity in Ballymun in 2006 just as the same towers are being pulled down – as essentially the two sides of the one coin that comprises the story of my extended family and of thousands of other Irish families caught up in successive waves of migration.

But when those siblings moved to Finglas in 1949, they had little sense that they were also the first wave of another massive wave of migration –

not abroad this time, but internally, as Dublin began to stretch out to encompass the surrounding countryside. Finglas would not be a small village for much longer. Soon, thousands of inner-city families from the crumbling Dublin tenements would be housed in a necklace of new estates that encircled the old main street.

People construct walls using all kinds of bricks, and place names can be among these. As these new Corporation estates were built, some of Finglas' more socially mobile residents began to incorporate Ballymun into their postal address. This was a way to discreetly distance themselves from the new arrivals, and to identify themselves with the new middle-class housing schemes being built on the nearby fields that were the first part of Ballymun to be developed.

This middle-class area was where Bono grew up. He once observed how, as a boy, he could go for a walk and the streets he passed through would change social class a half-dozen times in half an hour. Very soon, however, those richer Finglas inhabitants would stop trying to invoke Ballymun as part of their address because Ballymun was shortly to become an address that school-leavers were advised to avoid giving when attending job interviews. Indeed, soon after the towers were built, the middle-class part of Ballymun quickly pulled off the linguistic slight-of-hand of rebranding itself, by plebiscite, 'Glasnevin North'. Ballymun became a place name that stigmatised people, and came to represent Dublin's worst social nightmare.

Yet ironically, as a small boy, I can remember excursions on Sunday afternoons for picnics at the base of the towers as they were being built. In the newspapers of the time, there was a wave of euphoric hope that these technical wonders would be the panacea for Dublin's terrible housing crisis. Families came from miles (as described in the opening of *From these Green Heights*) to marvel at the dream suburb being planned, which would almost be as posh as America. Nothing would be too good for the chosen model tenants, who would survey the city they had left from 7 fifteen-storey-high blocks, with smaller blocks nestling nearby like clucking chicks around a mother hen.

I am glad that my first memories of Ballymun were of hope, because in the years that followed there seemed precious little hope about the place. I was slowly to become familiar with Ballymun from friends and acquaintances who lived there, but while it was a world I was close to, it was a world that I was not a part of.

The towers had been erected because of a housing crisis in 1963 when Dublin Corporation was forced to evacuate and condemn many old tenements following four deaths caused by collapsing buildings. Housing waiting lists doubled, with some families forced to sleep on the street. Already in Europe, high-rise schemes were being abandoned for having become 'vertical slums' whose inhabitants were socially isolated. This did not deter the Irish government from deciding that a prefabricated high-rise scheme represented 'an exciting alternative to the squalor of Dublin's tenements'. The original name for the towers – Ard Glas (Green Heights) – reflected official optimism. Impressive plans included an ultra-modern shopping centre and thirty-six acres of public gardens and play areas. In 1966, when the first families moved in, the government decided to name each block after an executed leader of the 1916 Rising.

The initial lettings were handed out almost as a reward to model tenants. The flats were large and had central heating. What they lacked was a thermostat. Tenants baked or froze, unable to turn their own heating on or off. Almost from the start, the lifts malfunctioned, with young families facing an ordeal to simply descend from their flats. Once on the ground floor, there was nowhere to go. It was three years before the first shop was built. Indeed, all the promised facilities were similarly absent. People had simply been taken from close-knit city communities and dumped amid the tower blocks and fields. Soon, tenants with financial resources were leaving, and gradually Ballymun came to serve as a dumping ground for problem tenants.

Not only was it a hell for some people, but it became a symbol of hell by being so visible in the Dublin skyline. Dublin possessed few high-rise buildings, and the towers stood out from miles away. For most Dubliners, a distant glimpse was as close as they came to witnessing life there. In time, a wall was erected, not just of names but of physical bricks between the private streets nearby and the flats, with mutual hostility on both sides. The early lyrics of Bono talk of seeing seven towers but no way out. He is not the only Irish artist who used Ballymun as a backdrop. *Family*, the television series by the Booker Prize-winning novelist, Roddy Doyle, caused controversy by its harsh portrayal of life there. The film *Into the West* showed two Traveller children keeping a horse in a high-rise flat there. If Dublin had certain official beauty spots, like the Ha'penny Bridge – which invariably appeared in folksy foreign-made films about Dublin – then, almost like a deliberate counterpoint, the Ballymun flats appeared in numerous independent Irish films, such as *Adam and Paul*.

But the first poet I know who depicted Ballymun from the inside was an elderly, good-natured and (it seemed to me) somewhat long-suffering man called Tom Casey. By 1978 I was running a writers' workshop in a basement in North Great George's Street. It cost thirty pence to attend, and the only warmth came from a single Super Ser heater, though the arguments there grew so heated at times that I was frequently able to reduce this to the lowest setting. Tom was a Dubliner who had known years of emigration in England before finding his way back to his native city and being housed in Ballymun. This was not an uncommon story, as the 1960s and early 1970s saw emigrants drawn back to Ireland only to find their hopes unfulfilled, with many being housed in Ballymun. I never met Tom's wife, though he sometimes referred to her as being bad with her nerves, but I got the impression that she felt imprisoned in the Ballymun tower in which they lived, where the lift seemed to never work, and she rarely went out.

Tom, in contrast, needed to be out and about. There seemed no part of Ballymun that he was not on the fringes of, jotting down rambling descriptions of everything he witnessed. He brought us these weekly dispatches from the front. They were convoluted, but invariably shot through with humour, humanity and hard-earned human experience. Sometimes, they were dispatches from hell – his tower block never seemed to sleep – but they were the writings of a man who had seen too much and yet had never lost his humanity and absolute decency.

I do not know what happened to Tom Casey after he left Ballymun. I just know that sometimes he haunts me still. Firstly, because he always spoke so touchingly about his wife, who – like many other women – found Ballymun hard, and felt cut off with the high-rise blues. Secondly, because the last report I had of him was hearing that he had been badly beaten up on the single-decker 36 bus to Ballymun. A fight had broken out on-board one afternoon, a number of youths attacking a younger boy in the back seat. Dublin was a changing city where, to survive, you needed to look the other way. Tom's humanity would not allow him to do this. He walked down the bus and intervened by trying to appeal to the youths' humanity, to their decency with the innate Dublin decency that was ingrained within him. He wound up with broken ribs.

The third thing that haunts me about Tom (and, indeed, about other writers, such as Pat Tierney, who lived in Ballymun and died too soon) is that he would have loved the axis arts centre that now exists there. He would have haunted the place. On some days the staff there would be busy and dread seeing him coming, and on other days they would have had time to be enthralled by his wealth of stories. Axis would not have turned Tom into a polished writer, but it would have give him his forum, and he would have been as astute observer of all that happened, quick to praise, yet unimpressed by any false note.

Maybe there seems too much detail here about Tom Casey – an elderly poet who published only one or two pieces in tiny magazines and broadsheets in the 1970s – but his story is important to me. Other essays here will hopefully deal with the practice and theory of public art, which are serious issues that need to be seriously addressed. But I am essentially a storyteller, and such issues are sometimes addressed in a language that I don't necessarily understand, or – to be more precise – that I don't allow myself to think in.

Most poets have an ideal reader – one poet whom I admire kept a picture of Beethoven on his desk, with his poems imaginatively addressed to him. You could do worse, and my respect for Beethoven knows no bounds. But when Ray Yeates and the arts team at axis in Ballymun asked me to write a trilogy of plays, I decided to keep the image of Tom Casey in my head as my ideal reader, because his story is one small but integral part of the tapestry of lives that makes up the collective experience of Ballymun. This is what my plays have attempted to tap into. The story of Tom and his wife became one verse in the litany of lives that make up my long poem, *The Ballymun Incantation*, which was the first piece I wrote for axis. It was performed at night in the open air as the centrepiece of the public wake to mark the destruction of the first tower. The casting was significant in mapping out how we intended to go on. There was Máire Ní Ghráinne, that acclaimed actress who had given a lifetime of service to the Abbey Theatre. There was a teenage Ballymun actress, Kelly Hickey, who represented the emerging talent being nurtured in Ballymun, and, finally, there was the late Derek Fitzpatrick, a dynamic and forceful Ballymun community activist.

> In Pearse Tower my wife grew shook,
> She was alone when the lift got stuck,
> She hated the squatters jarring her nerves,
> I can still see her shaking, reciting prayers.

That story of the lost figure of Elizabeth Meade from 1848 also weaves its way into a verse:

> Remember my name it is Elizabeth,
> In the local workhouse I faced my death,
> Cholera stole away on my only son,
> I burned him amid the fields of Ballymun.

But, there again, dozens of people – some of whom I had known personally and others whom I did not know – worked their way into the poem, just like their lives worked their way into *The Ballymun Trilogy*. This is because every character in a novel or play is essentially a composite of myriad lives and remembered stories – partly because fiction or drama exists in a parallel imaginative universe, which may hopefully reflect the real world, but by its nature simply cannot be reality.

As a writer, I have always been conscious that, while familiar with Ballymun, I remain an outsider. However, even if I had been born, bred and buttered in one of the towers, I still could not tell the full story of that place, because nobody owns the narrative of Ballymun – every experience there is valid, but every experience is personal and therefore totally different. The moment you begin to write, you start a process of selection. You have to filter out certain things to bring other things into focus, or otherwise your vision would merely be the unquestioning eye of the security camera, which can see everything and yet contextualise nothing.

When the American singer Sammy Cahn was once asked, 'What came first, the music or the lyrics?' he replied with the honesty of a professional: 'The phone call.' Similarly, *The Ballymun Trilogy* came about as the result of a phone call from somebody whom I deeply respected. I first came across Ray Yeates when he ran the tiny Chelsea Playhouse – a seventy-seat theatre in New York – and performed a one-man show of mine entitled *In High Germany*, which he later toured to other venues in the States. It was an uncompromising play that was never likely to make any actor's fortune, but his staging of it showed a commitment to saying awkward truths that impressed me. I liked what Yeates was doing in New York, and I liked that he seemed to understand what I was trying to do in Dublin.

When he returned to Ireland and proved to be an inspired choice as artistic director of axis, it was his phone call that lured me back into writing for the stage after a number of years when I had become disillusioned about just what type of audience the theatre was able to reach. Initially, we discussed just one play – that became *From these Green Heights* – but even one play that would cover four decades of Ballymun life seemed a daunting prospect. But it was also a chance to write for an audience that I had grown up alongside, and to work in a building whose ethos I admired.

Axis was originally meant as two distinct buildings: a community resource centre and an arts centre. However, the partnership of community groups and local artists who founded it discovered that they could only afford one building. This resulted in something even better, in that axis is now both an arts centre, which local residents feel they own, and a community resource centre, which has creativity central to its operation.

Axis contains a superb two-hundred-seat theatre, a dance studio/studio performance space, a gallery, an arts and crafts workroom, two music rehearsal rooms, a recording studio, conference centre facilities, office space for ten community development organisations, a crèche for thirty-five babies and toddlers, a café and an events bar. Every morning, children arriving at the crèche rub shoulders with community workers and actors arriving for rehearsal. Building workers sit in the axis café alongside lighting designers chatting with local residents.

Its core funder is Ballymun Regeneration Ltd (BRL), with the Arts Council, Pobal, Foras na Gaeilge, Cityjet and Dublin City Council important backers. What struck me as unique about the building was the sense of joint ownership, with a performance by local young rap artists seen as being as important as a play's world premiere, and where Tommy Tiernan wandered on stage after a local comic.

All this went against the grain of recent reports on social inclusion in the arts that point to the exclusion of virtually everyone from mainstream arts activity unless they are from a higher income graduate bracket. The axis arts team worked from the view that not only did the vast majority of people feel excluded from the arts, but that artists suffered greatly, too, from having this restricted audience, especially as many artists themselves come from this same excluded majority. As artists, we suffered because we only got a minority response to our work, and were denied responses from the vast majority of our fellow citizens, who felt utterly disconnected from the experience that we call art. This had a negative impact on the artist because being heard or read or seen is an integral part of the business of creation, and because the feedback between audience and artist is essential.

I had been trying various and often very unsuccessful techniques since the age of eighteen to try and bridge that gap between my work and the audience I most wanted to reach. I began by running a small arts movement in Finglas, sometimes using my father's living room as a gallery or venue for poetry and music when he was blissfully unaware, out at sea. In the late 1970s I remember trying to put up posters one night for the first ever Finglas Arts Festival, and within less than two minutes finding myself pinned against the back of a squad car with policemen shouting, 'Is it political? Is it political?' We staged events in corridors. We photocopied poems and sold them in pubs. In 1979 I gave my first Ballymun poetry reading in the grim basement of a tower block. Nobody present that night could have conceived that one day Ballymun would acquire an international reputation as the site of innovative art.

I was not alone in trying to make things happen. Other people were also taking the business of expression into their own hands. Local musician, Owen McQuill, recalls how in the 1980s 'You had to create your own job or emigrate. For those of us who stayed behind, music gave us a chance to rise above the low self-esteem infecting young people then. Finglas and Ballymun saw a surge in alternative bands rehearsing in garden sheds and kitchens.' While bands like Aslam were striding towards fame, McQuill would regularly push a supermarket trolley loaded with amps to Ballymun's St Pappin's hall with other members of his band, Perfect Blue, joining him at different street corners to form a convoy of supermarket trolleys. This experience of having nowhere to play led members of Perfect Blue to form the Peanut Club (generously hosted by singer Mark Adams) as a free platform to let talent show itself to the world and to encourage anyone with the dream of being on stage. Other groups of local writers, artists and musicians were also finding ways to be heard.

I had known basements and corridors and Ray Yeates had known the tiny precarious space of the Chelsea Playhouse, but when he approached me to write for axis, Yeates argued that this state of the art theatre space in the very heart of Ballymun could be an exception to the socially exclusive world of the arts. This was an ethos that was shared by his fellow members of the axis arts team – the arts development manager, Mark O'Brien, the original programme manager, Róisín McGarr, and the current programme manager, Niamh Ní Chonchubhair – who all seemed determined to achieve this difficult balancing act of being open, warm and inclusive on the one hand, while, on the other, retaining a high standard of excellence in all output.

For axis, the arts are precious in Ballymun because they are a sign of hope and of the tide turning. When they stage a rap project with a hundred local teenagers, they are affirming the artistic impulses already organic to the area. Therefore, it takes not just artistic ability to engage with local people but also the ability to mentor and a willingness to serve. I found that there was no separation within axis between its participatory programme and its arts-practice professional programme.

The axis mission statement sets out its aims to pursue an arts practice that strengthens the relationship between the vocational and professional, enhances the experience of audience, participant and practitioner, and provides an opportunity for artistic experience of an international standard in Ballymun. By embedding local people at every point of the artist's journey, it aims to provide visiting artists with a different type of relevance, engagement and challenge, and to build artistic capacity affirming artistic initiative within the Ballymun community.

The chance to work within such a framework made Yeates's request for a play a challenge impossible to resist, and it was an opportunity which only came about because of the fact that BRL had the unique vision to place the arts at the centre of its work. It was a bold and unprecedented move that has really paid off by making artistic participation and practice part of Ballymun life, and by making the arts in Ballymun part of a national arts scene. This vision of BRL was in sharp contrast to the environment in which I had taken my first tentative steps in the arts in Finglas two decades previously.

As I started to work on that first play, *From these Green Heights,* I recalled a day in the 1980s when a Ballymun friend showed me three different spots where he saw the bloody aftermath of falls from the towers. Some were suicides, others were children left unsupervised for a moment. That Ballymun of the 1980s was no place for anyone with depression or suicidal tendencies, especially when the Corporation began to brick up unoccupied flats to prevent large numbers of squatters from moving in. In 1985 they even introduced a 'surrender grant' that encouraged a mass exodus by tenants who could afford to leave.

This was a low point in Ballymun's history. Local unemployment was massive and heroin infested the area like a grey cloud, with dealers signalling their presence on the streets by tossing old pairs of runners over electricity cables overhead to let addicts know where to find them. Most shops closed, and the nadir seemed to be reached when Bank of Ireland decided to close the only bank there as non-profitable because it was used primarily for cashing unemployment cheques. Perhaps this deliberate snub – marking locals down as unprofitable consumers rather than citizens – helped to galvanise the community. Because amid the problems of the previous two decades, a great sense of comradeship had grown among those who had pledged their long term future to the area. People who had organised rent strikes when the Corporation refused to maintain the lifts, people who in 1974 had sat down together on the road to successfully block bulldozers trying to build a commercial development on the site of their promised swimming pool.

In *From these Green Heights* I wanted to capture something of this journey of individual families, from arriving with hope in the 1960s, through moments of personal happiness and despair, through emigration and return and love and birth and addiction, to a sense of finally feeling that they belonged to a place, and were determined to be part of shaping its future. *From these Green Heights* tracks the lives of two Dublin families over four decades. It moves from the 1960s when Dessie, as a child, first glimpses the Ballymun towers high-rise complex being built amid fields, to the night in 2004 when he helps his young daughter to pack up and leave the flat that has been his family home ever since.

There is now a Civic Plaza in front of axis, linking it to Main Street and making it highly visible, but when *From these Green Heights* was first staged, axis was still tightly hemmed in by the (by then) abandoned MacDonagh Tower, which was awaiting destruction. It was an eerie sensation for the audience, quite literally, to have to pass within a few feet of this empty block to reach the theatre. Some nights of the staging of *From these Green Heights* were both exciting and nerve-wracking for a playwright. We have all been at plays where a mobile phone goes off, but this was the first production where I actually watched a mobile call being made by an audience member. We did one afternoon production for the Drugs Taskforce Centre where, during the more intense moments, audience members would literally stand up and walk around, saying, 'I can't take this, this is doing my head in.' Yet afterwards they stayed for hours talking to the cast. Evening performances were obviously quieter, but there was a sense of people watching a version of their own lives on stage. As a playwright, there was nowhere to hide any false note, because this audience knew the play better than the playwright did. Their lives may have been on display, but in my head I was the one on trial.

It won the *Irish Times* ESB prize for best new Irish play, but this award was minor compared to winning the respect of that audience each night, to seeing people moved to tears or hear them sometimes unable to prevent themselves from commenting aloud on some line. On that opening night, I wanted Tom Casey to be there, and Pat Tierney, and others whom I had known in Ballymun.

In a strange way, the highlight for me of the staging of the second play in the trilogy, *The Townlands of Brazil*, was the fact that on the opening night the actual play was not the main focus of the building. There might have been a full house of theatre goers there, but the play was just one event among a dozen events occurring that evening in the teeming axis building. Taking a break from their dance classes, eleven-year-old ballerinas formed an impromptu line, and with elaborate bows and mock-posh accents, welcomed visitors to the axis toilets. Local committees bustled in and out of the lift. The play was part of what was happening that night, but only one part of it. There was a feeling that the Ballymun community had a definite sense of ownership of axis, that they were not just entering it as an audience but as active participants.

Compared to *From these Green Heights*, there was also a new quality to the silence within the theatre, to the actual listening, as a new audience grew more accustomed to theatre. I saw *Townlands* as a sort of sequel and pre-sequel to *Green Heights*. Its first act is set in 1963 in a landscape that Elizabeth Meade and her son might just have recognised – those fields still there, although now dotted with white crosses that marked the spots where the foundations for the towers were soon to be dug. It was – as Anne Enright described Glenn Patterson's novel, *The International*, set on the eve of the Northern Troubles – 'the moment before the blast'.

It was about the original local people who felt that their way of life was soon to be threatened by a sudden influx of 'foreigners' from Gardiner Street. It was a recreation of the lives that people led in Finglas before my parents moved there in 1949, and of the scattered lives in Ballymun in 1963 that were soon to be swept away. And in the emigration of the daughter to England for work, it reflected, as I say, the lives of my extended family. But so also did the stories within the second act, set in 2006, when virtually no character on stage is Irish. This act is about the babble of foreign voices on the building sites around Ballymun, in manual jobs in hotel kitchens, and on mushroom farms. It was about the loneliness of starting again in a place that is at best indifferent to you, and where there is as yet no sense of home.

In contrasting the life and dreams of this Irish girl forced to leave the townlands of Silloge and Balcurris in 1963 with a life and dreams of a young Polish girl who has come to Ballymun in search of money to support her daughter, it tries to link the two ends of the one experience. It also tries to show that the story of Ballymun did not just begin in 1963 when Dublin Corporation pushed ahead with the high-rise Ballymun scheme. Nor will it end when the last tower comes down, because if a place is truly alive then it is never finished. It is a constant work in progress, refreshed and enriched by the life experiences of those who come there and start the process of moving from being outsiders to slowly beginning in their hearts and minds to see a new place as home. It is also the story of those who become lost in that process and wind up belonging nowhere – those lives that are forgotten but which are an essential part of the secret history of any place.

Having tried to bring many Ballymun residents into the theatre for the first time with *Green Heights*, the staging of *Townlands* was an attempt by axis to reach out to the migrant communities starting to settle in Ballymun. I could no more truly capture the totality of their experience than I could capture all that had happened in Ballymun over the previous forty years, but for myself and axis, staging this play was putting down a marker that their lives had now become part of the collective history of Ballymun, and maybe hoping to nudge somebody in that audience into writing a better and more authentic account of their own experience.

Every night there were some people there who were Polish or Romanian, but another constituency remained even harder to lure out to axis. A mental apartheid still exists in parts of the Dublin arts world. Successive Dublin Theatre Festivals have turned down the chance to see all three parts of *The Ballymun Trilogy* staged as part of the festival in a way that would bring axis into the mainstream of theatre. Professional axis productions – featuring emerging Ballymun talent like the superb Kelly Hickey alongside nationally famous actors like Vincent McCabe – have now played in the US, Belgium, Britain and Poland. Yet axis shows never transfer to the mainstream Dublin venues, and some Irish critics refuse to attend the plays. To them, Ballymun remains a ghetto, but its isolation and its chance to start anew has made it a hotbed of innovative art.

The local acclaimed Roundabout Youth Theatre Company, energetically run by Louise Lowe, spawned the award-winning Performance Lab, an initiative of Ballymun Regional Youth Resource, which stages work in unconventional locations. In one fascinating show entitled *Baby Girl*, the audience was led up to the top floor of a Ballymun tower block, unsure of which people around them on the street were actors and who were simply passers-by. Inside the flat, the audience followed the action from room to room (furnished from other abandoned flats), with no separation between the young actors and audience.

Central to Ballymun's artistic flourishing has been Breaking Ground, BRL's Per Cent for Art programme, which launched some of Ireland's most challenging public art projects. These include Seamus Nolan's *Hotel Ballymun*, where the top floor of Clarke Tower opened its doors as a unique short-stay hotel, with artist Seamus Nolan and Ballymun's community groups collaborating to convert the former flats into hotel rooms that played host to events for guests and visitors.

The Townlands of Brazil opened doors internationally for axis, with an invitation for *Townlands* to play at the National Theatre of Poland, before Poland's National Theatre returned the compliment by bringing its acclaimed production of *Smycz* for its Irish debut at axis. This international dimension prompted a different play from me – *Walking the Road*. Before I completed the trilogy, I felt it important that axis should stage a play of mine that was quite deliberately not about Ballymun. This seemed a vital part of the maturing process for both the theatre and its audience, and axis had already branched out in this direction by commissioning a tour-de-force show about mental health – *The Mental* – written and performed by Little John Nee. Powerfully written and staged, it brought to light the story of Ireland's forgotten charges in institutions throughout the country. It was a groundbreaking production that addressed the stigma surrounding mental health issues, and portrayed that hidden world in a touching, humorous, poignant and ultimately human manner.

Walking the Road was commissioned under the In Context 3 Scheme – South Dublin County Council's Per Cent for Art programme – and produced by axis in association with the extraordinary In Flanders Fields Museum in Ieper, Belgium. It explored the life and death of the Irish poet Francis Ledwidge – a working-class Irish nationalist killed in a British uniform in 1917. It was premiered a few yards away from the site of the Ballymun tower named after his great friend, Thomas MacDonagh (two poets divided by uniforms and united by dreams), then played in the town-hall theatre in Ieper, only a mile or two away from where Ledwidge died, alongside many of the other lost Irishmen invoked in the play, from Finglas and Rathfarnham and other Irish streets and villages.

The Ballymun Trilogy is completed in the autumn of 2008, with *The Consequences of Lightning*, a play that is set in Ballymun mid-regeneration, with most of the towers down and new housing built. Yet, although modernity is everywhere, people are still trapped behind invisible walls of regrets, old hurts and unanswered questions. As Sam – the first tenant to move into the old tower blocks – dies, those touched by his life find themselves summoned to his bedside. Frank, his successful son who turned his back on him and on Ballymun to forge a new identity; Jeepers, the wayward surrogate grandson Sam tried to look out for; Katie, whose life once seemed destined to intertwine with Frank's; Anne, her young daughter whom Jeepers adores; Martin, a Jesuit in a torn jumper who has lived through every change in Ballymun.

Awkwardly thrown together, they bid farewell to a drunken father, a good neighbour, a recovered alcoholic and a friend. But they bid farewell also to the tangled history of Ballymun that Sam lived through. To do so, they finally need to address unrequited love and unforgiven wrongs, during one last night when they learn that truth is rarely simple and that a sense of belonging is neither easily gained nor easily shaken off.

The Consequences of Lightning attempts to explores a rebuilt Ballymun and the challenges that separate those who have – and those who have not – been able to face up to the consequences of the past and leave them truly behind. At the time of writing I have no idea of how it will be received. But this is part of the magic of theatre, the fact that from night to night you have no guarantee that a play will work. As a playwright all you can do is put your faith in the director, in the crew and in the extraordinary casts that Ray Yeates has assembled for my shows, in actors like Brendan Laird, Kelly Hickey, Vincent McCabe, Anne Kent, Ann O'Neill, Julia Kyrnke (who came from Poland to make her Irish debut in axis), Alan King, Melanie Grace, Colin O'Donoghue, Catherine Barry, Karen Brady, Doireann Ní Chorragáin, Georgina McKevitt, Michael Judd, Michael Byrne, Stephen Kelly and others who have allowed the phantoms of my imagination to become flesh and blood on the stage.

I hope that in the future when people read or see The Ballymun Trilogy they will in some small way catch a glimpse into the end of a vanished world and the start of an emerging new world. Into a community that was transported out to nowhere and had to fend and fight for itself; a world where some could not cope and sought death in long falls into oblivion and where others found love and partnership and started fresh lives with new hopes and dreams. Some of the towers have come down piece by piece. On other occasions explosives were placed in lift shafts and crowds gathered to cheer as the former homes imploded. But amid their cheers locals knew that they had lost something too, which these plays have tried to capture: a set of memories that held them together and set them apart, a backdrop to the births, deaths and loves of three decades. Memories that will never be erased by the new homes being built around them.

The National Memory Town

JOHN WATERS

From time to time, usually around Easter, public discussion nowadays drifts towards the question of how we should mark the one hundredth anniversary of the 1916 Rising, at the time of writing less than eight years away. The context has altered in recent years, not least because the settlement of the conflict in the North has removed one of the core strands of difficulty – the idea that any kind of celebration of the uprising that gave birth to the independent Ireland might be seen to give succour to one side of that most ugly and protracted conflict.

A dominant thought in all such deliberations must be of avoiding past mistakes. It has long since been clear that in 1966, the fiftieth anniversary, a naive sentimentality took hold of proceedings. That occasion was marked by an uncomplicated celebration of the militaristic elements of the Rising, with little thought given to other dimensions or to the complex social and cultural meanings to be reinforced by underscoring aspects of such a momentous and still contentious event. The result was a refuge in cliché, a formulaic reviewing-stand commemoration that ignored almost everything important about the Rising and its aftermath. There are those who attribute the outbreak of conflict in the North to the sense of nationalistic euphoria sparked off at that time, although this seems implausible unless you entirely ignore the conditions then endured by nationalists under the Stormont regime, and overlook that the initial rumblings of October 1968 were peaceful civil rights marches inspired by the student rebellions in Continental Europe earlier in the year.

Nevertheless, few can be in doubt that the hundredth anniversary will have to be approached with more subtlety and circumspection. This is all the more true since, in the years between 1966 and the present, an altogether more complex set of ideas has developed in Ireland about what constitutes self-determination. There is a sense now that the meaning of independence is more challenging and multifaceted, that it is not merely a matter of hoisting a different masthead and presenting for business under a new name. There is a sense now, far more than existed in 1966, that the project of national reconstruction is as much a psychological as a political one, that disengagement from a long process of colonisation entails far more than sticking guns out of windows and letting them off. There is a healthy awareness now that the process of radical interference suffered by the Irish nation had many complicated and profound effects, and that these, though existing in both the individuals' minds and collective mind of the society, have their roots in a relationship that did not end simply because, and as soon as, a new flag was raised.

The project of independence is more a ripening than anything. In the beginning, everything seems simple: surely you simply undo what has been done to you? It takes a long time to perceive that such undoing is impossible without causing everything to unravel. The indigenous culture, having been interrupted, lacks a definitive sense of its own nature or direction. It still exists, but in an altered form, and cannot simply be decontaminated and reconditioned for a new phase of existence. The collective mindset is affected by a series of paradoxical conditions. On the one hand, there is a desire to purge everything alien; on the other, there is the unavoidable fact that the mindset itself has been infiltrated by alien influences, the most insidious of which is a tendency to imitate. The native wishes to redefine himself, not merely in contradistinction to his historical abuser, but in a manner that will bear witness to his authentic self; and yet, this authentic self can no longer be located, because it has been altered by the influence of the coloniser, whom the native has been conditioned to perceive as the most worthy subject of emulation. The native has been convinced, unbeknownst to himself, that his authentic self is a worthless thing, and that his only salvation resides in imitating his master, whom, at a conscious level, he imagines himself to despise. Who, then, is in charge? What is the nature of authenticity? What is to be made of the liberated native's determination to again become himself, if his sense of direction is provided by the indoctrination he has received?

Somewhere along the way, between 1916 and 1966, such insights had been lost. It is not that they were never present. On the contrary, in the writings of Pádraic Pearse and some of the other leaders of the revolution, they are to be found in a clear and complex form. In the years coming up to the insurrection, Pearse had written several times about the coming moment and what it would mean. In his essay 'The Murder Machine' – about the effects of the English education system in Ireland – he had outlined what would be involved in the process of undoing the effects of this brutalisation, of the need to foster 'the elements of character native to a soul, to help to bring these to their full perfection rather than to implant exotic excellences'. True independence, he wrote in another essay, 'The Spiritual Nation', 'requires spiritual and intellectual independence as its basis, or it tends to become unstable, a thing resting merely on interests which change with time and circumstances.'

Such understanding of the true enormity of the task that lay ahead was lost to the work of the firing squads. What remained was the crudest possible understanding of what required to be done, and of the meaning and relevance of words like 'soul', 'spiritual', 'intellectual', as the fundamental processes of reinvention came to be bypassed in a misplaced over-emphasis on superficial concepts of independence.

The result was a failure of intellectual and psychological reintegration. In the absence of such integration, there emerged not one sense of Ireland but a mishmash of confused and inauthentic identities. On the one hand, driven by the unattainable desire for a reclaimed authenticity, there began an era defined by protectionism and backlash, a ritualistic purging of all that was alien and, therefore, allegedly false. At the other extreme – governed by the self-hatred inculcated by the coloniser – there developed a repugnance and mistrust of everything indigenous. Even more bizarre – unless you understand the psychological context – is that these strands can be perceived existing side by side in the formal policy of the state in the years between independence and the marking of the fiftieth anniversary of 1916. Few things in the Ireland of the past half-century have embodied these conditions as much as Ballymun.

Ballymun – at least as it was for four decades straddling the second and third millennia – was the creation of a people set up by history, a people whose sense of themselves had been interrupted and diverted, driven underground, a nation in retreat from itself and the stereotypes created by a mixture of condescension and interference.

The evidence is by no means as superficially circumstantial as the fact that the seven towers that used to dominate the skyline of North Dublin were named after the seven signatories to the 1916 Proclamation. More pertinent was the way in which the towers and the estates around them managed to embody the unacknowledged conditions of imitation and avoidance of reality that were in many respects at the heart of the failure of the first fifty years of independence.

From the early 1960s onwards, many things in what increasingly came to be referred to as 'modern' Ireland seemed to become defined by what they were not rather than by what they were. The mood of the time was defined by a seeking after things that would dramatise some coming-of-age as a recreated society, which seemed by definition to mean a retreat from traditional notions of life on the island. There was a sense of shifting rapidly away from a previously held version of Ireland, not primarily to go somewhere else, but, as a fundamental priority, to get away from the past. The 1943 St Patrick's Day radio address by the then Taoiseach, Eamon de Valera, had acquired in the national imagination a kind of negative motivating stimulus, simultaneously defining what we had been and wished to escape, and unwittingly staking out a new destination. The speech, which subsequently became known as the 'comely maidens dancing at the crossroads' speech – although it contained mention of neither – would become an unconscious totem of the ideology of the new Ireland. 'That Ireland which we dreamed of,' intoned the patriarch,

> would be the home of a people who valued material wealth only as the basis for right living, of a people who were satisfied with frugal comfort and devoted their leisure to things of the spirit – a land whose countryside would be bright with cosy homesteads, whose fields and villages would be joyous with the sounds of industry, with the romping of sturdy children, the contests of athletic youths and the laughter of happy maidens, whose firesides would be forums for the wisdom of

serene old age. It would, in a word, be the home of a people
living the life that God desires that man should live.

But somewhere deep in the unconscious of the nation, fed by the complex
interaction of post-colonial uncertainty and desire, a different idea was
taking root: the new destination would be as far as possible in the opposite
direction from Dev's vision. Ballymun was to become an unfortunate totem
of this new thinking.

Ballymun is, as well as being part of Dublin, also part of the psyche of
every Irish person who grew up or lived in Ireland during the second half
of the twentieth century. Even for someone coming, like myself, from the
deepest west, it came to signify something concrete and yet incommunicable,
stark and yet ambiguous. Although I never went there until the early 1990s,
it had formed part of my imagination for many years before that. I had seen
it on television in documentaries about drugs and urban decay, and retained
– apart from the feeling of vicarious vertigo induced by the towers, and the
strongest memory of dank claustrophobia gleaned from slow pans of
stairwells – images of horsebacked boys with freckled faces, hard accents and
a frightening self-confidence; or their pasty-faced teenage sisters pushing
prams containing more freckled-faced boys or more pasty-faced girls; or, in
documentaries about heroin and lifts that didn't work, the hopeless anger of
the boys' mothers as they fulfilled their role as token victims in a drama with
no conceivable ending. I remember no fathers.

Through the 1980s and 1990s, a come-of-age Ballymun fed the
prejudice of modern Ireland about the existence and nature of what we
had grandly come to call the Irish underclass. There were other ghettos in
Dublin and in other cities, which, back in the 1960s and 1970s, when most
of them were created, were likewise intended as declarations that we were
moving inexorably away from poverty and darkness by doing what was
obvious to any truly modern mind. Their names came to resonate in a
mass-media society greased by fear and mutual suspicion: Darndale,
Neilstown, Tallaght, Fatima Mansions, South Hill – addresses that
unleashed instant prejudices in the hearts of many citizens as readily as they
triggered platitudes from left-wing politicians and social workers. These
massive estates on the fringes of our cities had been intended to showcase
the new, urban, industrialised Ireland, and bear witness to the extent to

which we were becoming 'like other modern societies'. The irony that, already, 'other modern societies' were beginning to realise the mistake in such developments, was lost on the ideologues and social theorists seeking a way to declare a place that was no longer Ireland.

Conceived to a blueprint based on Hollywood B-movie notions of what modern living should be like, they were designed for the future blue-collar generations that would man the factories of the new Ireland. Within a few years, they had become as the dirt under the carpet of a new-fangled, spick and span Ireland, without any sense of the thought process that had created it.

Ballymun was, among such estates, a unique folly, an icon of the failed project of modernisation, a totem to the depth and density of official incoherence, a disaster on a scale proportionate to its visibility, the Mother of all Ghettos. The 7 fifteen-storey low-density tower blocks were to be Ireland's first high-rise apartment blocks, a showcase of modernity in accordance with the very latest imported thinking. One of the core absurdities of Ballymun was that its high-rise element was utterly, insanely superfluous, given that the towers and flat complexes ate up enough ground to house an equivalent number of people in conventional housing estates. This, more than anything, reflects the reality of Ballymun created as an urban utopia by a generation in exile from it roots in the land. The fact that, being constructed around the time of the fiftieth anniversary of the 1916 Rising, the seven towers were each given the name of a different revolutionary leader, was merely the tin hat on this living, ironic representation of the pathology of post-colonial confusion. Ballymun captured our helpless tendency towards imitation in the form of a monument to those who had died for what they hoped would be a complete and complex form of independence. Here, as a monument to our incoherence, were our seven Towers of Babel in the heart of a wasteland of imitation.

Ballymun was essentially a reservation. Many of the people who ended up there were only one or two generations removed from the land, a connection lost to them in the struggle for survival that had constituted most of the first fifty years of national independence. The people who lived here were largely unskilled workers, minimally educated, who, in times of high unemployment, were forced into dependency on the state. There was a high preponderance of single mothers. And in this reservation, a new type of Irish person emerged – urban but without strong urban roots, Irish but disconnected from the essentially natural identity of Ireland. It was as though these people had been put out here while we waited for something to happen, while we waited for modernity to take. The dominant motif was of a taming of the wilderness combined with the imposition of something unmistakably alien that, in a country endowed with both space and beauty, could only have arisen from some deep sense of self-doubt.

What was different about Ballymun was that it could not possibly have been an accident. The context of its creation made clear the presence of motive and opportunity to create something utterly incoherent. It was a purpose-built ghetto, a monument to the ignorance of a generation that imagined itself the quintessence of modernity. Ballymun will forever be associated with the then Fianna Fáil Minister for Local Government, Neil Blaney, from Donegal, and mythology had it that the towers had been strategically placed so that politicians, with a wave of the hand in the back of the state car, could indicate them to visiting dignitaries on the way in from the airport. It was not to be. In the wider economy, the Lemass boom of the early 1970s rapidly dissolved into a reprise of 1950s pessimism that lasted into the 1990s. Unemployment and the absence of even the most basic infrastructure ensured that this intended showcase of modern living turned into a nightmare ghetto, with none of the advantages of urban living and all of the disadvantages.

When the three-thousand-unit Ballymun project went to tender in 1964, the government specification required it to be constructed 'as speedily as possible, consistent with a high standard of layout, design and construction and to acceptable costs'. The towers and other apartment complexes were constructed from prefabricated concrete panels cast in an on-site factory. At the outset, flats in this showpiece development were in brisk demand, and prospective residents were subjected to assiduous interview to determine suitability. Problems soon began to manifest themselves, however, with poor maintenance leading to perennial tenant disgruntlement. The inefficient heating system, which could be regulated only by the opening of windows, was a prime focus of complaints, being both costly and inefficient, with poor insulation causing massive heat loss through the walls of the towers. The lifts were another source of grievance, and in one late-seventies year alone, two-and-a-half-thousand complaints under this heading were lodged with Dublin Corporation. The cumulative effect of these difficulties was the phenomenon of transient occupancy, which nurtured instability and fed an emerging drug culture.

Very soon, what Ballymun began to summon up in the psyche of modern Ireland was not modernity and progress, but poverty, deprivation and marginalisation. Ballymun was not the only poverty-saturated area in modern Ireland, but more than others seemed to embrace elements of senselessness and tragedy as an inevitable by-product of its own intrinsic absurdity. One way or another, it came to function as a cautionary example of something to be regarded as an unavoidable element of state-driven social intervention. It was a living, breathing, dizzying embodiment of the idea that the poor would always be with us, and a symbol, writ large and high on the Dublin skyline, of the condescension and dissociation that attended official thinking about the poor. In the final decades of the twentieth century, Ballymun came to be useful as an illustration for salutary messages about the urgency of doing something about poverty, deprivation and marginalisation. Ballymun became useful for journalists in search of pram-pushing teenage girls or freckled boys on horseback to illustrate articles about poverty and deprivation, but somehow these never led anywhere, as though the existence of such places was something unavoidable and, perhaps, in some backhanded way, a tribute to the modernity of Irish society.

When I came to Dublin in the mid-1980s, I had no idea where to find Ballymun and even less inclination to do so. By then, I had heard even more about the towers, in interviews with Bono about his growing up in Cedarwood Road in an area facing Ballymun at its southern end. These interviews seemed ambiguous, for it was clear even to me that Bono had not come from Ballymun, but from an adjacent area whose claim to fame was that it was Not-Ballymun and which was defined by its Not-Ballymunness. This was implicit, and more occasionally explicit, in everything Bono said about his childhood, but there was also, it seemed to me, a sense of trading off something perceived to be at once repulsive, exotic and more than faintly dangerous. This was understandable: he was, after all, a singer in a rock band.

When I moved to Dalkey in the early 1990s, on a clear day I could see Ballymun towers from my back window. I still had no idea how to get there. But then a friend of mine moved there, and over the course of a couple of years, I found myself occasionally ferrying her and her two children back there after occasional visits. They lived in a flat near the top of one of the towers, and I would carry their accoutrements up the stairwell because the lifts were still not working. I remember only the dankness which struck me as being utterly more intense than anything I could have intuited from television, and the smell of piss. Up in the flat, I remember big rooms with washing hanging in the balcony, and the vertigo, real now, from looking back at where we had come from.

I returned home, always, full of the deepest sadness, horror and guilt, having taken a young mother and her two beautiful children to their home in hell.

A couple of years later, I found myself back in the area again, having been commissioned to write a book about U2's relationship with Ireland. The concept was to write about the band in terms of what might have pre-existed it, culturally and otherwise, and therefore give the story a life that suggested the music as being unique to a place – a society, a community, a village. There was not a great deal to go on, not least because it had long been taken for granted that U2's connections with the Finglas/Glasnevin/Ballymun area, with Dublin and with Ireland in general, were minor elements in what was a simple story of a band that had broken big in the global rock marketplace and 'just so happened' to be from where they were from. This is not what I discovered. On the contrary, the story of the book I eventually wrote, *Race of Angels*, is the story of what happens when the possibilities for self-expression are all but extinguished. It is the story of what happens to human desire in the shadow of human hubris, and how the Tower of Babel – built by man to prove that he is the equal of God – will always cause that desire to become more insistent. In other words, it tells why, precisely, the origins of U2 were crucial to what they would become.

Interesting in terms of the mixed religious background of the four band members was the fact that the original impulse to build residential housing in what is now the Finglas/Ballymun area had arisen in the late 1940s when the Church of Ireland elected to build an estate for its working-class members. Before that, the area had been open countryside on the edge of the city, utterly oblivious to the future and what it would come to mean in a new Ireland not yet announced. Because there were not enough Protestants, however, the new development was thrown open to Catholics. As it grew, the area drew from a mixture of cultural as well as religious backgrounds, including resettled families from the inner city, young married couples seeking their first home, and boggers in search of a new life in the capital city. There is a sense of the broader area having become a kind of mini melting pot into which were deposited those who could find no secure place anywhere else. Quite apart from anything relating to tower blocks, this seems to have created a culture of alienation all by itself. The novelist and playwright Dermot Bolger, who in the 1960s grew up close to what was becoming Ballymun, employed his own home place as a backdrop to his 1990s novel, *The Journey Home*,[1] recently the subject of much-deserved renewed interest in the United States. Hano, the young protagonist, recalls his parents and other displaced culchies growing vegetables and keeping hens in their back gardens. His best friend, Shay, whose family moved out from the inner city, lived only a few streets away. 'You'd think we would share a background', he lamented. 'Yet somehow we didn't. At least not then, not till later when we found we were equally dispossessed. *The Children of Limbo* was how Shay called us once. We came from nowhere and found we belonged nowhere else.'

Dermot Bolger's older sister, June Considine, writing in *Invisible Dublin: A Journey through Dublin's Suburbs*,[2] recalled the origins of Finglas – to which her family moved from the country in the late 1940s – just a short distance from what is now Ballymun. She remembered Sunday afternoon walks during the 1950s down the Ballygall Road, nowadays seeming as though urbanised since the beginnings of time: 'We would walk past Craigie's land with its herd of grazing cattle while my mother gathered bunches of overhanging hawthorn blossom. The leaves cast filigrees of sun shadow before us and each rocky wall seemed to have a river trickling quietly behind it. They shimmered in the heart of every gully.'

During the 1950s and 1960s, Finglas was transmogrified into an urban sprawl, with purpose-built blocks of low-density housing, and the streams were buried under apartments, shopping centres and flat, open spaces. Already, it was as though one concept of Ireland had been buried under another, as though the nature of the landscape had been suppressed to make some kind of point, or maybe as a kind of vengeance on a land that had proved in so many ways inhospitable. The streams ran silently now, recalled Considine in her essay 'Buried Memories', 'neatly channelled under rows of suburban houses. A stream-lined dual carriageway, hot with the pulse of traffic, cuts a swathe through the memories of my childhood.'[3]

The image of burial was no fanciful metaphor. 'Sometime after we settled into our new home', she wrote, 'an underground tributary which had been buried underneath our estate defied its concrete grave and surfaced in a neighbour's living room. The excitement of the street was intense as its short-lived resurrection seeped through the new furnishings and fittings. Then it was grimly channelled back beneath the foundations of our lives.'

By the late 1960s, when Ballymun was being constructed, the wider locality was already a hotchpotch of private and Corporation housing in uneasy juxtaposition. There was deep mistrust between those who lived in the local authority estates and those from the 'purchased houses', a low cloud of mutual suspicion comprising equal elements of snobbery and fear. Each road had its own pretensions and illusions, creating micro apartheids based on house values and whatever there was of a residual sense of a former rootedness, already all but lost. Even people who lived just a few streets apart had utterly different senses of where they came from. As the building of Ballymun began, Finglas had already become such a dirty word that some neighbourhoods started changing their addresses to suggest themselves as belonging to Ballymun, though this was soon to change again. By then, the children of the first residents of Finglas had become teenagers, and gang warfare was a daily feature. Talking to Dermot Bolger in the 1990s, he recalled an area defined by a multiplicity of micro-identities. Even kids from up the road, he remembered, spoke about their home place in a way that sounded to his boy's ears as though they came from a foreign country. Bono, who was born on the faultline between Finglas and Ballymun, later told me: 'We didn't know what to call it. You went into Finglas and you might be surrounded by some skins who'd ask you where you came from – and you didn't know. We lived in this no-man's-land between, I suppose three tribes: the posher Glasnevin, then Finglas, then Ballymun. And it would be like a roll of the dice whether you said the right name. So that meant you had to change your identity in order to negotiate your way through the mêlée. And I did.'

'I can see seven towers, but I only see one way out,' he would later sing in 'Running to Stand Still', perhaps the most particular song he would write about this childhood in the shadow of the Irish Babel.

This, then, was Limbo, a place, at first, of banishment from the unfolding drama of modern Ireland, and at the same time a kind of prophecy of what was to come in a country in retreat from de Valera's notions of happy maidens and cosy homesteads, and yet lacking the faintest idea what it wished to become. To be born into such a place must have been strange indeed, like having a confused dream of visiting a house in the process of reconstruction while the life of the residents continued as though normal, and waking up to the realisation that you lived there, too.

Ballymun wasn't just towers, but it was the towers that set Ballymun apart. Gavin Friday, a friend of U2's singer Bono, and himself a member of the legendary Lypton Village collective from which U2 would emerge, later recalled the birth of the locality. 'I remember running around playing cowboys and Indians in the fields when the Ballymun flats were being built, and thinking they were great, real modern, y'know, "We're going to be like America!"'

Within a short time, however, this dream, too, had started to sour. 'Not being Ballymun,' remembered Dermot Bolger. 'That was the most important thing in your life.'

Ten years ago, at the outset of the regeneration project, the population of Ballymun was 16,556, having declined marginally through the 1990s. Women were in the majority, particularly in the twenty to forty age group. An incredible 37 per cent of households were lone-parent families, accounting for just under half of the children of Ballymun. Of residents of working age, 20 per cent were registered as unemployed at a time when national unemployment was approaching zero. Of these, two thirds had been unemployed for more than a year, although there had been a significant fall in unemployment in the previous twelve-month period. Registered unemployment among men was 31.5 per cent, despite the fact that the areas had significantly less men than women, and for men between twenty-five and forty-four, the rate was 40 per cent. Of Dublin Corporation tenants in Ballymun, 70.9 per cent depended on social welfare as their sole source of income. Surveys indicated that the vast majority of children left school at the earliest opportunity – usually at fifteen. Most adults had minimal education, and these patterns, and attendant attitudes, were being passed on to the young. In any given year, about two thousand five hundred pupils attended the eight primary schools in Ballymun, and about one third of these moved on to secondary level. Of the latter, only about half went on to complete second level, and the rate of progression to third level was negligible.

The story of Ballymun Regeneration Ltd and its now ten-year-old project of bringing fundamental human entitlements to this 760-acre site populated by nearly twenty thousand citizens is a story of, essentially, reparation. It is a snapshot of what is required for the restoration of balance, justice, coherence and sanity in a context where these values have been, for whatever reason, missing from the beginning. In particular, it is a parable of 'modern' Ireland and its capacity to face up to its pathologies, hubris and past mistakes.

The project was announced by the government in March 1997, in the earliest stages of the consciousness of the Celtic Tiger. The statement read:

> The aim of this major social project is to get Ballymun working as a town which caters for all social needs, attracts public and private investment, provides employment and secures a better mix of housing in a rejuvenated physical environment. Housing-based policies alone will not achieve this strategic aim but can act as the catalyst which will improve Ballymun for the people who live there, and those who will live and work there in the future.

In May 2008 I visited the new town of Ballymun, and was shown around by Ciarán Murray, the managing director of Ballymun Regeneration Ltd. Murray is a countryman with an understated outward air of what is clearly a dogged inward determination, who brings to the project a clear sense of human purpose, a traditional view of human dignity and a solid weight of common sense. He is deeply and justifiably proud of what is being achieved in Ballymun.

There is, unquestionably, something deeply moving about encountering the partly regenerated Ballymun, an inchoate sense of correspondence accountable for by a complex list of emotions. There is relief, a sense that a wrong is being put right, but, more, that a problem is being unpicked, a crime being atoned for. Already, the state has done ten years' community service in Ballymun, and looks set to do perhaps five or six more before it is finished.

And how sweet it is – after those years of being told that we must seek our future directions from the models offered by other societies – to learn that the new Ballymun may become a state of the art example of regeneration projects in the world.

In November 1997 a public consultation process concerning the future of Ballymun enabled two thousand local people to become involved in designing their own locality. A hallmark of the project from the beginning was that the masterplan for the regeneration of the area was to be developed in close consultation with local people and a wide range of local interests and community groups.

The challenges facing those undertaking the regeneration of Ballymun were many and obvious: as the opening statement-of-official-intent suggested, endemic issues like joblessness could only be tackled in the wider context of dealing with demographics, dependency culture, self-confidence, lack of education and basic skills, the unattractiveness of the environment, human isolation and dislocation, failure of official policy and public bodies, and lack of integration into the wider North Dublin communities.

The challenge was to jump-start the life of a community big enough to be deemed, by Irish standards, a small city. The emphasised elements were: quality of design, the creation of a vibrant town centre, quality homes, economic development and employment creation, social amenities, the fostering of commercial opportunities, the provision of health and education infrastructure, imaginative use of public space and the development of appropriate recreational facilities – all at all times with an eye to the maximisation of community involvement. This process would be paradoxical and complex: its success depended on the regeneration of a community, but this could only come about as a result of successful physical interventions. These latter were vital, but would lead nowhere fast unless the spirit of the human part of Ballymun was being lifted at the same time. Although the project includes elements of construction, demolition, design and renovation, the regeneration is only in the flimsiest sense a construction project. Much more is it a project aimed at the regeneration of life in an area where, in effect, culture had been perverted by bad planning, prejudice and condescension.

In pursuing such complex objectives, endless tangents and cul-de-sacs needed to be explored. The historical absence of basic infrastructure resulted in extraordinary complications when it came to reconstituting the locality. The dozens of container shops, for example, that had sprung up in the beginning as a consequence of the distances between many of the estates and local shops, meant that those running these informal corner-shops-without-corners had acquired rights of adverse possession which had to be addressed in a legal context. Some of the operators were motivated to become legitimate, but others opted to sit it out in the hope of windfall compensation, and one or two of these cases may yet end up in court.

In other respects, progress was more straightforward. The formless open spaces resulting from Ballymun's original design as a low-density, high-rise residential area posed challenges that have been addressed by the creation of parks, play areas and landscaped public spaces. A new town centre has been constructed, with a civic building, an arts centre, a health clinic and the Plaza that plays host to buskers, mime artists and a farmers' market. There has been an injection of commercial activity: hotels, shops and supermarkets, a leisure centre with a gym and swimming pool, and the massive IKEA complex which will soon be the focal point of the business end of the reconstituted Ballymun.

The new housing estates of Ballymun incorporate a careful mix of public and private and a number of estates which have been built as cooperatives of the residents. When complete, the new Ballymun will comprise some 4,751 housing units, including 2,228 public, 1,826 private, and 637 voluntary and affordable housing, including cooperatives. The new housing stock is remarkable in terms of its varied and attractive design features, but also because it seeks to create distinct and functioning communities as though they had occurred spontaneously. The phrase 'cosy homesteads' springs unprompted to mind.

About three quarters of the residential construction is now completed. The demolition process – requiring the levelling of thirty-six blocks of flats comprising 2,820 units – is continuing also, and will take several more years to complete. The project is somewhat behind schedule and over budget. Originally timed for completion in 2007, it is now unlikely to be finished before 2013, and may run later. The initial estimate of the overall cost was €442 million, but due to building-cost inflation and innumerable unforeseen difficulties, the final figure may be close to €1 billion. Considering that the project has involved, for example, 510 public procurement processes, 130 separate design projects, 108 individual planning applications (plus 21 planning appeals) and 10 court actions, this overrun is hardly surprising. But beyond such actuarial calculations, this project may yet prove, in human terms, the best billion euro we've ever spent.

All this means that Ballymun is no longer a reservation, a darkness on the edge of town, but an 'important strategic location' on the cutting edge of the capital city. Beside the airport, with direct access to the M50 and just four miles from the city centre, Ballymun was always well placed to participate in the economic life of the capital, and has been rendered even more so by the upgrading of the M50 and M1 road networks. It also has, in the immediate vicinity, a national third-level facility, Dublin City University (DCU), and is surrounded by land highly suited to development. These elements, combined with the forthcoming opening of the Ballymun light-rail link, may soon make Ballymun, for the first time in its history, a place with the potential to draw in the outside world, to become something enormously positive in the national imagination.

In a sense, what is being constructed here is a civilisation in microcosm by the application of lessons learned in the whirlwind of error that has constituted Irish independence thus far. Ballymun is therefore a symbol of what we can do when we put our minds to it, and its success or failure will be a measure of our capacity to call ourselves civilised.

What we surrendered as a society in creating monstrosities like Ballymun is the idea of the fundamental dignity of each human being. Regeneration, then, is only marginally a physical operation, but is essentially a religious project: the restoration of human freedom and human dignity – freedom to approach one's individual destiny and dignity in a place one can call home, and to have that journey honoured in its uniqueness by the outside world. This, in places like Ballymun, is what has long and fundamentally been denied, and is therefore the meaning of the grief I felt leaving those two boys and their mother back to Clarke Tower (I think it was Clarke Tower, though to me they were all the same) all those years ago. Poverty was never the primary problem, but the absence of hope arising from the denial of human reality.

In April 2005, about seven years into the regeneration project, I was back in Ballymun to meet a German artist called Jochen Gerz, whose area of specialisation was the creation of commemorative 'anti-monuments' to mark the sites of sundry human follies. Several of his previous projects had been directed against amnesia, like the Monument Against Fascism in Hamburg, a twelve-metre-tall lead-coated column which, over a period of seven years, was covered with the signatures of passing citizens and gradually lowered into the ground. Gerz had lately been working in the transforming Ballymun, the great sociological pratfall of 'modern' Ireland, with its seven towers of Babel casting their shadows far beyond the capital. By now, one by one, the towers were being toppled. With the aid of high-powered explosives, this unintentionally ironic monument to our obsession with modernity was being returned to dust. Commissioned to conceive a monument to announce the new Ballymun, Gerz proposed planting trees in the vicinity, with the names of the donors engraved on the pavement of the new town-centre Plaza. A local survey having found that, despite the overbearing presence of the towers, over 50 per cent of locals under thirty could not name a single signatory to the Proclamation, he was then extending his concept to construct what he called a National Memory Grove, a hectare of ground close by on which he proposed to plant four hundred oak trees to commemorate the patriots whose stories had begun to disappear, like the towers, from public view. Each tree would be donated by an individual or family and would have a plaque outlining the donor's reasons for subscribing. The text on each plaque would be by collaboration between artist and donor.

Gerz told me he wished the people of Ballymun, and of Ireland, to become the authors of their own story. 'Life is authorship. I don't say everybody is an artist, I say an artist is an author like everybody else.' The choice of trees as a motif of commemoration had many sides. To begin, a tree is a living entity. 'People are not an image,' Gerz insisted. 'We live a process life, we do not live a statue life.' The trees were intended to return Ballymun to nature, a kind of reparation to the place in advance of making reparation to its people. Eventually, the trees would die, and with them all they had come to mean – which was as it should be. 'Memories, oblivion, come and go,' Gerz explained. 'The need for art comes from the loss of life. It does not come from the size of archives, length of shelves, walls and lists.'

Jochen Gerz's idea for a National Memory Grove has since undergone some modification, although the trees remain a central motif in the new Ballymun. I saw many newly planted trees scattered through the area when I went there again just three years later to see how things were after ten years of the regeneration project.

We should, where possible, avoid further expressions of premature self-congratulation, but nevertheless there is something obvious in what is happening here that has not yet been publicly noted. While we scratch our heads in an attempt to find an occasion or a location by or in which to mark the centenary of the revolution that started the most recent stage of the Irish journey, the absolutely perfect thing is already under our noses. It is often lamented that the fruits of the recent boom have been wasted, but in Ballymun they have not. Here, unbeknownst to the vast majority of Irish taxpayers, our money is being spent in a way that has the potential one day soon to make us think a little differently about everything.

What does it lack, this slow but steady exercise in local-but-also-national reparation and renewal, that does not perfectly represent what needs to be represented in any celebration of what it means to be independent? What better cause for celebration than this hard-won triumph over myopia and stupidity? That the project looks set fair to be just about completed by 2015 is surely the result of someone or other trying to tell us something. For here is an opportunity not merely to nod to the reasons the towers were named after the Proclamation signatories in the first place, but also to acknowledge the ironies and the errors arising from this retrospectively self-satirising decision. Here, too, is an opportunity to celebrate the letter rather than merely the spirit of the Proclamation, a cherishing of some of the previously uncherished children of the nation as equal citizens of a free Ireland.

Deeper still, there are the essential themes of national remembering, the setting right of the pratfalls arising from post-colonial unknowing, and, above all, the exhilaration of discovering something about ourselves that, like Ballymun, we always knew about but never looked too closely at. Imagine, on the Easter Monday of 2016, taking the train with your children to a place reconstructed out of the hard-won lessons of the years of national independence, to participate in a celebration of what it is truly like to be a modern society which has come through the trauma of building and demolishing itself in the process of learning how to be properly human.

Ladies and gentlemen, citizens of the Republic, I give you – the National Memory Town.

NOTES AND REFERENCES

1   Dermot Bolger, *The Journey Home* (London, Viking, 1990).
2   June Considine, *Invisible Dublin: A Journey Through Dublin's Suburbs* (Dublin, Raven Arts Press, 1991).
3   Ibid.

About the Contributors

ROBERT BALLAGH's work is held in many important collections, including those at the National Gallery of Ireland, the Irish Museum of Modern Art, the Municipal Gallery in Cork and the Ulster Museum. As a graphic designer, he has designed book covers, posters, over seventy stamps for the Irish postal service and the last Irish banknotes produced by the Central Bank of Ireland. He is a member of Aosdána and president of the Ireland Institute, a centre for historical and cultural studies.

DERMOT BOLGER was reared in Finglas Park, a mile from Ballymun. His novels include *The Journey Home* and *The Family on Paradise Pier*, and he also devised the best-selling Finbar's Hotel collaborative novels. His debut play received The Samuel Beckett Award and the first of his Ballymun trilogy, *From These Green Heights*, staged by the axis arts and community resource centre in Ballymun, won the *Irish Times*/ESB award for best new Irish play of 2004. The author of eight volumes of poetry, he has been writer fellow in Trinity College Dublin and playwright in association with the Abbey Theatre.

CIARÁN CUFFE is an architect, planner and Dáil deputy. He was a city councillor representing Dublin's south inner city constituency from 1991 to 2002, and was first elected to the Dáil constituency for Dún Laoghaire in 2002. He has published legislation to protect Dublin Bay and control noise pollution, and has campaigned on transport, urban and environmental issues. A passionate advocate of urban life, he believes that architects and urban planners must ensure that urban design is used as a framework to provide for the needs of communities experiencing regeneration.

ANNA DAVIES was awarded her PhD on environmental values and the planning system from the University of Cambridge in 1999. After lecturing at King's College London she moved to Trinity College Dublin in 2001 where she became associate professor in environmental geography in 2007. She has published widely in the fields of environmental policy, politics and planning, and is currently working on a number of research projects, including the examination of grassroots sustainability enterprises and sustainable consumption.

DECLAN GORMAN is a playwright and theatre director with a background in community-engaged arts practice and policy. A past winner of the Stewart Parker Trust award for play-writing, he is currently associate artistic director of Upstate Theatre Project, Drogheda, and a chairperson of City Arts Dublin. He has been chair of the Abbey Theatre Outreach Education Working Group; a board member of Garter Lane Arts Centre and of Garage Theatre, Monaghan; and chair of an Arts Council steering group in support of research into networking and information exchange in participatory arts.

RONAN KING was appointed chairman of Ballymun Regeneration Limited in 2008. A chartered accountant and the immediate past president of the Dublin Chamber of Commerce, he is also chairman of Amethyst Investments Ltd. He was a lead member of the teams that prepared the original draft masterplan for the Dublin Docklands, and that advised Harland and Wolff on the development of the Titanic Quarter in Belfast. A firm believer in community service and corporate responsibility, he served as deputy chair of the 2003 Special Olympics World Games.

JOHN MONTAGUE is a freelance architectural historian and a part-time lecturer at Trinity College Dublin. He has lived in the flats in Ballymun since 1988, and has taken an active part in representing his area in community forums since the onset of the regeneration project. He has published widely in his field on subjects as diverse as the twelfth-century cathedral at Old Sarum (the precursor of Salisbury cathedral) and the Essex Street piazzas in eighteenth-century Dublin. In 2008 he completed a PhD on the subject of John Roque's 1756 map of Dublin.

RONNIE MUNCK works in the president's office of Dublin City University (DCU), where he coordinates the university's strategic foresight process and the civic engagement strategy. He is also visiting professor of sociology at the University of Liverpool. He has written a number of books on globalisation and its impact in terms of social exclusion, and others on regeneration in Liverpool. He is currently working with Deiric Ó Broin on DCU's next three-year strategic plan on civic engagement, designed to embed the strategy within all aspects of university life.

DEIRIC Ó BROIN is director of the regional think-and-do tank, NorDubCo, which is based at Dublin City University. He is also directly involved, with Ronnie Munck, in the development and implementation of the university's civic engagement strategy. He is a graduate of the Dublin Institute of Technology (DIT) and University College Dublin, where he completed a PhD. He lectures on local and regional economic development and EU policy in the School of Spatial Planning at DIT.

ANNE POWER is professor of social policy at the London School of Economics and Political Science, and is head of LSE Housing, a research and consultancy group within the Centre for Analysis of Social Exclusion. She is also a member of the British government's Sustainable Development Commission. From 1979 to 1989 she worked for the Department of the Environment and the Welsh Office, setting up Priority Estates Projects to rescue run-down estates. Since 1965 she has been involved in European and American housing and urban problems. She first visited Ballymun in 1968 and, since then, has been a valued advisor in the regeneration process.

DAVID PRICHARD led the multi-disciplinary team that created the masterplan for the regeneration of Ballymun. This masterplan went on to win the Irish Planning Institute's Planning Achievement Award. His other work includes the regeneration of the waterfront in Oslo, the regional plan for the Dead Sea Coast and the Cable and Wireless College, Coventry, which won the RFAC/*Sunday Times* building of the year award.

MICHELE RYAN is dean of the School of Community Studies at the National College of Ireland. Previously director of the Educational Opportunities Programmes Unit within the college, she has overseen the development of the college's collaborative, community-based learning initiatives since 1998. Before joining the college, she worked for ten years within the community and voluntary sectors. A founder member of the Ballymun Community Law Centre, she currently serves on its board of directors.

DUNCAN STEWART has been lecturing and practising as an architect for over thirty-five years. During this time he has won many architectural awards, particularly for his use of sustainable materials and his focus on sustainable design. His foremost passion is the environment and over the past fifteen years he has built as a career as a speaker and lecturer on conservation and environmental issues. As a broadcaster, presenter and producer, he has worked on many TV and radio shows including *Eco Eye* and *About the House*.

JOHN TIERNEY has been the Dublin City Manager since 2006. He contributes to the work of many different agencies and groups: his roles include chair of the Transport 21 Implementation Group, deputy chair of the Institute of Public Administration, director of the Affordable Homes Partnership Board and director of the Digital Hub Development Agency. He holds an MA in Public Management from the Institute of Public Administration.

JOHN WATERS is an author, journalist, magazine editor and columnist. His books include *Jiving at the Crossroads*, *An Intelligent Person's Guide to Modern Ireland* and *Lapsed Agnostic*. He has worked for the *Sunday Tribune*, the *Independent* newspaper group and RTÉ, and edited *Magill* and *In Dublin*. Throughout his journalistic career he has specialised in raising issues of public importance, including the repression of Famine memories and the denial of fathers' rights. He has written plays for radio and the stage including *Long Black Coat*, *Easter Dues* and *Adverse Possession*. He is an unmarried father of one daughter, Róisín Waters, now aged 12.

GERRY WHYTE is an associate professor at Trinity Law School and a fellow of Trinity College. The author and co-author of books on public interest law, constitutional law and trade union law, he has also edited books on aspects of law and religion and Irish social welfare law. He is active in a number of social justice and legal aid organisations and was the chairperson of Northside Community Law Centre from 1995–9.

PETER WYSE JACKSON is director of the National Botanic Gardens of Ireland. Currently the chairman of the Global Partnership for Plant Conservation, he has worked extensively throughout the world, helping to establish botanic gardens, especially in developing countries. His research interests include the flora of Ireland; he is working on a study of the uses of Irish wild plants, past and present. His publications include ten books, over two hundred scientific papers and a wide range of other articles. He is strongly committed to developing the relationship between the National Botanic Gardens of Ireland and Ballymun.

Index

Adam and Paul (film) 245
Adams, Mark 249
Adamstown 15
Ahrends Burton and Koralek
  (architects) 57
Albert College School of Agriculture
  51, 207
Allianz Business to Arts Awards 86
Amnesty International 129–30
Arnstein, Sherry 212
  A Ladder of Citizen Participation 212
Artists' Association 233
Arts Council 229, 233–4, 238, 248
axis arts and community resource
  centre 9, 14, 16, 38, 63, 83, 86,
  214, 219, 223, 225, 237–8, 246,
  248–56, 273

Bachelard, Gaston 55–6
  Poetics of Space 55
Ballyfermot 184
Ballygall Road (Dublin) 268
Ballymun
  area (land measurement) 2, 271
  Association of Horse Traders 32
  Balbutcher Lane 60, 63
  Balcurris 3, 11, 13, 24, 52, 64, 71,
    93, 100, 110, 127, 253
  Clarke Tower xi, 39, 254, 274
  community activism 11, 32, 48, 64,
    69, 214, 251
  Coultry 3, 10–13, 18, 24, 52, 61,
    64–5, 93
  design (1960s) x, 4, 6, 11, 28,
    46–8, 52–3, 55, 57, 59–61, 67,
    69, 80, 183–4, 207–10, 214–15,
    223–4, 226, 253, 264–6, 269
    Balency et Schuhl concrete system
      4, 52–3
    Lowton–Cubitt system 52
  Fairtrade town xi, 106
  farmers' market 14, 106, 196, 198,
    273
  MacDonagh Tower 252
  Men's Network 124

neighbourhood forums 11, 21, 61,
  85, 111, 127, 141, 143
  Balbutcher Forum 127
  Balcurris Forum 127
  Ballymun Partnership Forum 21
  Safer Ballymun 85
nomenclature 60, 244, 275–6
Pearse Tower 27, 32, 46, 247
Poppintree 3, 11, 13, 39, 49, 52, 64,
  93, 110, 127, 195–6, 211–12,
  216
  Poppintree Community Centre
    127
Plunkett Tower 60, 63, 69
population/demography x, 2, 8, 10,
  31, 34, 41, 48, 214, 241, 266,
  269–71
refurbishment (1990s) 5, 35–6, 60,
  63, 213
Scoil an tSeachtar Laoch 124
Shangan 3, 10–11, 52, 64, 93, 127,
  163
Silloge 3, 8, 10–11, 49, 52, 59, 64,
  93, 195, 253
St Pappin's hall 249
Woodhazel 64
Ballymun Area Partnership Company
  123
Ballymun Citizens' Information
  Centre 124, 156
Ballymun Community Action
  Programme 124
Ballymun Community Law Centre
  (BCLC) 40, 115, 120, 122–32,
  145–6
  Dublin City Council v. Fennell 128–9
  Fight for Your Rights 130
  Legal Education for All Project 130
  Mediation Ballymun 128
  Rehabilitation of Offenders Bill
    (2007) 131
  Spent Convictions Group 131
Ballymun Credit Union 32, 124
Ballymun Employment Centre 127
Ballymun Environmental Group 215

Ballymun Evaluation Report (2003)
    127
Ballymun Housing Task Force 62,
    124, 145, 211 *see also* Ballymun
    Neighbourhood Council
Ballymun Initiative for Third-level
    Education 146
Ballymun Library 16, 127, 216
Ballymun Neighbourhood Council
    145 *see also* Ballymun Housing
    Task Force
Ballymun Partnership 124
Ballymun Regeneration Ltd (BRL)
    establishment of x, 2, 4–5, 36, 62,
        124, 184, 210, 225
    logo xii, 3
    masterplan
        arterial strategy 5–8, 10–12, 14,
            18, 24, 63, 90–1, 210
        budget/costs/funding 25, 30,
            36–7, 43, 63, 159, 212–13,
            273–4
        built-environment strategy 6, 9,
            14, 18–19, 37, 63, 89, 216–17,
            237, 272
            Ballymun Civic Plaza
                (objectives of) 14, 16, 63,
                273
        community development/support
            strategy 40, 85
        community facilities strategy
            24, 37
            arts 3, 16–17, 23, 38–9, 83, 86,
                225, 233, 237–9, 246, 248,
                250, 252, 273 *see also*
                axis arts and community
                resource centre
                Breaking Ground 17, 22–3,
                    39, 86, 225, 237, 239,
                    254
            childcare 5, 10, 84
            civic 3, 8–9, 15–16, 37, 63, 67,
                83, 174
            community/meeting rooms
                5, 10, 16, 64, 214
            health care 3, 16, 83
            leisure/sport 3, 9, 13–14, 63,
                85, 90, 273
            parks/recreation areas 5, 7,
                12–13, 19, 37, 61, 64, 85,
                90, 185, 189, 273
            retail xii, 5, 8–10, 14–16, 41,

            63–4, 83, 210, 216–17,
                272–3
            youth facilities 39–40
                Aisling project 39–40
        community identity strategy 7, 9,
            11–12, 19, 36–7, 66
        consultation strategy 2–5, 11–12,
            21–2, 36, 38, 62–3, 69, 81,
            185, 189, 210, 212, 272
        ecological/environmental strategy
            5, 21, 39–40, 87, 103, 109–12,
            185–8, 191–2, 194–201,
            211–12, 216, 218–19
            Ballymun Composting Project
                88, 103
            Ballymun Gardens
                Competition 97–100, 107
            *Biodiversity Action Plan for
                Ballymun* 97, 109–10, 112
            Rediscovery Centre 39, 88,
                191–2, 194–8, 200–1
        economic/commercial
            development strategy xii, 3, 6,
            8–9, 14–16, 82–4, 90, 167–81,
            211–12, 214, 217, 271–4
        education strategy 84 *see also*
            Dublin City University (DCU)
        employment strategy xii, 15–16,
            24, 82–3, 127, 167, 173, 178,
            180, 191, 195, 217, 271–2
        energy strategy 5, 10, 20–1, 39,
            43, 87, 185–7, 218–19
        exit strategy 22–3
        housing strategy (planning,
            design) 11–12, 17–19, 24–5,
            36, 64–7, 89, 185–6, 189,
            216–18, 225, 272–3
        housing tenure strategy ix, 21–2,
            37, 41–2, 83, 214–15, 271,
            273
        infrastructure strategy ix, 7, 67,
            82, 175–7, 179–80
        landscaping strategy 5, 7, 12–13,
            19, 24, 61, 97, 108–10, 185,
            189, 217–18, 237, 273, 276
            Garden Action Team 97
        management strategy 13, 16,
            19–21, 23, 43
        partnership with Ballymun
            Community Law Centre *see*
            Ballymun Community Law
            Centre (BCLC)

partnership with Dublic City
University (DCU) *see* Dublin
City University (DCU)
partnership with National College
of Ireland *see* National College
of Ireland (NCI)
partnership with National Botanic
Gardens 100 *see* National
Botanic Gardens
partnership with Vocational
Educational Council (VEC) *see*
Vocational Educational
Council (VEC)
public transport strategy 8–9, 40,
82, 90, 175, 184, 211, 217,
219
bus services 7–8, 10, 40, 90–1,
171, 188
LUAS 8, 14, 90, 211
Metro North xii, 6, 8–9, 15, 22,
83, 90, 161, 179, 188, 211
security/safety strategy ix, 13,
37–8, 85–6
spatial strategy 5, 7, 16, 61, 69, 90
tax designation benefits 4, 14, 82
town identity strategy 3, 5, 7–8,
11–12, 19, 24, 63–4, 79, 83,
89, 189
nomenclature 12, 37
Ballymun Regional Youth Resource
254
Performance Lab 254
Baby Girl (play) 254
Ballymun Task Force 21
Ballymun Women's Resource Centre
124, 145
Barrett, Jim 211
Barry, Catherine 256
Basildon 4
Bealtaine (arts group) 232
Belfast 173, 225, 230–2
Belton, Paddy 207
Beresford, Christina 126
Bin Lids (play) 230
Birmingham 42
Birmingham Street tenement collapse
(Dublin) ix–x
Blaney, Neil 51, 207, 265
Board of Works 53
Bolger, Dermot xi, 38, 268–70
From these Green Heights (play) xi,
243, 248, 251–3

In High Germany (play) 248
The Ballymun Incantation (poem) 246
The Ballymun Trilogy (play) 241,
247, 254–6
The Consequences of Lightning (play)
255–6
The Journey Home (novel) 268
The Townlands of Brazil (play) 242,
252–4
Walking the Road (play) 255
Bolton Street tenement collapse
(Dublin) ix–x, 50, 207
Bono 243, 266, 269–70
Booterstown 217
Bow Housing Action Trust 4
Bradford 42
Brady, Karen 256
Burke, Christy 236
Burnham, Daniel 219
Byrne, John 237, 239
Byrne, Linda 50
Byrne, Michael 256

Cahill, Gerry 209–10
Back to the Street 210
CAIRDE (NGO) 163
Cardiff Bay 17
Casey, Tom 245–6, 252
Castlethorn Construction Ltd 15
Church Street (Dublin) 61
Citizens' Information Service 40, 127
Cityjet 248
City Quay (Dublin) 234
Clondalkin 123
Cocking, Simon 95
Codema (advisory agency) 20
Collinstown (Dublin) airport (design
of) 53
Commission for Architecture and
Built Environment (UK) 13
Start with the Park 13
Committee on Civil Legal Aid and
Advice *see* Pringle Committee
(Committee on Civil Legal Aid
and Advice, 1977)
Community and Family Training
Agency (CAFTA) 142, 145–6
Considine, June 268–9
'Buried Memories' 269
*Invisible Dublin: A Journey through
Dublin's Suburbs* 268

Coolock Community Law Centre 123–4
Corbusier *see* Le Corbusier, Charles
Coventry 57
Craig Gardner Report (1993) 63, 123, 210, 213
Cubitt (construction firm) 52
Cubitt Haden Sisk (construction consortium) 52

Dangerous Buildings Emergency (1963) x, 51
Darndale 263
Department of Local Government 51
Department of the Environment, Heritage and Local Government 21, 47–8, 88
Changing Our Ways 193
Sustainable Developments – A Strategy for Ireland 21
Waste Management Act 193
de Valera, Eamon 262–3, 270
Divis (Belfast) 225
Doyle, Roddy 244
Family 244
Drugs Taskforce Centre 252
Dublin Bus 91, 171
Dublin Chamber of Commerce 174–5
Developing a Knowledge City Region 175
Dublin City Council
Access Dublin 83
Achieving Liveable, Sustainable New Apartment Homes For Dublin City 4, 88
and Ballymun regeneration 4–5, 78–9, 81–4
as Ballymun planning authority 2, 14
Biodiversity Action Plan 87
Climate Change Strategy 87
Energy Action Plan 87
Integrated Area Plan 82, 90, 213
Local Authority Sale Scheme 89
Making Neighbourhoods 83
Maximising the City's Potential: A Strategy for Intensification and Height 1
Parnell Square plan 86
Retail Cores Plan 82
Dublin City University (DCU) 84, 107, 124, 129, 153–6, 159, 161–4, 178, 185, 274

Citizenship and Community Engagement Strategy 162
DCU in the Community 162–3
DCU Science Shop 163
Leadership through Foresight strategy 162
Dublin Corporation *see* Dublin City Council
Dublin Docklands 173–4
Dublin Health Authority x
Dublin Housing Action Committee 226
Dublin Naturalists' Field Club 111
Dublin North West Citizens' Information Service 127
Dublin Theatre Festival 254
Dundalk Institute of Technology 187

Eastern Health Board 124
ECO (Environmental Community Organisation) 195
Elliot, Eamonn 67
Ellis, Dave 124
Elmpark (Booterstown) 217–18
Emerald Housing Co-op 186
Enneclann 146
Enterprise Ireland 155
Environmental Protection Agency 102
Environmental Research Technological Development and Innovation Programme 102, 195
European Union
Image programme 87
Regan Link project 20

Family Mediation Service 40
Family Support Agency 128
FÁS (Foras Áiseanna Saothair) 195–8
Fatima Mansions 2, 4, 213, 220, 263
Feasta (NGO) 215
Fenian Street tenement collapse (Dublin) ix–x, 50, 207, 209
Fingal County Council 2, 217
Finglas 184, 241–3, 249–50, 253, 255, 267, 269
Finglas Arts Festival 249
Fire Station Studios (Dublin) 234
First Programme for Economic Expansion (Whitaker report) 207
Fitzgerald, Desmond 53
Fitzpatrick, Derek 247
Foras na Gaeilge 248

Free Legal Advice Centres (FLAC)
    119–20, 122–4, 126, 129
Friday, Gavin 270
Further Education and Training
    Awards Council (FETAC) 130

Garda Síochána, An 9, 16, 30, 32,
    37–8, 83, 85, 124, 128, 171, 249
Gardiner Street (Dublin) 253
Gerz, Joachim 237, 275–6
    Monument Against Fascism in
        Hamburg 275
    National Memory Grove 275–6
Gifford, Warren 238
Glasgow 55, 57
Glasnevin 7, 93, 106, 243, 267, 269
Global Action Plan 87, 188, 194
Gorbals (Glasgow) 55
Gormley, Anthony 234
Grace, Melanie 256
Gregory, Tony 236
Guillemot, Robert 215

Haden (engineering) 52
Haughey, Charles 235
Health Service Executive 9, 16, 85,
    171, 237
Hewson, Paul see Bono (Paul Hewson)
Hickey, Kelly 246–7, 254, 256
Higher Education Authority 155
Holland, Hannen & Cubitt
    (construction) 53
Homeless Initiative 85
Hugh Lane Municipal Gallery 86
Humphries, Gerard 238
    Our National Games 238
Hutchesontown Area C (Glasgow) 55

Ieper (Ypres, Belgium) 255
    In Flanders Fields Museum 255
IKEA xii, 3, 6, 41, 83, 161, 180, 217,
    273
Industrial Development Authority
    (IDA) 155
Into the West (film) 244–5
Iveagh Trust 219

Jacobs, Jane 208, 210
    The Death and Life of Great American
        Cities 208
Johansen, John 57
Jones, Marie 230
Judd, Michael 256

Kavanagh, Paddy 237–8
Keating, Justin 209
Kelly, Stephen 256
Kent, Anne 256
Kilbarrack 232
King, Alan 256
KLEAR Project (Kilbarrack) 232
Kyrnke, Julia 256

Laird, Brendan 256
Law Reform Commission 130–1
Le Corbusier, Charles 31, 55, 208,
    210, 216–18
Ledwidge, Francis 255
Legal Aid Board 40, 115, 119, 124–7,
    132
Lemass, Seán 207, 265
Levitt Bernstein Associates 4
Lewisham 17
Liberties (Dublin) 210
'Local Agenda 21' 194
London Docklands 4
Lowe, Louise 254
Lowton Construction Group Ltd 52
Lynott, Maureen 170
Lypton Village collective 270

MacCormac Jamieson Prichard
    (architects) 210
Mackay, David 211
Maher, Nina 126
Maine, John 17
Manchester 42
Maples, John 50
Maples, May 50
Marino (Dublin) 61
Marseilles 55
McBride, Aideen 237–8
McCabe, Vincent 254, 256
McCarthy, C.J. 61
McConnell, Ronnie 107
McDonagh, Thomas 255
McGarr, Róisín 250
McKevitt, Georgina 256
McQuill, Owen 249
Meade, Elizabeth 241, 247
Merrion Square (Dublin) 235
Milton Keynes 4
Molloy, Bobby 209
Money Advice and Budgeting Service
    (MABS) 124–6
Moyross (Limerick) 213

Muir Associates 14
Muir, Jenny 212
Murphy, Frank 126
Murray, Ciarán 271

National Botanic Gardens 39, 93, 95,
    99–109, 111
  Sustainability Week 106, 108
National Building Agency 51, 208
National College of Ireland (NCI) 84,
    124, 126, 129, 137–42, 145,
    147–9
  Active Citizenship for Local
    Development Programme 145
  Centre for Educational Opportunity
    142
  Discovering University 146
  Educational Opportunity
    Programmes unit 142
  Employment Law 146
  Family and Community Support
    146
  Family Law Matters 146
  Housing Advice and Advocacy 146
  Neighbourhood Renewal
    Programme 145
  Oral History Projects and Practice
    146
  Parents in Education 146
  School of Business 142
  School of Community Studies 142
  Transition Programme 142–5
National Development Plan 199
  Transforming Ireland – A Better
    Quality of Life for All 199–200
National Discover Primary Science
    initiative 88
National Institute for Higher
    Education 52
National Roads Authority 171
National Theatre of Poland 254
  Smycz (play) 254
National Tidy Towns competition ix,
    23, 39, 87
National University of Ireland, Galway
    129
Nee, Little John 255
  The Mental (play) 255
Neilstown 263
New Hall (Essex) 25
Ní Chonchubhair, Niamh 250
Ní Chorragáin, Doireann 256

Niemeyer, Oscar 218
Ní Grainne, Máire 246
Nolan, Seamus ix, 39, 254
  Hotel Ballymun (art installation) ix,
    39, 254
NorDubCo 156
North City Centre Community
    Action Project 228
North Dublin Workhouse 241
North King Street (Dublin) 210
Northside Community Law Centre
    115, 120, 129

Oasis (sculptural project) 235
O'Brien, Mark 250
O'Donoghue, Colin 256
O'Hare, Danny 170
O'Mahony Pike Architects 3
O'Neill, Ann 256
O'Siochru, Emer 215

Peanut Club 249
Pearse, Pádraic 261
  'The Murder Machine' 261
  'The Spiritual Nation' 261
Pepper, David 199
Per Cent for Art Scheme ix, 17, 23,
    39, 86, 233, 255
  In Context 3 Scheme 255
Perret, August 55
Pobal 248
Pollard Thomas Edwards 4
Power, Anne x, 67
  Estates on the Edge x, 36
Power, Sinéad 67
Pringle Committee (Committee on
    Civil Legal Aid and Advice,
    1977) 115–16, 129, 132
Priority Estates Projects (UK) 30, 33
Public–Private Partnerships (PPP) 4,
    158, 236

Radburn (New Jersey) 59
Rafferty, Mick 228, 236
Raheny 235
Railway Procurement Agency 8, 171
Rathfarnham 255
Rice, Peter 53, 64
Robin Hood Gardens (London)
    48–9, 55
Rocque, John 49
Roundabout Youth Theatre Company
    254

Rowntree, Joseph, Charitable Trust 126
Royal Dublin Society (RDS) Student Innovation Awards 178
Ryan, Ray 218

Santry 7, 10, 49
Scanlon, Patricia 125
Science Foundation Ireland 155
Scott, Michael 59
Seán McDermott Street (Dublin) 228
Sheriff Street (Dublin) 228
SIPTU 124
Sisk (construction firm) 52, 227
Slattery, David 227
Smithson, Alison 49, 55
Smithson, Peter 49, 55
Somerville-Woodward, Robert 48
South Dublin County Council 255
South Hill (Limerick) 263
South Inner City Community Development Association 210
Spence, Sir Basil 55
St Anne's Park (Raheny) 235
Stormanstown House (Ballymun) 141, 150
Surrender Grant Scheme 29, 47–8, 209
Sustaining Progress (social partnership agreement) 199
Swift, Arthur, and Partners 57

Tallaght 123, 263
Taskforce on Active Citizenship 147

Team 10 (architects) 49, 55
Temple Bar 82, 86
Tenant Purchase Scheme 29
Threshold 48, 124, 126–7
Tiernan, Tommy 248
Tierney, Pat 246, 252
Titanic Quarter (Belfast) 173
Towards 2016 (social partnership agreement) 199
Treasury Holdings Ltd 14–15
Trinity College Dublin 57

U2 46, 267, 270
  'Running to Stand Still' 46, 270
Unité d'Habitation (Marseilles) 55, 208, 217
University College Dublin 51
Urban Renewal Act 1998 82
Urban Splash (UK) 42
Urban Task Force Report (UK) 215–16
Urrus 124

Vardy, Marie 50
Vocational Educational Committee (VEC) 85, 162

Warrington 4
Welfare Rights Group 124
Whitaker, T.K. 207
White, Conleth 230

Yeates, Ray 238, 246–8, 250, 256
Youth Action Programme 124